CODE BASED SECRET SHARING SCHEMES

Applied Combinatorial Coding Theory

CODE BASED SECRET SHARING SCHEMES

Applied Combinatorial Coding Theory

Selda Çalkavur
Kocaeli University, Turkey

Alexis Bonnecaze
University of Aix-Marseille, France

Romar dela Cruz
University of the Philippines Diliman, Philippines

Patrick Solé
University of Aix-Marseille, France

W⊜ World Scientific

NEW JERSEY · LONDON · SINGAPORE · BEIJING · SHANGHAI · HONG KONG · TAIPEI · CHENNAI · TOKYO

Published by

World Scientific Publishing Co. Pte. Ltd.
5 Toh Tuck Link, Singapore 596224
USA office: 27 Warren Street, Suite 401-402, Hackensack, NJ 07601
UK office: 57 Shelton Street, Covent Garden, London WC2H 9HE

Library of Congress Control Number: 2022011655

British Library Cataloguing-in-Publication Data
A catalogue record for this book is available from the British Library.

CODE BASED SECRET SHARING SCHEMES
Applied Combinatorial Coding Theory

ISBN 978-981-124-832-0 (hardcover)
ISBN 978-981-124-833-7 (ebook for institutions)
ISBN 978-981-124-834-4 (ebook for individuals)

For any available supplementary material, please visit
https://www.worldscientific.com/worldscibooks/10.1142/12585#t=suppl

Desk Editors: Vishnu Mohan/Rok Ting Tan

Typeset by Stallion Press
Email: enquiries@stallionpress.com

Printed in Singapore

Foreword

I am very happy that my colleagues from ATI team at "Institut de Mathématiques de Marseille" (I2M), Alexis Bonnecaze and Patrick Solé, asked me to write a foreword their book on *Code-Based Secret Sharing Schemes* (SSS).

Both Alexis and Patrick are experts in Coding Theory, with a life-long interest in cryptography. To speak about their two coauthors: Selda is a young Turkish cryptographer, and Romar is a young mathematician from Manila.

The book focuses on the interplay between Coding Theory and SSS. While the first and most popular SSS (Shamir scheme) was written in the language of polynomial interpolation over finite fields, it transpired soon that it was in fact related to Reed Solomon codes, the most famous class of codes after the Hamming codes. In subsequent years, research developed in several directions related to combinatorics of codes and designs. The concept of minimal code is an example related to Massey scheme. There are also some application to the so-called real world-like image processing.

The book collects classical applications and gives some examples of research related to the authors practice. I recommend it as a friendly introduction to a domain at the crossroads of mathematics, computer science and engineering.

Marseilles
July 24th 2021

Robert Rolland
Emeritus Professor at Aix-Marseille University
President of ACRYPTA

Preface

A pirate wants to disclose the secret of a treasure location to his crew. To avoid that the greedy sailors compete and fight for the secret, he dissects the map of the location into several pieces, and gives a piece to each crew member. One single piece of the map is not enough to locate the treasure. Several pieces are needed to find it. This small tale is a toy example of a *secret-sharing scheme*.

Secret-sharing schemes form one of the most important topic in Cryptography. These protocols are used in many areas, applied mathematics, computer science, engineering, etc. A secret-sharing scheme is an encryption method. A secret s is divided into n pieces called shares. Each piece has no information about the secret, but it is retrieved by a specified of combination of these pieces. Specifically, a secret-sharing scheme is called a (k, n)-threshold scheme if the following property holds. Any k out of n pieces can reach the secret s but $k-1$ or fewer pieces have no information about s. The k elements that are capable of recovering the secret are called minimal access elements. A central entity, called the dealer, distributes the pieces to the participants. This distribution phase constitutes the first step of the protocol. In a second step, the recovery phase, coalitions of participants can pool their respective shares, and, if they are authorized, run an algebraic algorithm to reconstruct the secret.

Secret-sharing schemes were introduced independently by Shamir [25] and Blakley [6] in 1979. Shamir scheme uses polynomial interpolation over finite fields. It remains the most popular scheme in industrial applications today. Blakley scheme relies on geometric ideas (arrangements of hyperplanes) that work better in characteristic zero than over finite fields [19]. Massey [22, 27] used linear codes to construct the secret-sharing schemes and explained the relationship between the access structure and the minimal codewords of the dual code of the main code. It was shown later that Shamir scheme can be interpreted as an instance of Massey scheme when the underlying code is a Reed–Solomon code [23].

The aim of this book is twofold. First, we give a self-contained exposition of these classical protocols, and their various generalizations. This is the topic of Chapter 1: Foundations. Next, we give some examples of the research that these classical methods trigerred. Massey scheme (Chapter 2) led to research on the combinatorics of self-dual codes [21, 24], and on the support of codewords [2–4]. Blakley scheme (Chapter 3) was studied in [1, 9, 16, 19]. Alternative schemes, that are different from the above three (Chapter 4), were studied in [8, 15, 18, 20]. Some practical applications, in particular to image processing [14] key management in MANETs [5] and to trusted timestamping [7] are given in Chapter 5.

References

[1] A. Alahmadi, A. Altassan, A. AlKenani, S. Çalkavur, H. Shoaib and P. Solé. A multisecret-sharing scheme based on LCD codes. *Mathematics*, 8:272, 2020.

[2] A. Alahmadi, R.E.L. Aldred, R. dela Cruz, P. Solé and C. Thomassen. The maximum number of minimal codewords in long codes. *Discret. Appl. Math.* 161(3):424–429, 2013.

[3] A. Alahmadi, R.E.L. Aldred, R. dela Cruz, P. Solé and C. Thomassen. The maximum number of minimal codewords in an [n, k]-code. *Discret. Math.* 313(15):1569–1574, 2013.

[4] A. Alahmadi, R.E.L. Aldred, R. dela Cruz, S. Ok, P. Solé and C. Thomassen. The minimum number of minimal codewords in an [n, k]-code and in graphic codes. *Discret. Appl. Math.*, 184:32–39, 2015.

[5] A. Bonnecaze and A. Gabillon. On key distribution in MANETs. In *SITIS*, pp. 363–368, 2009.

[6] G.R. Blakley. Safeguarding cryptographic keys. In *AFIPS 1979 Nat. Computer Conf.*, Vol. 48, pp. 313–317, 1979.

[7] D.-P. Le, A. Bonnecaze and A. Gabillon. A secure round-based timestamping scheme. In *ICISS'08*, 2008.

[8] S. Çalkavur. Secret-sharing schemes and syndrome decoding. *J. Math. Statist. Sci.*, 2016:741–750, 2016.

[9] S. Çalkavur and F. Molla. The Blakley based secret sharing approach. *Sigma J. Eng. Natural Sci.*, 37(2):489–494, 2019.

[10] S. Çalkavur. Some secret sharing schemes based on the finite fields. *Comput. Technol. Appl.*, 7:269–272, 2016, doi: 10.17265/1934-7332/2016.06.001.

[11] S. Çalkavur. A secret sharing scheme based on residue class ring. *Appl. Math. Inform. Sci.*, 9(4):1–3, 2015.

[12] S. Çalkavur. A study on minimality of the codewords in the dual code of the code of a symmetric (v, k, λ)-design. *Appl. Math. Inform. Sci.*, 9(6):1–4, 2015.

[13] S. Çalkavur. Secret sharing schemes based on the dual code of the code of a symmetric (v, k, λ)-design and minimal access sets. *Comput. Technol. Appl.*, 6:95–100, 2015.

[14] S. Çalkavur and F. Molla. An image secret sharing method based on Shamir secret sharing. *Current Trends Comput. Sci. Appl.*, 1(2):19–22, 2018.

[15] S. Çalkavur and P. Solé. Multisecret-sharing schemes and bounded distance decoding of linear codes. *Int. J. Comput. Math.* 94(1):107–114, 2017.

[16] S. Çalkavur and P. Solé. Some multisecret-sharing schemes over finite fields. *Mathematics*, 8:654, 2020, doi:10.3390/math8050654.

[17] S. Çalkavur and P. Solé. Secret sharing, zero sum sets, and hamming codes. *Mathematics*, 8:1644, 2020, doi:10.3390/math8101644.

[18] S. Çalkavur, P. Solé and A. Bonnecaze. A new secret sharing scheme based on polynomials over finite fields. *Mathematics*, 8(8):1200, 2020, https://doi.org/10.3390/math8081200.

[19] S. Çalkavur and P. Solé. Some multisecret-sharing schemes over finite fields. MDPI, *Mathematics*, 8(5):654, 2020.

[20] S. Çalkavur. Secret sharing schemes based on extension fields. *European J. Pure Appl. Math.*, 11(2):410–416, 2018.

[21] S.T. Dougherty, S. Mesnager and P. Solé. Secret-sharing schemes based on self-dual codes. In *ITW 2008*, pp. 338–342, 2007.

[22] J.L. Massey. Minimal codewords and secret sharing. In *Proc. 6th Joint Swedish-Russian Workshop on Information Theory*, Mölle, Sweden, pp. 276–279, 1993.

[23] R.J. McEliece and D.V. Sarwate. On sharing secrets and Reed–Solomon codes. *Comm. ACM* 24:583–584, 1981.

[24] R. dela Cruz, A. Meyer and P. Solé. An extension of Massey scheme for secret sharing. In *ITW 2010*, pp. 1–5, 2010.

[25] A. Shamir. How to share a secret. *Comm. ACM*, 22(11):612–613, 1979.

[26] H. Yamamoto. On secret sharing systems using (k, L, n)-threshold scheme. *IECE Trans.*, J68-A(9):945–952, 1985 (in Japanese), English translation: *Electron. Commun. Japan, Part I*, 69(9):46–54, Scripta Technica, Inc., 1986.

[27] H. Yamamoto. Some applications of coding theory. In *Cryptography, Codes and Ciphers: Cryptography and Coding IV*, pp. 33–47, 1995.

Contents

Chapter 1

Foundations

The notion of secret sharing was independently introduced in 1979 by Shamir [36] and Blakley [7]. A secret-sharing scheme (also called SSS) is a method by which one can distribute shares of a secret to a set of participants in such a way that only specified groups of participants can reconstruct the secret by pooling their shares. Secret-sharing schemes are widely used in cryptographic protocols. In particular, it is common in the field of key management and key distribution that keys are shared in fragments to make an attack more difficult. For example, it may be useful for a node A in a network to obtain a private key. This key can be given to him by a trusted third party who then becomes key escrow. In some networks such as *ad hoc* networks, which do not have a trusted third party, this key may be provided by a set of nodes, each of which provides a fragment of the key. Thus, in the absence of collision of these nodes, only node A will know its key which will be a function of the fragments.

There are many other applications to secret sharing, like secure multiparty computation which is perhaps the application with the most potential. Secure Multiparty Computation (SMPC) is a cryptographic technique that allows multiple parties to jointly and securely compute a function while keeping their inputs private. This can be useful, for example, to create secure, privacy-preserving machine learning. It has been introduced in the early 1980s by Yao [45] as a solution to the famous Millionaires' problem: two millionaires want to determine who is the richest without revealing their personal wealth. With theoretical constructs dating back to the 1980s, there have been

1

substantial improvements in algorithmic and engineering designs over the past decade to improve performance in terms of computation times [18]. In fact, ARPA mentions that the overall performance of sMPCs has increased by four to five orders of magnitude in the last decade alone, representing drastic improvements. As a result, applications of sMPCs are no longer relegated to theoretical designs and are now firmly rooted in the practical world. Another important cryptographic application, which can be related to sMPC, is the so-called oblivious transfer [23]. In such a protocol, a sender transmits an information, selected among several possible sendings, to a recipient, without the sender being able to know the choice of the recipient, nor the recipient being able to know the information he did not request.

In general, secret-sharing schemes are used in many security protocols, and still have great potential both theoretically and practically. Thus, the theoretical appeal and the profusion of applications explain the interest of researchers in the domain.

We are interested, in this document, in a large family of schemes called linear and which have the advantage of being able to use the tools of linear algebra. There are several approaches to building linear secret-sharing schemes. One can for example quote those based on matroids [44]. Matroids can be used to obtain specific properties of secret-sharing schemes. In this book, we will focus on constructions based on error correcting codes defined over the finite field $\mathbb{F}_q$, q being a prime power.

In this chapter, we set the notations that will be used throughout the book and we give the general definitions related to secret-sharing scheme and coding theory. We consider the two main constructions of secret-sharing schemes based on linear codes. For both constructions, we analyze the properties of the underlying codes that allow us to obtain the secret-sharing schemes with the desired parameters. In particular, we show the importance of the so-called Maximum Distance Separable (MDS) codes. Then, we introduce the most popular schemes which can be constructed using a linear code: Shamir [36], Massey [31, 32] and Blakley [7] secret-sharing schemes. Shamir scheme, the best-known secret-sharing scheme, is often presented in terms of univariate polynomials. But we will see that it can also be constructed using a code-based construction, in this case a Reed–Solomon code.

Finally, we introduce multisecret-sharing schemes that can be seen as generalizations of secret-sharing schemes in the sense that these schemes share m arbitrarily related secrets among a set of n participants. It is thus possible to define many thresholds, depending on the secrets. The study of these schemes has been the subject of numerous studies (see for example [1, 4, 11, 13, 13, 14]).

Specific properties of these schemes are detailed in the following chapters.

1.1. Access Structures

A secret-sharing scheme (SSS) involves a *dealer* who detains a *secret*. This dealer distributes its secret to a set of *participants* (also called users or shareholders) in order that each party holds a *share* (or fragment) of that secret. Some special subsets of participants can reconstruct the secret while the other cannot. The groups that can reconstruct the secret are called *qualified* (or sometimes authorized) and the other groups are called *rejected* (or sometimes forbidden).

Let $\mathcal{P} = \{p_1, \ldots, p_n\}$ be a set of participants. A collection $\mathcal{A} \subseteq 2^{\mathcal{P}}$ is *monotone increasing* if $A \in \mathcal{A}$ and $A \subseteq B$ imply that $B \in \mathcal{A}$. This means that any superset of A is also in $\mathcal{A}$. Similarly, a collection $\mathcal{B} \subseteq 2^{\mathcal{P}}$ is *monotone decreasing* if for each set B in $\mathcal{B}$ also each subset of B is in $\mathcal{B}$. A monotone increasing set $\mathcal{A}$ can be efficiently described by the set $\mathcal{A}^-$ consisting of the minimal elements (sets) in $\mathcal{A}$, i.e. the elements in $\mathcal{A}$ for which no proper subset is also in $\mathcal{A}$. Similarly, the set $\mathcal{B}^+$ consists of the maximal elements (sets) in $\mathcal{B}$, i.e. the elements in $\mathcal{B}$ for which no proper superset is also in $\mathcal{B}$.

Let $\mathcal{A} \subseteq 2^{\mathcal{P}}$ be the set of qualified groups of participants and $\mathcal{B} \subseteq 2^{\mathcal{P}}$ be the set of rejected groups. The tuple $(\mathcal{A}, \mathcal{B})$ is called an *access structure* if $\mathcal{A} \cap \mathcal{B} = \emptyset$. It is called monotone if $\mathcal{A}$ is monotone increasing and $\mathcal{B}$ is monotone decreasing. In this case, $(\mathcal{A}^+, \mathcal{B}^-)$ generates $(\mathcal{A}, \mathcal{B})$. Most of the access structures are monotone. However, there are situations where it is more appropriate to consider non-monotone access structures (see for example [29]). In this book, we will only consider monotone access structures which is a natural assumption. In this case, if the set $\{a, b\}$ is qualified to initiate an action, then any superset is also able to do so and on the other hand, if the group composed of a and b is rejected, then participant a (respectively, b) is rejected.

If $\mathcal{A} = \emptyset$, then the secret will remain secret and no one will receive a share. When $\mathcal{A} \cup \mathcal{B} = 2^{\mathcal{P}}$, the access structure is called *complete* and can simply be denoted by $\mathcal{A}$ and $\mathcal{B} = \mathcal{A}^c$, the complement of $\mathcal{A}$.

The dual access structure $(\mathcal{A}^{\perp}, \mathcal{B}^{\perp})$ for $(\mathcal{A}, \mathcal{B})$ is such that

$$\mathcal{A}^{\perp} = \{A \ : \ A^c \in \mathcal{B}\} \quad \text{and} \quad \mathcal{B}^{\perp} = \{A \ : \ A^c \in \mathcal{A}\}.$$

It is easy to see that if $\mathcal{A}$ is a complete access structure defined on $\mathcal{P}$, then the dual access $\mathcal{A}^{\perp}$ is the collection of sets $A \in \mathcal{P}$ such that $\mathcal{P} \setminus A = A^c \in \mathcal{B}$. Moreover, we have $(\mathcal{A}^{\perp})^{\perp} = \mathcal{A}$ and $(\mathcal{B}^{\perp})^{\perp} = \mathcal{B}$.

1.2.   Secret-Sharing Schemes and Examples

After having introduced the notion of access structure, it is time to look at the notion of secret-sharing scheme. To do so, we rely on examples.

Suppose a company may want to require the collaboration of (at least) one deputy director and one manager to be able to obtain the key to spend an amount that exceeds a certain threshold. Suppose the key s belongs to $\mathbb{Z}_q$, q being an integer. Let $d_1, \ldots, d_2$ be the deputy directors and let $m_1, \ldots, m_2$ be the managers. Then we have

$$\mathcal{A} = \{\{d_1, m_1\}, \{d_1, m_2\}, \{d_2, m_1\}, \{d_2, m_2\}, \{d_1, m_1, m_2\},$$

$$\{d_2, m_1, m_2\}, \{d_1, d_2, m_1\}, \{d_1, d_2, m_2\}, \{d_1, d_2, m_1, m_2\}\}$$

and

$$\mathcal{B} = \{\emptyset, \{d_1\}, \{d_2\}, \{m_1\}, \{m_2\}, \{d_1, d_2\}, \{m_1, m_2\}\}.$$

The pair $(\mathcal{A}, \mathcal{B})$ is an access structure since $\mathcal{A} \cap \mathcal{B} = \emptyset$. This access structure is monotone and complete. Suppose it is given to each deputy director the share a (randomly chosen in $\mathbb{Z}_q$) and to each manager the share $s + a$. Then, we can see that all the elements of $\mathcal{A}$ are able to compute s while no element of $\mathcal{B}$ is able to do so. In fact, since a is randomly chosen in $\mathbb{Z}_q$ and is independent of s, share $a + s$ is uniformly distributed over $\mathbb{Z}_q$. This means that $a + s$ takes on every value with equal probability and therefore $a + s$ gives no information on s. On the other hand, a group containing shares a and $a + s$ is able to compute the key s by subtracting share a to share $a + s$.

This scheme can be viewed as a pair (Share, Reconstruct) of protocols (or phases). The sharing phase consists for the dealer P_0 to share the secret s to the participants (here, the deputy directors and the managers each receives a share) and the reconstruction phase consists for the participants to try to reconstruct s. Note that the participants of any set of $\mathcal{B}$ learn nothing about the secret s and moreover the key s can be computed by any set of participants $A \in \mathcal{A}$. Note also that the size of a share is exactly the size of the secret.

This pair of protocols along with the two aforementioned properties realize what we call a secret-sharing scheme (SSS) based on the access structure $(\mathcal{A}, \mathcal{B})$. More generally, we can state the definition of an SSS.

Definition 1.2.1. A *secret-sharing scheme* based on an access structure $(\mathcal{A}, \mathcal{B})$ is a pair (Share, Reconstruct) of protocols such that the protocol Share consists for the dealer to compute the shares of a secret and to distribute them to the participants and the Reconstruct protocol consists for groups of participants to try to reconstruct the secret from their shares. Moreover, the scheme must have the following properties:

- *Privacy*: the participants of any element of $\mathcal{B}$ learn nothing about the secret s.
- *Correctness*: the key s can be computed by any group of participants $A \in \mathcal{A}$.

Note that when $\mathcal{B}^c = \mathcal{A}$ (i.e. the access structure is complete), the secret-sharing scheme is called *perfect*.

A qualified group is *minimal* if none of its proper subset is qualified. A secret-sharing scheme is to be *t-democratic* if every group of t participants is in the same number of minimal qualified groups, where $t \geq 1$. A participant is called a *dictator* if she/he is a member of every minimal qualified group.

An important efficient parameter in secret-sharing scheme is *the size* of the shares compare to the size of the secret. In any perfect secret-sharing scheme, the size of each share is greater than the size of the secret. On the contrary, in non-perfect schemes the size of each share can be smaller than the size of the secret. This can be an advantage for some applications. A complete access structure $\mathcal{A}$ providing an *ideal* secret-sharing scheme is a scheme such that any participant has only one share with size equal to the size of the secret.

Let us now construct a more complex SSS based on the previous example and similar to [38]. Suppose that the company may want to require the collaboration of at least two deputy directors or at least three managers to be able to obtain the key. It is also required that a deputy director should act as a manager. Therefore, two managers and one deputy director form a qualified group. There are m managers counted from 1 to m and d deputy directors counted from $m + 1$ to $m + d$. The director chooses randomly the key $s \in \mathrm{GF}(q)$, where $\mathrm{GF}(q)$ is the Galois field of order q (q being a prime power). To share s among the deputy directors and the managers, the director first selects non-zero distinct elements $\alpha_1, \ldots, \alpha_m \in \mathrm{GF}(q)$. Then he selects $\alpha_{m+1}, \ldots, \alpha_{m+d} \in \mathrm{GF}(q)$ such that they are distinct and different from all values

$$\alpha_i \alpha_j (\alpha_i + \alpha_j)^{-1}, \quad 1 \le i < j \le m.$$

Of course, this can happen only if $q \ge 1 + m + m(m-1)/2 + d$ since otherwise the number of elements in the field is not sufficient. The director stores these $m + d$ elements in a public directory. In the next step, the director chooses randomly $a, b \in \mathrm{GF}(q)$, and transmits the share

$$s_i = s + a\alpha_i + b(\alpha_i)^2, \quad \text{where } 1 \le i \le m$$

to the ith manager, and share

$$s_i = s + a\alpha_i, \quad \text{where } m + 1 \le i \le m + d$$

to the ith deputy director. The elements a and b are kept secret by the director.

There are three kinds of groups that are qualified. The groups containing at least two deputy directors, the groups containing two managers and one deputy directors and the groups containing three managers. Suppose managers i and j together with the deputy director k combine their shares in order to compute the key s. They use the public directory of the director to construct the matrix

$$G = \begin{pmatrix} 1 & 1 & 1 \\ \alpha_i & \alpha_j & \alpha_k \\ (\alpha_i)^2 & (\alpha_j)^2 & 0 \end{pmatrix}$$

and its inverse G^{-1} which exists since $\det(G) = -(\alpha_k(\alpha_j)^2) + (\alpha_k(\alpha_i)^2) + (\alpha_i(\alpha_j)^2) - (\alpha_j(\alpha_i)^2) = (\alpha_i - \alpha_j)(\alpha_k(\alpha_i + \alpha_j) - \alpha_i\alpha_j) \neq 0$.
Then they compute

$$(s_i, s_j, s_k)G^{-1} = (s, a, b),$$

in order to obtain s.

The combination of three managers uses the matrix

$$G = \begin{pmatrix} 1 & 1 & 1 \\ \alpha_i & \alpha_j & \alpha_k \\ (\alpha_i)^2 & (\alpha_j)^2 & (\alpha_j)^2 \end{pmatrix}$$

which also has a non-zero determinant since G is the transpose of a Vandermonde matrix and the α_i are all distinct.

The combination of two deputy directors uses the matrix

$$G = \begin{pmatrix} 1 & 1 \\ \alpha_i & \alpha_j \end{pmatrix},$$

which again has a non-zero determinant.

Now, if two managers i and j combine their shares, can they obtain s? Their shares are given by the entries of the vector

$$s(1,1) + (a,b) \begin{pmatrix} 1 & 1 \\ \alpha_i & \alpha_j \\ (\alpha_i)^2 & (\alpha_j)^2 \end{pmatrix}.$$

The information about the value of s contained in this vector is equal to the information about the value of s contained in the vector

$$s(1,1) \begin{pmatrix} \alpha_i & \alpha_j \\ (\alpha_i)^2 & (\alpha_j)^2 \end{pmatrix}^{-1} + (a,b).$$

We know that the director has chosen a and b randomly in $\mathrm{GF}(q)$ and that s, a and b are statistically independent. Therefore, two deputy directors cannot obtain any information about s. It can be proved in a similar way that a deputy director and a manager cannot collude to obtain s.

It is interesting to note that the construction of the shares makes use of a matrix. In fact, the transformation from the vector (s, a, b) to the shares $(s_1, \ldots, s_{m+d})$ is linear. It means that for any two secrets s and s' and respective share s_i and s'_i (where $1 \leq i \leq m + d$), the shares $s_i + s'_i$ and λs_i are valid shares for the secrets $s + s'$ and λs, respectively. This property is very common and leads us to state the following definition.

Definition 1.2.2. A secret-sharing scheme is said to be *linear* if for any two secrets s and s' and respective share vectors $(s_1, \ldots, s_n)$ and $(s'_1, \ldots, s'_n)$, the vectors $(s_1 + s'_1, \ldots, s_n + s'_n)$ and $(\lambda s_1, \ldots, \lambda s_n)$ are valid share vectors for the secrets $s + s'$ and λs, respectively.

The vast majority of secret-sharing schemes are linear. This is particularly the case when these schemes are based on linear error correcting codes as we will see later.

1.3.   Alternative Definitions

There are many definitions of a secret-sharing scheme which are each adapted to a specific objective or mathematical vision. In what follows, we give two more definitions. The first one makes use of the notion of distribution scheme and can be found in [3].

Definition 1.3.1. A *distribution scheme* $\Sigma = \langle \Pi, \mu \rangle$ with domain of secrets K is a pair, where μ is a probability distribution on some finite set R called the set of random strings and Π is a mapping from $K \times R$ to a set of n-tuples $K_1 \times K_2 \times \cdots \times K_n$, where K_j is called the domain of shares of p_j. A dealer distributes a secret according to Σ by first sampling a random string $r \in R$ according to μ, computing a vector of shares $\Pi(k, r) = (s_1, \ldots s_n)$, and privately communicating each share s_j to party p_j. For a set $A \subseteq \{p_1, \ldots, p_n\}$, we denote $\Pi(s, r)_A$ the restriction of $\Pi(s, r)$ to its A-entries.

In a practical implementation of an SSS, it is important for security and efficiency reasons, to keep the size of the shares as small as possible. In order to measure the amount of information that must be given to the participants, we can use the worst-case *information ratio*, which is the ratio between the maximum size of the shares and the size of the secret. The information ratio of a distribution scheme is

$$\frac{\max_{1 \leq j \leq n} \log |K_j|}{\log |K|}.$$

We can also use the *average information ratio* which is the ratio between the arithmetic mean of the size of all shares and the size of the secret. It is defined as

$$\frac{\sum_{1 \leq j \leq n} \log |K_j|}{n \log |K|}.$$

The *information rate* is defined as the inverse of the information ratio.

Definition 1.3.2. Let K be a finite set of secrets, where $|K| \geq 2$. A distribution scheme $\langle \Pi, \mu \rangle$ with domain of secrets K is a secret-sharing scheme realizing an access structure $(\mathcal{A}, \mathcal{B})$ if the following requirements hold:

- *Correctness*: The secret k can be reconstructed by any qualified set of participants. That is, for any set $A \in \mathcal{A}$ (where $A = \{p_1, \ldots, p_{|A|}\}$), there exists a reconstruction function $\text{Reconstr}_A : K_{i_1} \times \cdots \times K_{i_{|A|}} \to K$ such that for every $k \in K$,

$$\Pr[\text{Reconstr}_A(\Pi(k, r)_A) = k] = 1. \qquad (1.3.1)$$

- *Privacy*: Every rejected set cannot learn anything about the secret (in the information theoretic sense) from their shares. Formally, for any set $B \in \mathcal{B}$, for every two secrets $k_1, k_2 \in K$, and for every possible vector of shares $\langle s_j \rangle_{p_j \in B}$:

$$\Pr[\Pi(k_1, r)_B = \langle s_j \rangle_{p_j \in B}] = \Pr[\Pi(k_2, r)_B = \langle s_j \rangle_{p_j \in B}]. \qquad (1.3.2)$$

This definition can be qualified as "strong" in the sense that correctness of the reconstruction with probability 1 is required and distributions $\Pi(k_1, r)_B$ and $\Pi(k_2, r)_B$ must be equal. Indeed, there exist more flexible definitions that simply require that the correctness hold with a high probability and that the distributions be very close.

Secret-sharing schemes can also be defined using the *entropy function* [25]. For this, we assume that a probability distribution over the domain of secrets is known. So let us consider such a probability distribution together with a distribution scheme Σ. This induces, for any set $A \subseteq \{p_1, \ldots, p_n\}$, a probability distribution on the vector of shares corresponding to the participants in A.

The random variable taking values according to this probability distribution is denoted S_A, while S is the random variable denoting the secret. Next, we will see that the privacy and correctness requirements can be formalized using the entropy function. For this, we first need to introduce the notions of entropy.

Let X be a random variable. The support of X, denoted $\mathrm{supp}(X)$, is the set of values x such that $\Pr[X = x] > 0$ and the *entropy* of X is defined as

$$H(X) := \sum_{x \in \mathrm{supp}(X)} \Pr[X = x] \log 1/\Pr[X = x].$$

Intuitively, $H(X)$ measures the amount of uncertainty in X. If X is known, its entropy is equal to 0. Here the notation log means a logarithm of arbitrary base. Very often, the information is represented as bit sequences and logarithm base 2 is used.

Example 1.3.3. Let X be a discrete random variable taking 3 values a, b and c such that $\Pr[X = a] = 1/2$, $\Pr[X = b] = 1/4$, $\Pr[X = a] = 1/4$. Then $H(X) = 1/2 \log_2(2) + 2 * (1/4) \log_2(4) = 1.5$. This also means that encoding X takes 1.5 bits and that the uncertainty of X is of 1.5 bits. Note that in this example we use the logarithm base 2 in order to consider the bit as the information unit.

If X is uniformly distributed over $\mathrm{supp}(X)$, then

$$H(X) = \log |\mathrm{supp}(X)|$$

and in general we have $0 \leq H(X) \leq \log |\mathrm{supp}(X)|$.

Now, if we consider two random variables X and Y, *the joint entropy* $H(X, Y)$ is a measure of the uncertainty associated with the set of the two variables X and Y. It is defined as

$$H(X, Y) = -\sum_{x \in X} \sum_{y \in Y} Pr(X = x, Y = y) \log[Pr(X = x, Y = y)],$$

where $Pr(X = x, Y = y)$ denotes the joint probability of x and y occurring together. This definition can be generalized to more than two variables but this generalization is useless for our purpose.

The *conditional entropy* $H(X|Y)$ measures the amount of information needed to describe the outcome of a random variable X given that the value of another random variable Y is known. It is defined as

$$H(X|Y) = H(X, Y) - H(Y).$$

If the two variables are independent, we have $H(X|Y) = H(X)$.

Another definition of secret-sharing scheme, equivalent to Definition 1.3.2, is now given using conditional entropy.

Definition 1.3.4. A distribution scheme is a secret-sharing scheme realizing an access structure $(\mathcal{A}, \mathcal{B})$ with respect to a given probability distribution on the secrets, denoted by a random variable S, if the following conditions hold.

- *Correctness*: For every qualified set $A \in \mathcal{A}$,

$$H(S|S_A) = 0.$$

- *Privacy*: For every rejected set $B \in \mathcal{B}$,

$$H(S|S_B) = H(S).$$

Note that the security offered by this model is *unconditional*. This means that it is independent of the amount of computing time and resources that are available when attempting to obtain information about the secret by some unauthorized means.

Blundo *et al.* [10] proved that if a scheme realizes an access structure with respect to one distribution on the secrets, then it realizes the access structure with respect to any distribution with the same support.

We recall that an ideal secret-sharing scheme is a scheme in which the size of the share of each party is exactly the size of the secret. We will see that this is the case of Shamir scheme which is in addition an example of *threshold scheme*. A (k, n) threshold scheme is a scheme for which the qualified sets are all the sets whose size is above a certain *threshold* $k \leq n$, where n is the number of participants.

The notion of *ramp scheme* generalizes that of threshold scheme. A (k, t, n) ramp scheme is such that the qualified sets are all the sets whose size is greater than t. Moreover, any subset of participants of size at most $k-1$ should get no information about the secret and the subsets of participants of size between k and $t-1$ might get some information about the secret.

1.4. Security Models

In order to analyze the security of a secret-sharing scheme with an access structure $(\mathcal{A}, \mathcal{B})$, it is necessary to define the conditions under which the scheme is used. We assume that each participant is connected to a broadcast medium and that the system is synchronized, i.e. the participants can access a common global clock. Moreover, there are secure channels between every two participants and between the dealer and every participant. We also assume that each participant has a local source of randomness. This communication model is called secure-channel and was introduced in [5, 16].

The collaborating participants are asked to execute the protocol correctly but this rule may not be followed. An adversary may corrupt some of the participants subject to certain constraints, for example an upper bound on the total number of corrupted participants. One can distinguish between *passive* and *active* corruption, see Fehr and Maurer [21] for recent results. Passive corruption means that the adversary obtains entire information held by the corrupted participants while they are executing the protocol correctly. These participants are also called *honest* but *curious*. Active corruption means that the adversary takes full control of the corrupted participants. In this case, the protocol may not be correctly executed by some corrupted participants. To be more precise, let D be the set of all the corrupted participants and let $A \subseteq D$ be the set of actively corrupted participants. The set $D \setminus A$ is the set of honest but curious. The adversary is characterized by a *privacy structure* $\mathcal{A} \subseteq 2^P$ and an *adversary structure* $\mathcal{A}_A \subseteq \mathcal{A}$. The adversary can corrupt participants passively or actively as long as they belong to the set D. Active corruption is strictly stronger than passive corruption.

When the set of corrupted participants is chosen once and for all before the protocol starts, the adversary is called *static*.

When the set of corrupted participants is not static, the adversary is called *adaptive*. This means that the adversary can at any time during the protocol choose to corrupt a new participant based on the information he has (as long as this participant belongs to the set of corrupted participants). This model is known as the *mixed* adversary model.

Standard secret-sharing schemes, like for example Shamir schemes, that will be presented in the following section, assume that all participants perform the protocol correctly. Therefore, their security does not include active attacks. However, there are schemes that allow participants to verify their shares. More formally, *verifiable secret sharing* ensures that even if the dealer is malicious there is a well-defined secret that the participants can later reconstruct. The concept of verifiable secret sharing (VSS) was first introduced in 1985 by Chor *et al.* in [17]. All the schemes considered in the following are standard schemes and therefore assume that the protocol is executed correctly.

1.5. Shamir Scheme and Applications

Shamir's threshold secret-sharing scheme [36] is probably the most known secret-sharing scheme and perhaps the most used. It has been introduced by Shamir in 1979 and is still used in many security or network protocols, generally to distribute keys.

The qualified sets are all the sets whose size is greater than a certain *threshold* $t \leq n$, where n is the number of participants. The scheme is usually called Shamir's (t, n)-threshold scheme and its access structure is defined as

$$\mathcal{A} = \{A \subseteq \{p_1, \ldots, p_n\} : |A| \geq t\}.$$

The idea of Shamir is smart albeit very simple: it is based on the fact that a univariate polynomial $y = f(x)$ of degree $t - 1$ is uniquely defined by t points (x_i, y_i) with distinct x_i. The knowledge of less than t points gives no information on the polynomial. The secret is the constant term of the polynomial and the shares are the points of the polynomials. The reconstruction of the secret uses *Lagrange interpolation*.

Protocol 1 details the scheme for a prime field (generalization for any field is straightforward).

Protocol 1: Shamir's (t, n) threshold Scheme (in $\mathbb{Z}_p$)

Input: a trusted dealer distributes shares of a secret S to n participants.
Goal: any group of t participants which pool their shares can recover S.

1. **Setup.** The trusted dealer T distributes a secret integer $S \geq 0$ to n participants.
   (a) T chooses a prime $p > \max(S, n)$, and set $a_0 = S$.
   (b) T defines the polynomial $f(x)$ over $\mathbb{Z}_p$ as $f(x) = \sum_{j=0}^{t-1} a_j x^j$, where $a_j \in_R \mathbb{Z}_p$ for $j \neq 0$ and $a_0 = S$.
   (c) T computes the n shares $s_i = f(i) \mod p$ for distinct $i \in \mathbb{Z}_p$ and securely transfers them to party p_i.
2. **Pooling of shares.** Any group of at least t participants pool their shares, providing enough distinct points to compute coefficients a_j by Lagrange interpolation. The secret is $f(0) = a_0$.

Starting from the t points, the secret $S = a_0$ is recovered using a formula that can be deduced from Lagrange interpolation:

$$S = \sum_{i=1}^{t} c_i s_i, \text{ where } c_i = \prod_{1 \leq j \leq t, j \neq i} \frac{s_j}{s_j - s_i}.$$

This scheme has the following properties:

1. *Perfect privacy* is preserved since given the knowledge of any $t-1$ or fewer shares, all values $0 \leq S \leq p - 1$ of the shared secret remain equally probable.
2. It is *ideal*: the size of a share is equal to the size of the secret.
3. It is *extendable*: new shares can be computed and distributed without affecting existing shares. This means that the number of participants can be increased if needed.
4. It is possible to *vary the level of control* by providing multiple shares to one party.

5. The *security of the scheme is theoretical* and does not rely on a "hard problem" (like many asymmetric cryptographic algorithms).
6. It is a *linear scheme.*

The simplicity of its access structure mainly brings two disadvantages. First, participants are all equal in rights and it is not possible to privilege some over others. Yet in real life, there are often hierarchies between people. However, it is still possible to assign several shares to a single participant in order to increase its power. The second drawback comes from the density of the structure: any group with a size above the fixed threshold is qualified. This does not simplify the tracing to identify the group that has obtained the secret. When this tracing property is required, it may be a good idea to use a sparse access structure. Suppose we have a $(5, 2)$-access structure. Even if we have identified a participant who did not participate in the reconstruction of the secret, there are still six possible pairs. Now, if we consider a sparse access structure, for example $\{1, 2\}$, $\{1, 3\}$, $\{1, 4\}$, $\{2, 3\}$, $\{2, 4\}$, we know that if the participant 1 did not participate in the reconstruction of the secret, then participant 2 did it and he can possibly reveal the identity of the other participant.

Shamir scheme has many direct applications but also indirect applications as for example secure multiparty computation (SMPC) which allows parties to jointly compute a function over their inputs while keeping those inputs private. It is thus a question of protecting participants' privacy from each other. This problem is difficult and started to be studied in the 1970s [37]. Several protocols have been developed since then. For more about multiparty computation, one can consult for example [27]. The following example presents a very simple example of SMPC.

Example 1.5.1. Alice, Bob and Iwan want to know the total sum of their salaries without disclosing theirs. To do this, each participant constructs a polynomial (that is kept secret) of degree 2 with random coefficients except for the constant term which is equal to the participant's salary. Let P_1, P_2, P_3 be the respective polynomials of Alice, Bob and Iwan. Thus, $P_1(0)$ is equal to the salary of Alice, $P_2(0)$ is equal to the salary of Bob and so on.

Now Alice evaluates its polynomial at three defined values (say 1, 2, 3) i.e. $P_1(x)$ for $x = 1$, 2, 3, while Bob and Iwan evaluate their own polynomial at the same values. Then, Alice sends $P_1(2)$ to Bob and $P_1(3)$ to Iwan, Bob sends $P_2(1)$ to Alice and $P_2(3)$ to Iwan and Iwan sends $P_3(1)$ to Alice and $P_3(2)$ to Bob. At this stage, Alice knows

$$P_1(1), \ P_2(1), \ P_3(1),$$

Bob knows

$$P_1(2), \ P_2(2), \ P_3(2),$$

and Iwan knows

$$P_1(3), \ P_2(3), \ P_3(3).$$

This means that each participant knows the (public) value $P(i)$ with $P = P_1 + P_2 + P_3$ for respectively $i = 1$, 2, 3 by just adding their shares. The polynomial P of degree 2 can be constructed with these 3 values using an interpolation and $P(0)$ gives the sum of the three salaries. In fact, this protocol can also be used for different other applications like anonymous voting. The security of the scheme relies on the fact that P_i are kept secret and that each participant keeps one of its three evaluations secret. Moreover, the participants must execute the protocol correctly without cheating.

In the following sections, we will consider secret-sharing schemes that are constructed using linear codes. In particular, we will see that Shamir scheme can also be constructed from special linear codes called Reed Solomon codes.

1.6. Basics of Coding Theory

We briefly introduce the main notions of error correcting block codes. For more details about this topic, see [30], Let $\mathbb{F}_q$ be the finite field of order q, where q is a prime power. Any non-empty subset C of $\mathbb{F}_q^n$ is called a *code* and the parameter n is called the length of the code. Each vector in C is called a codeword of C. The *Hamming weight* wt(v) of a vector v in $\mathbb{F}_q^n$ is the number of its non-zero coordinates. The *Hamming distance* between two vectors of $\mathbb{F}_q^n$ is the number of coordinates that differ between these two vectors. The *minimum distance* of a code C is the smallest of all Hamming distances between different codewords in C. It follows from this definition that a code with minimum distance $d_{\min}$ can correct $e := \lfloor (d_{\min} - 1)/2 \rfloor$ errors, since spheres of radius e are pairwise disjoint. The number e is called the *packing radius* or *error correction capability* of the code. If $d_{\min}$ is even the code can detect $d_{\min}/2$ errors, meaning that a received vector cannot have distance $d_{\min}/2$ to one codeword and distance less than $d_{\min}/2$ to another one. It may however have distance $d_{\min}/2$ to more codewords. Notice that for a subspace $V \subset \mathbb{F}_q^n$, the minimum distance of V can be computed by linearity as the minimum non-zero Hamming weight in V that is

$$d_{\min}(V) = \min\{\mathrm{wt}(v) | v \in V \setminus \{0\}\}.$$

The notion of error can be completed by the notion of *erasure*. We use the term erasure when there is an ambiguity on the value of a coordinate at a given position in the received vector. Thus erasures can be considered as errors in known positions. A code can decode errors and erasures simultaneously. If C is a code of length n with minimum distance $d_{\min}$ then it can correct b errors and c erasures as long as $2b + c < d_{\min}$. In other words, the transmitted codeword should be retrievable if during the transmission at most c of the symbols in the word are erased and at most b received symbols are incorrect.

Definition 1.6.1. An $[n, k, d]$ *linear code* C is a linear subspace of $\mathbb{F}_q^n$, where k is the dimension and $d = d_{\min}(C)$ is the minimum Hamming weight.

A *generator matrix* G for a code C is a matrix whose rows form a basis for C. For any linear code C, we denote by $C^\perp$ its *dual* under the usual inner product. A code C is said to be *self-orthogonal* if $C \subseteq C^\perp$ and it is *self-dual* if $C = C^\perp$. Whenever d is used to denote the minimum distance of C, $d^\perp$ is used to denote the minimum distance of $C^\perp$. The standard inner product of two vectors x and y is denoted $x \cdot y$.

Example 1.6.2. Let $\mathcal{C}$ be a $[5, 2, 2]$ linear binary code with generator matrix

$$G = \begin{pmatrix} 0 & 1 & 1 & 0 & 0 \\ 0 & 0 & 0 & 1 & 1 \end{pmatrix}.$$

This code is self-orthogonal since all its codewords are orthogonal to each other. It is not self-dual since the vector $v = (11100) \notin \mathcal{C}$ belongs to the dual code. Let d be the minimum distance of $\mathcal{C}$, then the fact that $\mathcal{C} \subseteq \mathcal{C}^{\perp}$ implies that $d^{\perp} \leq d$. It is easy to see that $d = 2$ and $d^{\perp} = 1$ (because the vector $(10000) \in \mathcal{C}^{\perp}$).

A linear complementary dual code also called *LCD* is such that $C \cap C^{\perp} = \{0\}$.

As seen before, the support of v is given by $\mathrm{supp}(v) = \{i : v_i \neq 0, 1 \leq i \leq n\}$. A vector v_2 covers a vector v_1 if the support of v_2 contains that of v_1.

Definition 1.6.3. A non-zero codeword of C is called *minimal vector* if its support does not properly contain the support of another non-zero codeword.

The *covering problem* of a linear code is to determine the set of all its minimal vectors.

Definition 1.6.4. A linear code C is minimal if every non-zero codeword of C is a minimal vector.

Example 1.6.5. The binary Simplex code of parameters $[7, 3, 4]$ is minimal since it is a one weight code.

A linear code C can also be defined by its parity check matrix H. This is a matrix which describes the linear relations that the components of a codeword must satisfy. The matrix H is the generator matrix of the dual of C. This means that a codeword c is in C if and only if $cH^T = 0$. Thus, we have $HG^T = GH^T = 0$.

For any $[n, k, d]$-code, the following inequality known as the Singleton bound holds, $d \leq n - k + 1$. In case of equality, the code is called maximum distance separable (MDS). The most famous MDS codes are Reed–Solomon codes which are used in many applications, and in particular in secret-sharing schemes. Some properties of MDS codes are recalled in the following lemma.

Lemma 1.6.6. *Let C be an $[n, k, d]$-code. Then, the following statements are equivalent:*

(1) *the minimum distance $d_{\min}$ of C is such that $d_{\min} = n - k + 1$;*
(2) *any k columns of a generator matrix of C are linearly independent;*
(3) *$C^\perp$ is an $[n, n - k, k + 1]$-MDS code.*

1.7. Code-Based Constructions of Secret-Sharing Schemes

McEliece and Sarwate [34] were the first to observe a connection between secret-sharing and error-correcting codes. Then some general relationships between linear codes and secret-sharing schemes were established by Massey [31] and Blakley and Kabatianskii [8].

In terms of vector spaces, Brickell [12] studied also this kind of secret-sharing schemes. A generalization of this approach was given by Bertilsson [6] and then by van Dijk [41].

Two approaches can be considered for the construction of secret-sharing schemes based on linear codes. These two constructions can be described as follows.

1.7.1. Construction 1

The first construction uses an $[n, k, d]$ linear code C over $\mathbb{F}_q$ ($k \geq 2$) with generator matrix $G = (g_0, \ldots, g_n)$. Recall that G is a $k \times n$ matrix, thus, g_i are vectors of length k. Let P_0 be the dealer and $P_i, 1 \leq i \leq n$, be the participants. The dealer chooses a vector $u = (s = u_0, \ldots, u_{k-1}) \in \mathbb{F}_q^k$ whose first coordinate is the secret s and the other coordinates are chosen randomly. He calculates the codeword $y = (s_0, \ldots, s_{n-1}) \in \mathbb{F}_q^n$ corresponding to this information vector u as $y = uG$. The dealer P_0 gives the share s_i to participant P_i. Notice that the vector of shares y is a linear combination of the rows of the generator matrix of the code G. We have

$$(s, u_1, \ldots, u_{k-1})G = (s_1, \ldots, s_n).$$

Moreover, it is easy to see that a set of shares $\{s_{i_1}, s_{i_2}, \ldots, s_{i_m}\}$ determines the secret s if and only if the vector $e_1 = (1, 0, \ldots, 0)^T$ is a linear combination of $g_{i_1}, g_{i_2}, \ldots, g_{i_m}$, where g_i is the ith column of G. Furthermore, the secret-sharing scheme is perfect and ideal.

The secret recovering procedure goes as follows. Given a set of shares $\{s_{i_1}, s_{i_2}, \ldots, s_{i_m}\}$ which can determine the secret, the group of m participants solves the equation

$$e_1 = \sum_{j=1}^{m} x_j g_{i_j}$$

to obtain the combination of the columns of G which is equal to e_1. Then the secret is

$$s = u \cdot e_1 = \sum_{j=1}^{m} x_j u \cdot g_{i_j} = \sum_{j=1}^{m} x_j s_{i_j}.$$

Thus, we can state the following theorem.

Theorem 1.7.1. *Let C be an $[n, k, d]$-code over $\mathbb{F}_q$ with generator matrix $G = [g_1, \ldots, g_n]$. The access structure of the secret-sharing scheme based on G with respect to the first construction is given by*

$$\mathcal{A} = \left\{ \{P_i \; : \; i \in \mathrm{supp}((x_1, \ldots, x_n))\} \; : \; e_1 = \sum_{j=1}^{m} x_j g_{i_j} \right\}.$$

This theorem shows that the access structure depends on the choice of the underlying generator matrix G.

Secret-sharing schemes based on MDS codes over $\mathbb{F}_q$ with respect to the first construction were investigated by Renvall and Ding in [35]. Their access structures are known and documented in the following theorems.

Theorem 1.7.2. *Let G be a generator matrix of an $[n, k, n-k+1]$-MDS code C defined over $\mathbb{F}_q$. In the secret-sharing scheme based on G with respect to the first construction, any k shares determine the secret.*

Theorem 1.7.3. *Let G be a generator matrix of an $[n, k, n-k+1]$-code C defined over $\mathbb{F}_q$ such that its ith column is a multiple of e_1.*

In the secret-sharing scheme based on G with respect to the first construction, a set of shares determines the secret if and only if it contains the ith share or its cardinality is no less than k.

Theorem 1.7.3 is interesting because it describes an access structure which can have some useful applications. For example, in a company, any group containing the director can obtain the secret. Moreover, if a group does not contain the director, it must contain at least k participants to obtain the secret. In fact it is always possible to form a generator matrix whose one column is e_1 by taking adequate linear combinations of some rows of the matrix.

Theorem 1.7.4. *Let G be a generator matrix of an $[n, k, n-k+1]$-code C over $\mathbb{F}_q$ such that e_1 is a linear combination of g_1 and g_2, but not a multiple of any of them, where g_i denotes the ith column vector of G. The access structure of the secret-sharing scheme based on G with respect to the first construction is then described as follows:*

(1) *any set of k shares determines the secret;*
(2) *a set of shares with cardinality $k-2$ or less determines the secret if and only if the set contains both s_1 and s_2;*
(3) *a set of $k-1$ shares $\{s_{i_1}, s_{i_2}, \ldots, s_{i_{k-1}}\}$*

  • *determines the secret when it contains both s_1 and s_2;*
  • *cannot determine the secret when it contains one and only one of s_1 and s_2;*
  • *determines the secret if and only if $\text{Rank}(e_1, g_{i_1}, \ldots, g_{i_{k-1}}) = k-1$ when it contains none of s_1 and s_2.*

Theorem 1.7.5. *Let G be a generator matrix of an $[n, k, n-k+1]$-code C over $\mathbb{F}_q$. The secret-sharing scheme based on G with respect to the first construction is a (k, n)-threshold scheme if and only if e_1 is not a linear combination of any $k-1$ columns of G.*

The following theorem, also presented in [35], gives a relation between access structure and the minimum distance of the code when considering the first construction.

Theorem 1.7.6. *Let G be a generator matrix of an $[n, k, n-k+1]$-code C over $\mathbb{F}_q$. In the secret-sharing scheme based on G with respect to the first construction, if each of two sets of shares $\{s_{i_1}, \ldots, s_{i_l}\}$ and*

$\{t_{j_1}, \ldots, t_{j_m}\}$ *determines the secret, but no subset of any of them can do so, then*

$$|\{i_1, \ldots, i_l\} \cup \{j_1, \ldots, j_m\}| - |\{i_1, \ldots, i_l\} \cap \{j_1, \ldots, j_m\}| \geq d^\perp,$$

where $d^\perp$ is the minimum distance of the dual code C.

The access structure of a secret-sharing scheme built using the first construction may be very complex. Few investigations have been made on the subject.

Shamir scheme: We already saw that Shamir secret-sharing scheme has originally been presented in terms of polynomials. We show that it is in fact a scheme based on a linear code which is MDS.

Consider the information vector (which is kept secret) $a = (a_0, a_1, \ldots, a_{k-1})$, where $a_0 = s$ and the other coordinates are chosen randomly in the considered field. This vector defines a polynomial $f(x) = a_0 + a_1 x + \cdots + a_{k-1} x^{k-1}$. The vector of shares is the codeword $c = (f(\alpha_1), f(\alpha_2), \ldots, f(\alpha_n))$, where all the α_i are distinct. Let G be the generator matrix of this $[n, k]$-code

$$G = \begin{pmatrix} 1 & 1 & 1 & \cdots & 1 \\ \alpha_1 & \alpha_2 & \alpha_3 & \cdots & \alpha_n \\ \alpha_1^2 & \alpha_2^2 & \alpha_3^2 & \cdots & \alpha_n^2 \\ \vdots & \vdots & \vdots & \vdots & \vdots \\ \alpha_1^{k-1} & \alpha_2^{k-1} & \alpha_3^{k-1} & \cdots & \alpha_n^{k-1} \end{pmatrix}.$$

We have

$$c = aG.$$

The matrix G is the transpose of a Vandermonde matrix whose determinant is known to be non-zero (since all α_i are distinct). Thus, any k columns in G are linearly independent. By Lemma 1.6.6, this means that the minimum distance of the code is $d = n - k + 1$ (i.e. the code is MDS) and the code can correct $d - 1 = n - k$ erasures. Thus participants are able to obtain the full codeword as soon as they know k coordinates.

We can also consider the $[n + 1, k]$ code of generator matrix $G' = (e_1, G)$, where $e_1 = (1, 0, \ldots, 0)^T$. This latter code is also

MDS with parameters $[n + 1, k, d + 1]$. The generated codeword is $(f(0), f(\alpha_1), f(\alpha_2), \ldots, f(\alpha_n))$, where $f(0)$ is the secret and the other coordinates are the shares. Now, if participants know k coordinates, they can retrieved the full codeword including the secret which is in the first coordinate.

In fact, we can notice that there is an equivalence between the existence of a (k, n)-linear threshold secret-sharing scheme and a $[n + 1, k]$ MDS code.

Remark 1.7.7. The code used to construct the Shamir secret-sharing scheme is a Reed–Solomon code, as was observed in [34].

Blakley scheme: Blakley scheme can be presented in terms of hyperplane geometry: to implement a (t, n)-threshold scheme, each of the n users is given a hyper-plane equation in a t-dimensional space over a finite field such that each hyperplane passes through a certain point. The intersection point of the hyperplanes is the secret. The secret can be retrieved by any group of t participants.

An affine hyperplane in a t-dimensional space with coordinates in a field $\mathbb{F}_q$ can be described by a linear equation of the following general form:

$$a_1 x_1 + a_2 x_2 + \cdots + a_t x_t = b.$$

The intersection of any t of these hyperplanes gives the intersection point. The secret can be any of the coordinates of the intersection point or any function of the coordinates. We take the secret to be the first coordinate of the point of intersection.

Let $x = (x_1, \ldots, x_n) \in \mathbb{F}_q^n$ be the secret point whose first coordinate is the secret (i.e. $x_1 = s$) and the other ones are random. The dealer construct randomly the $t \times n$ matrix G with coordinates $a_{ij} \in \mathbb{F}_q$. Then he considers the linear system $Gx = y$, where $y = (s_1, \ldots, s_n)$. The dealer sends to the ith participant the value s_i along with the ith row of G. In fact, the whole matrix G can also be made public once and for all. Any group $S = \{i_1, \ldots, i_t\}$ of t participants can retrieve the secret by forming the matrix G_S and solve the equation $G_S x = s_S$, where s_S is the vector of shares of the t participants. The secret is the first coordinate of x. In order to get a solution G_S must be invertible which is the case if a Vandermonde matrix is chosen.

Blakley's scheme is less space-efficient than Shamir's; while Shamir's scheme is ideal, Blakley's shares are t times larger than the secret, where t is the threshold number of players. Blakley's scheme can be tightened by adding restrictions on which planes are usable as shares. The resulting scheme is equivalent to Shamir's polynomial system.

1.7.2. Construction 2

Secret-sharing schemes based on codes with respect to the second construction were considered by Massey. The two constructions may seem different but they are related. In the first approach all the shares form a complete codeword of the code, while in the second one all the shares form only part of a codeword. But as remarked by Van Dijk [42] we can switch from the second method to the first one since the generator matrix of the first method is obtained by puncturing the generator matrix of the second method.

In 1993, James Massey [31, 32] showed that a perfect and ideal secret-sharing scheme can be constructed using a linear code C. He introduced the notion of minimal codewords of a code and pointed out the relationship between access structures and minimal codewords of $C^{\perp}$.

The second construction uses an $[N = n + 1, k, d]$ linear code C over $\mathbb{F}_q$ (all the codes considered in this chapter are defined over $\mathbb{F}_q$). Let $G = (g_0, g_1, \ldots, g_n)$ be a generator matrix of C (it is a $k \times (n+1)$ matrix). The secret is denoted $s \in \mathbb{F}_q$ and the participants are $P_1, P_2, \ldots, P_n$.

The dealer computes the shares by randomly choosing a vector

$$u = (u_0, \ldots, u_{k-1}) \in \mathbb{F}_q^k$$

such that

$$s = u g_0.$$

In practice, the dealer can randomly select $k - 1$ coordinates and then compute the kth in order to obtain the right property. Thus, there are q^{k-1} possible such u. This vector u is seen as an information vector and the dealer computes the codeword

$$y = uG = (s, s_1, \ldots, s_n).$$

The first coordinate of y is the secret s and the other coordinates are the shares corresponding to the secret.

Then the dealer P_0 gives the share s_i to participant P_i, $(1 \leq i \leq n)$.

The vector of shares y is a linear combination of the rows of G. Moreover, any group $S = \{P_{i_1}, \ldots, P_{i_m}\}$ of m participants can retrieve the secret if and only if g_0 is a linear combination of $g_{i_1}, \ldots, g_{i_m}$. Therefore, the access structure of the scheme is

$$\mathcal{A} = \left\{ \{P_{i_1}, \ldots, P_{i_m}\} : \begin{array}{c} 1 \leq i_1 < \cdots < i_m \leq n \text{ and} \\ g_0 \text{ is a linear combination of } g_{i_1}, \ldots, g_{i_m} \end{array} \right\}.$$

If g_0 is not a linear combination of $g_{i_1}, \ldots, g_{i_m}$, the set of shares $\{s_{i_1}, \ldots, s_{i_m}\}$ gives no information about s. Thus, the secret-sharing scheme is perfect.

Suppose m participants pool their shares $t_{i_1}, \ldots, t_{i_m}$. This set is qualified if and only if there exists in the dual code $\mathcal{C}^\perp$ a codeword

$$c^* = (1, 0, \ldots, 0, \lambda_{i_1}, 0, \ldots, 0, \lambda_{i_m}, 0, \ldots, 0)$$

of Hamming weight at least 2. Equivalently, we have

$$g_0 = -\sum_{j=1}^{m} \lambda_{i_j} g_{i_j}.$$

Since $s = ug_0$, the secret s can be computed as

$$s = ug_0 = -\sum_{j=1}^{m} \lambda_{i_j} ug_{i_j} = -\sum_{j=1}^{m} \lambda_{i_j} t_{i_j}.$$

The scheme being monotone, a group covering a qualified group is also qualified. Thus, the set of qualified groups can be deduced from the set of minimal qualified groups (which is a spanning set of the set of qualified groups). This means that in order to obtain the access structure it is sufficient to determine the set of minimal qualified groups.

In order to find minimal qualified groups, we introduce the notion of minimal codewords:

Definition 1.7.8. A codeword $c \in \mathcal{C}$ is called a *minimal codeword* if its first coordinate is 1 and covers no other codeword whose first coordinate is 1.

Remark 1.7.9. Notice that the notion of minimal codeword is more stringent than that of minimal vector.

Example 1.7.10. Consider again Example 1.6.2. The dual code $\mathcal{C}^{\perp}$ is a $[5, 3, 1]$ linear binary code with generator matrix

$$G = \begin{pmatrix} 0 & 1 & 1 & 0 & 0 \\ 0 & 0 & 0 & 1 & 1 \\ 1 & 0 & 0 & 0 & 0 \end{pmatrix}.$$

The codeword (11111) is not a minimal codeword since it covers 2 other codewords: (11100) and (10011). Indeed, the minimal codewords of $\mathcal{C}^{\perp}$ are (11100) and (10011).

In order to find the set of qualified groups, it is enough to find the set of minimal qualified groups. In fact, Massey shows in [31] that there is a one-to-one correspondence between the set of minimal qualified groups and the set of minimal codewords of $\mathcal{C}^{\perp}$. Therefore, searching for the access structure of the scheme means determining the minimal codewords of $\mathcal{C}^{\perp}$. In other words, the set of groups A such that

$$A = \{P_i : i \in \text{supp}(c) : c \text{ is a minimal codeword of } \mathcal{C}^{\perp}\}$$

is a spanning set for the set of qualified groups. We can see that, unlike the first construction, the access structure of the secret-sharing scheme is independent of the choice of the generator of the code.

Example 1.7.11. Let C be a $[6, 4, 2]$-linear code over $\mathbb{F}_5$ with generator matrix

$$G = \begin{pmatrix} 1 & 0 & 0 & 0 & 4 & 0 \\ 0 & 1 & 0 & 0 & 4 & 1 \\ 1 & 0 & 1 & 0 & 3 & 1 \\ 0 & 0 & 0 & 1 & 0 & 4 \end{pmatrix}$$

and parity-check matrix

$$H = \begin{pmatrix} 1 & 0 & 0 & 1 & 1 & 1 \\ 0 & 1 & 1 & 4 & 0 & 4 \end{pmatrix}.$$

Suppose the secret is $s = 3 \in \mathbb{F}_5$. The dealer chooses $u = (1123)$ and computes the codeword $t = uG = (312340)$. Thus, t_0 is the secret and the shares are $t_1 = 1$, $t_2 = 2$, $t_3 = 3$, $t_4 = 4$, $t_5 = 0$. The dealer then sends the share t_i to participant p_i. The set of codewords whose first coefficient is 1 is

$$\{(100111), (111010), (122414), (133313), (144212)\}$$

and the set of minimal codewords is

$$\{(100111), (111010)\}.$$

Therefore, the set $\{\{p_3, p_4, p_5\},\ \{p_1, p_2, p_4\}\}$ is a spanning set for the set of qualified groups.

Unfortunately, determining the minimal codewords is hard for general linear codes, which means that obtaining the access structures of a scheme based on general linear codes is also hard [19, 28]. Renvall and Ding [35] show that the minimum distance $d^\perp$ of $C^\perp$ gives a lower bound on the size of any minimal qualified group in the secret-sharing scheme based on C.

Theorem 1.7.12. *Let C be an $[n, k, d]$-code. In the secret-sharing scheme based on C with respect to the second construction, any set of $d^\perp - 2$ or fewer shares do not give any information on the secret, and there is at least one set of $d^\perp$ shares that determines the secret.*

The following theorem, due to Ding and Yuan in [19], describes the access structure of the secret-sharing scheme based on the dual of a minimal linear code.

Theorem 1.7.13. *Let C be an $[n + 1, k, d]$-code, and let $H = [h_0, h_1, \ldots, h_n]$ be its parity-check matrix. If $C^\perp$ is minimal, then in the secret-sharing scheme based on C with respect to the second construction, the set of participants is $P = \{P_1, P_2, \ldots, P_n\}$, and there are altogether q^{n-k} minimal qualified groups.*

- *When $d = 2$, the access structure is as follows. If h_i is a multiple of h_0, $1 \le i \le n$, then participant P_i must be in every minimal qualified group. If h_i is not a multiple of h_0, $1 \le i \le n$, then participant P_i must be in $(q - 1)q^{n-k-1}$ out of q^{n-k} minimal qualified groups.*

- When $d \geq 3$, for any fixed $1 \leq t \leq \min(n - k, d - 2)$ every group of t participants is involved in $(q - 1)^t q^{n-k-t}$ out of q^{n-k} minimal qualified groups.

Example 1.7.14. Let C be the binary code of length $n + 1 = 15$, dimension $k = 11$, minimum distance $d = 3$ and generator matrix

$$G = \begin{pmatrix}
1 & 0 & 0 & 0 & 0 & 0 & 0 & 0 & 0 & 0 & 0 & 1 & 1 & 0 & 0 \\
0 & 1 & 0 & 0 & 0 & 0 & 0 & 0 & 0 & 0 & 0 & 0 & 1 & 1 & 0 \\
0 & 0 & 1 & 0 & 0 & 0 & 0 & 0 & 0 & 0 & 0 & 0 & 0 & 1 & 1 \\
0 & 0 & 0 & 1 & 0 & 0 & 0 & 0 & 0 & 0 & 0 & 1 & 1 & 0 & 1 \\
0 & 0 & 0 & 0 & 1 & 0 & 0 & 0 & 0 & 0 & 0 & 1 & 0 & 1 & 0 \\
0 & 0 & 0 & 0 & 0 & 1 & 0 & 0 & 0 & 0 & 0 & 1 & 0 & 1 \\
0 & 0 & 0 & 0 & 0 & 0 & 1 & 0 & 0 & 0 & 0 & 1 & 1 & 1 & 0 \\
0 & 0 & 0 & 0 & 0 & 0 & 0 & 1 & 0 & 0 & 0 & 0 & 1 & 1 & 1 \\
0 & 0 & 0 & 0 & 0 & 0 & 0 & 0 & 1 & 0 & 0 & 1 & 1 & 1 & 1 \\
0 & 0 & 0 & 0 & 0 & 0 & 0 & 0 & 0 & 1 & 0 & 1 & 0 & 1 & 1 \\
0 & 0 & 0 & 0 & 0 & 0 & 0 & 0 & 0 & 0 & 1 & 1 & 0 & 0 & 1
\end{pmatrix}.$$

Its dual is generated by

$$H = \begin{pmatrix}
1 & 0 & 0 & 0 & 1 & 0 & 0 & 1 & 1 & 0 & 1 & 0 & 1 & 1 & 1 \\
0 & 1 & 0 & 0 & 1 & 1 & 0 & 1 & 0 & 1 & 1 & 1 & 1 & 0 & 0 \\
0 & 0 & 1 & 0 & 0 & 1 & 1 & 0 & 1 & 0 & 1 & 1 & 1 & 1 & 0 \\
0 & 0 & 0 & 1 & 0 & 0 & 1 & 1 & 0 & 1 & 0 & 1 & 1 & 1 & 1
\end{pmatrix}$$

and contains 16 codewords. This code is equivalent to the binary Hamming code of length 15. The $2^{n-k} = 8$ minimal qualified groups are

$$\{4, 7, 8, 10, 12, 13, 14\}, \quad \{1, 5, 8, 9, 11, 13, 14\}, \quad \{1, 2, 6, 9, 10, 12, 14\},$$
$$\{2, 4, 5, 6, 7, 11, 14\}, \quad \{2, 3, 4, 5, 9, 12, 13\}, \quad \{1, 2, 3, 7, 10, 11, 13\},$$
$$\{1, 3, 5, 6, 7, 8, 12\}, \quad \{3, 4, 6, 8, 9, 10, 11\}.$$

We can see that every participant is involved in four minimal qualified groups, every group of two participants is involved in two minimal qualified groups and every group of three participants is involved in one minimal qualified group.

Example 1.7.15. Let C be the binary cyclic code of length $n + 1 = 9$, dimension $k = 7$, minimum distance $d = 2$ and generator matrix

$$G = \begin{pmatrix} 1 & 0 & 0 & 0 & 0 & 0 & 0 & 1 & 1 \\ 0 & 1 & 0 & 0 & 0 & 0 & 0 & 1 & 0 \\ 0 & 0 & 1 & 0 & 0 & 0 & 0 & 0 & 1 \\ 0 & 0 & 0 & 1 & 0 & 0 & 0 & 1 & 1 \\ 0 & 0 & 0 & 0 & 1 & 0 & 0 & 1 & 0 \\ 0 & 0 & 0 & 0 & 0 & 1 & 0 & 0 & 1 \\ 0 & 0 & 0 & 0 & 0 & 0 & 1 & 1 & 1 \end{pmatrix}.$$

Its dual is generated by

$$H = \begin{pmatrix} 1 & 0 & 1 & 1 & 0 & 1 & 1 & 0 & 1 \\ 0 & 1 & 1 & 0 & 1 & 1 & 0 & 1 & 1 \end{pmatrix}.$$

Since $h_3 = h_6 = h_0$, participants P_3 and P_6 are dictators: they are involved in all qualified groups.

The second construction has been studied in many different works. We can mention the work of Anderson, Ding, Helleseth and Kløve [2] which deals with codes having few words and the relations between t-designs and access structures. In 2005, Carlet, Ding and Yuan [15] used perfect nonlinear functions to construct several classes of linear codes and analyze the access structures of the secret-sharing schemes based on the dual of these codes. In 2008, Dougherty, Mesnager and Solé [20] considered self-dual codes to construct secret-sharing schemes. Secret-sharing schemes based on additive codes over $\mathbb{F}_4$ and their connections with t-designs were considered by Kim and Lee in [26].

1.8. Multisecret-Sharing Schemes

A *multisecret-sharing scheme* is a protocol to share m arbitrarily related secrets $s_1, \ldots, s_m$ among a set of n participants $\{P_1, \ldots, P_n\}$. It is an important variant of secret-sharing scheme which arises when multiple secrets must be distributed with different thresholds to the participants [4, 11, 40, 43]. Jackson *et al.* [24] studied the case where each secret s_i is associated with a threshold t_i. In this scheme, called *multisecret threshold schemes*, only a group of more than t_i participants can recover s_i. Blundo *et al.* [11] have shown that in order to obtain unconditional security for multisecret threshold schemes, the size of each share must be, at least, linear in the number of secrets. These lower bounds have been supplemented by more recent work from Masucci [33] who presented a weaker notion of security for multisecret sharing schemes in unconditional settings, and gave some lower bounds for the size of each share. Herranz *et al.* [22] then proved that each share in multisecret threshold schemes must be linear in the number of secrets. Multisecret sharing scheme is always very studied as shown by very recent articles on the subject (see for example [1, 13, 14]).

We assume that each element of the secret space S_i is equally likely to be the ith secret for each i such that $1 \leq i \leq k$. The share space is denoted T_i for $1 \leq i \leq n$. We consider the case where both spaces are equal to $\mathbb{F}_q$. Let $S = S_1 \times \cdots \times S_k$ and $T = T_1 \times \cdots \times T_n$ be product spaces.

Definition 1.8.1. Let $s = (s_1, \ldots, s_k)$ be the vector consisting of k secrets and $t = (t_1, \ldots, t_n)$ be the set of the shares. A (k, m, n)-multisecret sharing scheme consists of two protocols, Share and Reconstruct.

The Share function

$$f : S \to T$$
$$f(s) = t$$

is a function that constructs the n shares from the k secrets. Share t_i is given to the ith participant.

The Reconstruction phase consists in recovering the secret from the shares. In fact, any group of m shares is able to reconstruct secret s_j but no group of strictly less than m shares is able to reconstruct the secret.

A multisecret-sharing scheme is said to be *linear* if for all $a, a' \in \mathbb{F}_q$ and all $s, s' \in S$, $f(as + a's') = af(s) + a'f(s')$. The scheme is called *affine* if there is a constant λ such that $f - \lambda$ is linear. In fact, if the scheme is linear, it must be of the form $f(s) = sG$, where G is $k \times n$ matrix with rank k. Then whenever we define such a scheme, we define an $[n, k, d]$-code over $\mathbb{F}_q$ and the Share function is just an encoding mapping of a linear code.

For a group of m participants, recovering the secret is equivalent to solving a linear equation. Suppose the group knows the shares $t_{i_1}, \ldots, t_{i_m}$ ($m \leq n$) and let G' be a submatrix of G consisting of the t_{i_1}th, $\ldots, t_{i_m}$th columns of G. The linear equation is

$$sG' = (t_{i_1}, \ldots, t_{i_m}) \tag{1.8.1}$$

and solving this equation is not difficult, for example using Gaussian elimination method.

We consider here the particular case $m = k$ which is adapted to construct linear multisecret-sharing schemes based on MDS codes.

Theorem 1.8.2. *A multisecret-sharing scheme is a $[k, k, n]$-threshold scheme if and only if*

(1) *the linear code C with generator matrix G is MDS and*
(2) *any set of $k-1$ column vectors of G generates a $[k, k-1, 2]$-MDS code.*

This means that in order to obtain a $[k, k, n]$-threshold scheme, we need a $[n, k, n-k+1]$-code and k codes with parameters $[k, k-1, 2]$.

In a $[k, k, n]$-multisecret-sharing scheme, each share contains the same amount of information about the multisecret, and two groups of shares give the same amount of information about the multisecret if and only if these two groups have the same number of shares.

We can use a Reed–Solomon code to construct such a scheme. Let $\alpha = (\alpha_1, \ldots, \alpha_n)$, where α_i are distinct element of $\mathbb{F}_q$. It is well known that the following generator matrix:

$$G = \begin{pmatrix} 1 & 1 & 1 & \cdots & 1 \\ \alpha_1 & \alpha_2 & \alpha_3 & \cdots & \alpha_n \\ \alpha_1^2 & \alpha_2^2 & \alpha_3^2 & \cdots & \alpha_n^2 \\ \vdots & \vdots & \vdots & \vdots & \vdots \\ \alpha_1^{k-1} & \alpha_2^{k-1} & \alpha_3^{k-1} & \cdots & \alpha_n^{k-1} \end{pmatrix}$$

generates an MDS $[n, k, n-k+1]$-code. In order that condition (2) of Theorem 1.8.2 holds, we have to choose α_i such that: any $(k-1) \times (k-1)$ submatrix of G has rank $k-1$ if and only if for any set of indices $1 \le i_1 < \cdots < i_{k-1} \le n$ we have

$$\sum_{1 \le u_1 < \cdots < u_j \le k-1} \alpha_{i_{u_1}} \alpha_{i_{u_2}} \cdots \alpha_{i_{u_j}} \ne 0 \quad \text{for all } j = 1, 2, \dots, k-2.$$

Then using Eq. (1.8.1), we can obtain the vector of shares.

Example 1.8.3. We consider the code of parameters $[5, 3, 3]$ over F_{13} with generator matrix

$$G = \begin{pmatrix} 1 & 1 & 1 & 1 & 1 \\ 1 & 2 & 4 & 8 & 3 \\ 1 & 4 & 3 & 12 & 9 \end{pmatrix}.$$

In this matrix, condition (2) of Theorem 1.8.2 is met. Therefore, G provides a $[3, 3, 5]$-multisecret threshold scheme.

References

[1] A. Alahmadi, A. Altassan, A. AlKenani, S. Çalkavur, H. Shoaib and P. Solé. A multisecret-sharing scheme based on LCD codes. *Mathematics*, 8:272, 2020, doi:10.3390/math8020272.

[2] R.J. Anderson, C. Ding, T. Helleseth and T. Kløve. How to build robust shared control systems. *Des. Codes Cryptography*, 15(2):111–124, 1998.

[3] A. Beimel. Secret-sharing schemes: a survey. In Chee Y.M. *et al.*, editor, *Coding and Cryptology. IWCC 2011.* Lecture Notes in Computer Science, Vol. 6639. Springer, Berlin, https://doi.org/10.1007/978-3-642-20901-7_2.

[4] A. Beimel, A. Ben-Efraim, C. Padro and I. Tyomkin. Multilinear secret-sharing schemes. In *Theory of Cryptography-TCC 2014*, pp. 394–418, 2014.

[5] M. Ben-Or, S. Goldwasser and A. Wigderson. Completeness theorems for non-cryptographic fault-tolerant distributed computation. In *STOC'88*, pp. 1–10, 1988.

[6] M. Bertilsson, Linear codes and secret sharing, PhD thesis, Linköping University, 1993.

[7] G. Blakley. Safeguarding cryptographic keys. *AFIPS Conf. Proc.*, 48:313–317, 1979.

[8] G. Blakley and G. Kabatianskii. *Linear algebra approach to secret sharing schemes.* Selected Papers from the Workshop on Information Protection, Error Control, Cryptology, and Speech Compression, Springer-Verlag, Berlin, Heidelberg, December 1993.

[9] K. Bozkurt, K. Kaya, A. Selçuk and A. Güloğlu. Threshold cryptography based on blakley secret sharing, *ICS*, 2008.

[10] C. Blundo, A. De Santis and U. Vaccaro. On secret sharing schemes. *Inform. Process. Lett.*, 65(1):2532, 1998.

[11] C. Blundo, A.D. Santis, G.D. Crescenzo, A.G. Gaggia and U. Vaccaro. Multi-secret sharing schemes. In *CRYPTO '94*, pp. 150–163, 1994.

[12] E. Brickell. Some ideal secret sharing schemes. In Quisquater J.J. and Vandewalle J. editors, *Advances in Cryptology, EUROCRYPT '89. EUROCRYPT 1989.* Lecture Notes in Computer Science, Vol. 434. Springer, Berlin, 1989, https://doi.org/10.1007/3-540-46885-4_45.

[13] S. Çalkavur and P. Solé. Multisecret-sharing schemes and bounded distance decoding of linear codes. *Int. J. Comput. Math.*, 94(1):107–114, 2017.

[14] S. Çalkavur and P. Solé. Some multisecret-sharing schemes over finite fields. *Mathematics*, 8:654, 2020, doi:10.3390/math8050654.

[15] C. Carlet, C. Ding and J. Yuan. Linear codes from perfect nonlinear mappings and their secret sharing schemes. *IEEE Trans. Inform. Theory*, 51(6):2089–2102, 2005.

[16] D. Chaum, C. Crepeau and I. Damgard. Multi-party unconditionally secure protokols. In *STOC'88*, pp. 11–19, 1988.

[17] B. Chor, S. Goldwasser, S. Micali and B. Awerbuch. Verifiable secret sharing and achieving simultaneity in the presence of faults. In *FOCS85*, pp. 383–395, 1985. doi:10.1109/SFCS.1985.64.

[18] R. Cramer, I.B. Damgard and J.B. Nielsen. *Secure Multiparty Computation and Secret Sharing.* Cambridge University Press, 2015, https://doi.org/10.1017/CBO9781107337756.

[19] C.S. Ding and J. Yuan. Covering and secret sharing with linear codes. In *Discrete Mathematics and Theoretical Computer Science*, Lecture Notes in Computer Science, Vol. 2731. Springer-Verlag, pp. 11–25, 2003.

[20] S.T. Dougherty, S. Mesnager and P. Solé. Secret-sharing schemes based on self-dual codes. In *Proc. 2008 Information Theory Workshop*, pp. 338–342. IEEE Press, 2008.

[21] S. Fehr and U. Maurer. Linear VSS and distributed commitments based on secret sharing and pairwise checks. In *CRYPTO'02*, Lecture Notes in Computer Science, Vol. 2442, pp. 565–580, 2002.

[22] J.J. Herranz, A. Ruiz and G. Saez. New results and applications for multi-secret sharing schemes. *Des. Codes Cryptography*, 73(3):841–864, 2014.

[23] Y. Ishai and E. Kushilevitz. Private simultaneous messages protocols with applications. In *Proc. of ISTCS'97*, IEEE Computer Society, pp. 174–184, 1997.

[24] W.-A. Jackson, K.M. Martin and C.M. O'Keefe. Multisecret threshold schemes. In *CRYPTO 1993*, pp. 126–135, 1993.

[25] E.D. Karnin, J.W. Greene and M.E. Hellman. On secret sharing systems. *IEEE Trans. Inform. Theory*, 29(1):3541, 1983.

[26] J.-L. Kim and N. Lee. Secret sharing schemes based on additive codes over GF(4). *Appl. Algebra Eng. Commun. Comput.*, 28(1):79–97, 2017.

[27] Y. Lindell. Secure multiparty computation (MPC), Cryptology ePrint Archive, Report 2020/300, 2020, https://eprint.iacr.org/2020/300.

[28] Z.H. Li, T. Xue and H. Lai. Secret sharing schemes from binary linear codes. *Inform. Sci.*, 180:4412–4419, 2011.

[29] J. Liu, S. Mesnager and L. Chen. Secret sharing schemes with general access structures. In Lin, D., Wang, X., Yung, M., editors, Information Security and Cryptology. Inscrypt 2015. Lecture Notes in Computer Science, Vol. 9589. Springer, Cham, 2016.

[30] F.J. MacWilliams and N.J.A. Sloane. *The Theory of Error Correcting Codes*. North-Holland, Amsterdam, 1977.

[31] J.L. Massey. Minimal codewords and secret sharing. In *Sixth Joint Swedish-Russian Workshop on Information Theory*, pp. 276–279, 1993.

[32] J.L. Massey. Some applications of coding theory in cryptography. In *Cryptography and Coding IV*, Formara Ltd, England, 1995.

[33] B. Masucci. Sharing multiple secrets: Models, schemes and analysis. *Des. Codes Cryptography*, 39(1):89–111, 2006.

[34] R.J. McEliece and D.V. Sarwate. On sharing secrets and Reed-Solomon codes. *Comm. ACM*, 24(9):583–584, 1981.

[35] A. Renvall and C. Ding. The access structure of some secret sharing schemes. In *Information Security and Privacy*, Lecture Notes in Computer Science, Vol. 1172, pp. 67–78. Springer, 1993.

[36] A. Shamir. How to share a secret. *Commun. ACM*, 22:612–613, 1979.

[37] A. Shamir, R. Rivest and L. Adleman. "Mental Poker", Technical Report LCS/TR-125, Massachusetts Institute of Technology, April 1979.

[38] G.J. Simmons. An introduction to shared secret and/or shared control schemes and their application. In *Contemporary Cryptology*, IEEE Press, New York, pp. 441–497.

[39] Y. Song and Z. Li. Secret sharing with a class of minimal linear codes. Preprint arXiv 1202.4058, 2012.

[40] C. Tartary, J. Pieprzyk and H. Wang. Verifiable multi-secret sharing schemes for multiple threshold access structures. In *Information Security and Cryptology, Third SKLOIS Conf., Inscrypt 2007*, Xining, China, August 31–September 5, 2007, Revised Selected Papers, pp. 167–181, 2007.

[41] M. van Dijk. A linear construction of secret sharing schemes. *Des. Codes Cryptography*, 12:161–201, 1997. https://doi.org/10.1023/A:1008259214236.

[42] M. van Dijk. *Secret key sharing and secret key generation*, Ph.D. thesis, TU Eindhoven, 1997.

[43] M. van Dijk, W.-A. Jackson and K.M. Martin. A general decomposition construction for incomplete secret sharing schemes. *Des. Codes Cryptography*, 3:301–321, 1998.

[44] D. Welsh. *Matroid Theory*. Academic Press, London, 1976.

[45] A. Yao. Protocols for secure computations. In *FOCS. 23rd Annual Symp. Foundations of Computer Science (FOCS 1982)*, pp. 160–164. doi:10.1109/SFCS.1982.88.

Chapter 2

Massey Scheme

2.1. On the Number of Minimal Codewords

This chapter focuses on the maximum and minimum number of minimal codewords in binary linear codes. Minimal codewords have been used in decoding algorithms and in secret sharing schemes. Massey showed that in a secret sharing schemes based on linear code, there is a one-to-one correspondence between the minimum authorized groups and certain minimal codewords of the dual code with a non-zero first coordinate.

2.1.1. Introduction

Given a linear code, it is important to know its minimal codewords. However, in general, this is a very hard task and it is completed only for a few classes of codes. In this section, C denotes a binary linear code of length n and dimension k. We define $M(C)$ to be the number of its minimal codewords. We are interested with the following question:

What is the maximum and minimum number of minimal codewords a code C can have?

Answering this question may give us an idea on which access structures can be realized by a scheme based on linear codes. For example, suppose we are given the number of minimal groups in an access structure. If this number exceeds the maximal number for some n and k, then we know that this access structure cannot be realized by an SSS based on an $[n, n - k]$ binary linear code.

This question have been considered before in the setting of graphs and matroids. If C is the cycle code of a connected graph G with m vertices and n edges, then C is a binary $[n, n - m + 1]$ linear code. The minimal codewords of C are exactly the characteristic vectors of the cycles in G. Hence, the question above can be stated in terms of cycles in connected graphs. This problem was studied by Entringer and Slater in [16] where they showed that a connected graph with m vertices and n edges cannot have 2^{n-m+1} cycles. In [15], Dósa, Szalkai and Laflamme investigated the maximum and minimum number of circuits of matroids given the size and rank. The question above is a special case of this problem since the minimal codewords of C are the circuits of the matroid represented by the parity-check matrix of C.

The material in this section can be found in [2–4].

2.1.2. Maximum number of minimal codewords

Let $\mathbf{C}[n, k]$ denote the set of all binary codes of length n and dimension k. We define

$$M(n, k) = \max\{M(C) \; : \; C \in \mathbf{C}[n, k]\},$$

that is, $M(n, k)$ is the maximum of $M(C)$ over all $[n, k]$-codes.

2.1.2.1. *Upper bounds*

We note that if C is of dimension k, then $M(C)$ is at most $2^k - 1$. Hence,

$$M(n, k) \leq 2^k - 1.$$

We will call this bound the *trivial upper bound*. It implies the bound for the number of cycles in a connected graph by Entringer and Slater.

A binary linear code C is *intersecting* if the supports of any two non-zero codewords are not disjoint. The trivial upper bound is met with equality for intersecting codes.

Lemma 2.1.1. *A binary linear code C of dimension k is intersecting if and only if $M(C) = 2^k - 1$.*

Proof. Suppose C is not intersecting. Then there exist two codewords u, v whose supports are disjoint. It follows that the sum $u + v$ is non-zero and is not a minimal codeword. Thus, $M(C) < 2^k - 1$. Conversely, suppose C has a non-minimal codeword u. Then there exists a codeword v such that $\operatorname{supp}(v) \subset \operatorname{supp}(u)$. This implies that the codewords v and $u + v$ have disjoint supports. □

The following theorem was proved in [15] and we present here a short independent proof.

Theorem 2.1.2. *If $\mathcal{M}$ is a matroid on n elements and of rank r, then $\mathcal{M}$ has at most*

$$\binom{n}{r+1}$$

circuits (that is, minimal dependent sets).

Proof. The proof is by induction on n. Let B be a basis of $\mathcal{M}$. If $B = M$, then $r = n$ and the number of circuits is

$$0 = \binom{n}{r+1}.$$

So assume there is an element a not in B. Then $M - a$ has rank r, and has therefore, by induction, at most

$$\binom{n-1}{r+1}$$

circuits.

As all bases of $M - a$ have cardinality r, there are at most

$$\binom{n-1}{r}$$

bases of $M - a$. For each such basis B, $B \cup \{a\}$ has precisely one circuit (a so-called fundamental circuit). Every circuit containing a

is the fundamental circuit for some basis. Hence $\mathcal{M}$ has at most

$$\binom{n-1}{r}$$

circuits containing a. Therefore the total number of circuits is at most

$$\binom{n-1}{r+1} + \binom{n-1}{r} = \binom{n}{r+1}. \qquad \square$$

It is not difficult to see that the inequality in Theorem 2.1.2 is an equality if and only if the matroid $\mathcal{M}$ is uniform, that is all sets of cardinality r are maximal independent.

Corollary 2.1.3. *For all $1 \leq k \leq n$ we have $M(n,k) \leq \binom{n}{k-1}$.*

Proof. The minimal codewords of an $[n,k]$-code C are exactly the circuits of the matroid on n elements and rank $n - k$ associated with its dual code. $\qquad \square$

We refer to this bound as the *matroid bound*. This bound is tight for $k = 1, n$, and also for $k = n - 1$ as the dual of the repetition code shows.

We can also derive Corollary 2.1.3 from the following theorem.

Theorem 2.1.4. *For all $1 \leq k \leq n$, we have*

$$M(n,k) \leq M(n-1,k-1) + \binom{n-1}{k-1}.$$

Proof. Let H be the parity-check of C that realizes $M(n,k)$, and H' the matrix with column n removed. Assume, up to column reordering, that there is a basis of the column space not containing column n, or equivalently that the rank of H' is $n - k$. This is always possible if $k \geq 1$. Let x be a non-zero minimal codeword in C and discuss according to the value of x_n.

If $x_n = 0$, then the projection x' on the first $n - 1$ coordinates is a minimal codeword in $\ker(H') = \{y \in \mathbb{F}_2^{n-1} : H'y^T = 0^T\}$, an $[n-1, k-1]$ code. Therefore, there are at most $M(n-1, k-1)$ such vectors.

If $x_n = 1$, then the set of columns where the projection x' on the first $n - 1$ coordinates is non-zero form an independent set of the column space of H', because of the minimality property of x. There are at most

$$\binom{n-1}{n-k} = \binom{n-1}{k-1}$$

possible such x'. □

Note that Corollary 2.1.3 also follows from Theorem 2.1.4 by induction on k. Clearly, the bound is true for $k = 1$, since $M(n, 1) = 1 = \binom{n}{0}$. Assuming $M(n - 1, k - 1) \leq \binom{n-1}{k-2}$, the induction step is completed using Pascal's triangle.

Finally, we state, as Theorem 2.1.5, a bound for $M(n, k)$ from [1]. We refer to this bound as the *Agrell bound*.

Theorem 2.1.5. *For $\frac{k-1}{n} > \frac{1}{2}$ we have*

$$M(n, k) \leq \frac{2^k}{4n(\frac{k-1}{n} - \frac{1}{2})^2}.$$

2.1.2.2. Lower bounds

A random coding lower bound was proved in [5], namely

$$M(n, k)2^{n-k} \geq \sum_{j=0}^{n-k+1} \binom{n}{j} \prod_{i=0}^{j-2}(1 - 2^{-(n-k-i)}).$$

Another lower bound is as follows. Denote by $d(n, k)$ the largest minimum distance of an $[n, k]$-code. The following proposition is a direct consequence of [6].

Proposition 2.1.6. *For all $n \geq k \geq 1$, we have*

$$\sum_{i=1}^{\lfloor n/d(n,k) \rfloor} \binom{M(n, k)}{i} \geq 2^k - 1.$$

Proof. Let C be an $[n, k, d]$-code. By induction, it can be seen that every non-zero codeword can be written as a sum of at most

$\lfloor n/d \rfloor$ minimal codewords with pairwise disjoint supports. Hence, enumeration of such sums yields

$$\sum_{i=1}^{\lfloor n/d \rfloor} \binom{M(C)}{i} \geq 2^k - 1.$$

The result follows by choosing C such that $d = d(n, k)$. $\square$

This result shows that good codes cannot have too few minimum codewords. It is not very sharp. We only get $M(8, 4) \geq 5$, whereas the example of the extended Hamming code (an $[8, 4, 4]$-code) shows that $M(8, 4) \geq 14$.

2.1.2.3. *Tabulating $M(n, k)$*

Monotonicity properties: It is not difficult to show that $M(n, k) \leq M(n + 1, k)$ by adding a zero column to a code realizing $M(n, k)$. This trivial observation provides better bounds than the random coding bound for $k = 4$ and $n = 7, 8$, as well as for $k = 5$ and $n = 7, 8, 9$ and so on. It is not the case that $M(n, k) \leq M(n, k + 1)$ as the values of $M(4, k)$ already show. We conjecture, but cannot prove, that $M(n, k)$ is an unimodal function of k for fixed n.

Proposition 2.1.7. *For binary codes C, D, we have $M(C \oplus D) = M(C) + M(D)$.*

Proof. If u and v are minimal codewords of C and D, respectively, then $(u, 0)$ and $(0, v)$ are minimal codewords of $C \oplus D$. Conversely, we claim that all minimal codewords of the latter code arise in that way. Indeed, if (u, v) is a minimal codeword of $C \oplus D$, with both u and v non-zero, then $(u, v) = (u, 0) + (0, v)$ contradicting the minimality. $\square$

Using Proposition 2.1.7, we see that $M(n, k)$ is superadditive:

$$M(n + m, k + j) \geq M(n, k) + M(m, j).$$

Exact values: Trivial values are $M(n, 1) = 1$, and $M(n, n) = n$ for all $n \geq 1$. $M(n, n - 1)$ is already known from Corollary 2.1.3 but a direct elementary proof is tedious.

Proposition 2.1.8. $M(n, n - 1) = \binom{n}{2}$ *for $3 \leq n$.*

Proof. We claim that

$$M(n, n-1) = \max\left\{ \binom{x}{2} + (n-x) \; : \; 1 \le x \le n \right\}.$$

Denote for $x \ge 2, y \ge 1$ by P_x the $[x, x-1]$-parity-check code, and by U_y the $[y, y]$-universe code. By convention, we let $P_1 = \{0\}$, the zero code. It is immediate that $M(P_x) = \binom{x}{2}$, with the convention $\binom{1}{2} = 0$. Also $M(U_y) = y$ because minimal codewords have weight one. We see that, by Proposition 2.1.7, $M(P_x \oplus U_{n-x}) = \binom{x}{2} + (n-x) =: f(x)$. The quadratic function $f(x)$ is increasing for $x \in [1, n]$. Since $f(n) = \binom{n}{2}$, we are done. $\qquad\square$

An exact value for $M(n, n-2)$ is possible for n a multiple of 3.

Theorem 2.1.9. *If $\mathcal{C}$ is an $[n, n-2, 2]$-code, then*

$$M(\mathcal{C}) \le \frac{n^3}{27} + 3\binom{\frac{n}{3}}{2},$$

with equality if n is a multiple of 3.

Proof. Let $\mathcal{C}$ be an $[n, n-2, 2]$-code. Since $2 \times 2 > n - (n-2) + 1$, the minimal codewords are by [1] those of weight 2 or 3. Let $a + b, a + c, b + c$ be the non-zero dual weights with $a + b + c = n$. Direct counting shows that the number of codewords of weight 3 is abc, and the number of codewords of weight 2 is $\binom{a}{2} + \binom{b}{2} + \binom{c}{2}$. Let

$$ub(a, b, c) = abc + \frac{a^2 - a + b^2 - b + c^2 - c}{2}.$$

The function ub being a symmetric function of the three *real* variables $a, b, c \ge 0$ is maximized under the constraint $a + b + c = n$, when $a = b = c = \frac{n}{3}$. Since $M(\mathcal{C}) \le ub(a, b, c)$, with a, b, c integers the result follows. $\qquad\square$

Corollary 2.1.10. *If $n \ge 3$, then*

$$M(n, n-2) \le \frac{n^3}{27} + 3\binom{\frac{n}{3}}{2},$$

with equality if n is a multiple of 3.

Table 2.1. $g(n)$ for $3 \leq n \leq 15$.

n	3	4	5	6	7	8	9	10	11	12	13	14	15
$g(n)$	2	2	2	3	3	3	4	4	4	4	5	5	6

Proof.   Proof by induction on n. Clearly $M(3,1) = 1$. If $\mathcal{C}$ is an $[n, n-2, d]$-code, then $d \leq 2$. If $d = 2$, the bound follows by Theorem 2.1.9. If $d = 1$, let u be a codeword of weight 1. Assume that $u_1 = 1$. Denote by $\mathcal{C}'$ the code shortened at coordinate 1. Thus $\mathcal{C} = \{0,1\} \oplus \mathcal{C}'$. We know by Proposition 2.1.7 that $M(\mathcal{C}) = 1 + M(\mathcal{C}')$. But $\mathcal{C}'$ is a $[n-1, n-3]$-code. The bound follows in that case by induction hypothesis.

If n is a multiple of 3, it is easy to construct $\mathcal{C}^{\perp}$ with single non-zero weight $2n/3$ such that no coordinate is zero ensuring that $\mathcal{C}$ has minimum distance at least 2. Minimum distance 3 is impossible by the Hamming bound. $\square$

Intersecting codes: We recall that a linear binary code meets the trivial bound with equality if and only if it is intersecting. Following [33], denote by $f(k)$ the shortest length of a binary linear intersecting code. Equivalently, there is a function $g(n)$ such that if $k \leq g(n)$, then there is an intersecting $[n, k]$-code; and there is not such a code if $k > g(n)$; thus, if $k \leq g(n)$, then $M(n, k) = 2^k - 1$, and if $k > g(n)$, then $M(n, k) \leq 2^k - 2$. The function $g(n)$, the inverse of f, is known exactly for $1 \leq n \leq 15$ [33] and given in Table 2.1.

Table of $M(n, k)$:   The symbols t, m, a in Tables 2.2 and 2.3 mean that the bounds are obtained as follows:

- t — The trivial bound;
- a — The Agrell bound;
- x — The bound of Corollary 2.1.10.

When the trivial bound is met with equality, the t is omitted. Empty entries correspond to $k > n$ in which case $M(n, k)$ is undefined. The lower bounds are derived by explicit constructions of codes $\mathcal{C}$ derived from the so-called Betten list of indecomposable codes [7], followed by an application of rule G or rule H of [1] to derive $M(\mathcal{C})$. Computations were done using MAGMA [10]. The codes realizing

Table 2.2. $M(n,k)$ for $3 \leq n \leq 15, 1 \leq k \leq 9$.

n/k	1	2	3	4	5	6	7	8	9
3	1	3	3						
4	1	3	6	4					
5	1	3	6	10	5				
6	1	3	7	11	15	6			
7	1	3	7	14	17	21	7		
8	1	3	7	14	$22\text{–}30^t$	25	28	8	
9	1	3	7	15	$26\text{–}30^t$	$33\text{–}62^t$	36	36	9
10	1	3	7	15	30	$42\text{–}62^t$	$48\text{–}126^t$	48	45
11	1	3	7	15	30	$52\text{–}62^t$	$66\text{–}126^t$	$69\text{–}254^t$	63
12	1	3	7	15	30	$54\text{–}62^t$	$90\text{–}126^t$	$103\text{–}254^t$	$95\text{–}384^a$
13	1	3	7	15	31	$58\text{–}62^t$	$94\text{–}126^t$	$151\text{–}254^t$	$149\text{–}510^t$
14	1	3	7	15	31	62	$106\text{–}126^t$	$159\text{–}254^t$	$245\text{–}510^t$
15	1	3	7	15	31	63	$108\text{–}126^t$	$171\text{–}254^t$	$245\text{–}510^t$

Table 2.3. $M(n,k)$ for $10 \leq n \leq 15, 10 \leq k \leq 15$.

n/k	10	11	12	13	14	15
10	10					
11	55	11				
12	82	66	12			
13	$130\text{–}532^a$	$102\text{–}103^x$	78	13		
14	$217\text{–}896^a$	$175\text{–}796^a$	$126\text{–}127^x$	91	14	
15	$385\text{–}1022^t$	$308\text{–}1228^a$	$221\text{–}1253^a$	155	105	15

$M(n,k)$ do not in general have the largest minimum distance, but they are in general indecomposable.

Cycle codes of graphs: Let $M_g(n,k)$ be the maximum number of minimal codewords over the set of all $[n,k]$ cycle codes, i.e. it is obtained by restricting $\mathbf{C}[n,k]$ to cycle codes in the definition of $M(n,k)$. The values for $M_g(n,k)$, $1 \leq k \leq 10$, $3 \leq n \leq 15$, are shown in Table 2.4. These values were obtained using MAGMA [10] and NAUTY, the graph generation program of B. McKay [23].

2.1.2.4.   *Asymptotic analysis*

We consider bounds on $M(n,k)$ for families of binary linear codes of lengths going to infinity and with rates approaching R. We define $\mu(R)$ as the asymptotic exponent of $M(n,k)$ for families of codes C

Table 2.4. $M_g(n,k)$ for $1 \leq k \leq 10$, $3 \leq n \leq 15$.

n/k	1	2	3	4	5	6	7	8	9	10
3	1									
4	1									
5	1	3								
6	1	3	7							
7	1	3	7							
8	1	3	7	13						
9	1	3	7	15	22					
10	1	3	7	15	24	37				
11	1	3	7	15	26	39				
12	1	3	7	15	29	42	63			
13	1	3	7	15	29	46	69	91		
14	1	3	7	15	29	51	75	108	133	
15	1	3	7	15	29	57	82	123	156	197

with rates approaching R, where R is the limsup of k/n. Formally,

$$\mu(R) = \limsup_{n\to\infty} \frac{1}{n} \log_2 M(n, \lceil Rn \rceil).$$

If, in this definition, we replace $\mathbf{C}[n,k]$ by the cycle codes of graphs with p vertices and q edges (where $n = q$, and $k = q - p + 1$), we obtain $\mu_g(R)$.

By the trivial upper bound, $\mu(R) \leq R$. The matroid bound implies that $\mu(R) \leq H(R)$, where H is Shannon's binary entropy function defined for $x \in [0,1]$ by

$$H(x) = -x \log_2 x - (1-x) \log_2(1-x).$$

The matroid bound is better than the trivial upper bound for $R > R_0 \approx 0.77$ where $H(R_0) = R_0$.

By averaging arguments (random coding), it was shown in [5] that for $R < 1/2$, we have

$$\mu(R) \geq R,$$

and for $R > 1/2$, we have

$$\mu(R) \geq H(R) - 1 + R.$$

We will prove an upper bound for the number of cycles in a graph with p vertices and q edges. This upper bound will then be used to determine $\mu_g(R)$.

Consider a path with vertices $v_1, v_2, \ldots, v_p$. A *multipath* is obtained from a path by replacing some edges with multiple edges. Let $f(q,p)$ denote the maximal number of paths from v_1 to v_p in a multipath with p vertices and q edges. This maximum is attained if no two edge multiplicities differ by more than 1 where the *multiplicity of an edge* is the number of multiple edges sharing the same end vertices.

Lemma 2.1.11. *If x, y are vertices in a graph G with p vertices and q edges, then G has at most $f(q,p)$ paths from x to y.*

Proof. The proof is by induction on p. If $p = 2$, the statement is trivial. So assume $p > 2$. Let d denote the degree of x, and let $x_1, x_2, \ldots, x_d$ be the neighbors of x. (Some of these neighbors may be identical.) By induction, $G - x$ has at most $f(q - d, p - 1)$ paths from x_i to y, for each $i = 1, 2, \ldots, d$. So G has at most $df(q - d, p - 1)$ paths from x to y. As $f(q - d, p - 1)$ is the number of paths between the ends in a multipath with $p - 1$ vertices and $q - d$ edges, we may interpret $df(q - d, p - 1)$ as the number of paths between the ends in a multipath with p vertices and q edges, where the first edge multiplicity in the multipath is d. By the maximum property of $f(q,p)$, we have

$$df(q - d, p - 1) \leq f(q,p),$$

which completes the proof. □

Theorem 2.1.12. *Let p, q be natural numbers ≥ 2. There exists a graph with p vertices, q edges, and at least $f(q - 1, p)$ cycles. If G is any graph with p vertices and q edges, then G has at most*

$$qf(q - 1, p)$$

cycles.

Proof. By the definition of f, there exists a multipath with p vertices, $q - 1$ edges, and precisely $f(q - 1, p)$ paths between the ends. If we add an edge between the ends, we get a graph with p vertices, q edges, and at least $f(q - 1, p)$ cycles.

To prove the last statement, consider any edge $e = xy$ in G. The number of cycles in G containing e is the number of paths in $G - e$

from x to y. By Lemma 2.1.11, this number is at most

$$f(q-1, p).$$

This completes the proof.   □

Theorem 2.1.13. *For $0 < R \le 0.5$,*

$$\mu_g(R) = R.$$

If R is of the form $1 - 1/t$ where t is a natural number ≥ 2, then

$$\mu_g(R) = -(1-R)\log_2(1-R).$$

The function $\mu_g(R)$ is continuous and linear in each closed interval from $1 - 1/t$ to $1 - 1/(t+1)$, where t is a natural number ≥ 2.

Proof.   Assume first that $0 < R < 0.5$. Let tC_p be the cycle of length p where each edge has been duplicated t times. For any two natural numbers p, r, we let $C_{p,r}$ be obtained from $2C_p$ by subdividing one edge r times. Then $C_{p,r}$ has $p + r$ vertices and $n = 2p + r$ edges. Thus, the dimension of the cycle code is $k = p+1$, and the rate of the cycle code is $k/n = (p+1)/(2p+r)$. For each natural number p, we let r be the largest natural number such that $k/n = (p+1)/(2p+r) \ge R$. Then $k = \lceil Rn \rceil$. Also, $r = \lfloor (p+1)/R - 2p \rfloor$. Recall that the number of cycles in $2C_p$ and hence also in $C_{p,r}$ is $> 2^p$. Substituting these values in the definition of μ_g and letting p tend to infinity, we conclude that $\mu_g(R) \ge R$.

The trivial upper bound shows that this inequality is, in fact, an equality.

Consider next the case where $R = 1 - 1/t$ for where t is natural number ≥ 2. The graph tC_p has p vertices and $q = pt$ edges. The number of cycles in this graph is

$$t^p + p\binom{t}{2},$$

the first term counting cycles of length p and the second cycles of length 2. The graph is regular of degree $2t$. Hence it has $n = pt$ edges and has rate $(pt - p + 1)/pt = 1 - 1/t + 1/pt$. Hence its cycle code is an $[n, Rn + 1]$-code. If we delete an edge, then we get an $[n - 1, \lceil R(n - 1) \rceil]$-code. Deleting an edge reduces the number of cycles only slightly. Letting p and hence also n tend to infinity, we conclude that

$$\mu_g(R) \geq -(1 - R)\log_2(1 - R).$$

Now assume that $1 - 1/t < R < 1 - 1/(t + 1)$, where t is a (fixed) natural number ≥ 2. Then we let $G(p, R, r)$ denote the graph obtained from tC_p by adding r edges between neighboring vertices such that all edge multiplicities are t or $t + 1$. The resulting graph $G(p, R, r)$ has p vertices and $n = pt + r$ edges. Thus, the dimension of the cycle code is $k = p(t - 1) + r + 1$, and the rate of the cycle code is $k/n = (p(t - 1) + r + 1)/(pt + r)$.

We first choose any p so large that the rate of tC_p, which is $(pt - p + 1)/pt = 1 - 1/t + 1/pt$, is smaller than R. Then we let r be the largest natural number such that the rate of $G(p, R, r)$, which is $(p(t - 1) + r + 1)/(pt + r)$, is smaller than or equal to R. That is, $r = -pt + \lfloor (p - 1)/(1 - R) \rfloor$. Then the cycle code of $G(p, R, r)$ is an $[n, \lceil Rn \rceil]$-code, where $n = pt + r = \lfloor (p - 1)/(1 - R) \rfloor$ is the number of edges of $G(p, R, r)$.

The number of cycles in $G(p, R, r)$ is greater than $t^{p-r}(t + 1)^r$.

If we substitute these values in the definition of μ_g and let p tend to infinity, then we conclude that

$$\mu_g(R) \geq ((1 - R)(1 + t) - 1)\log(t) + (-t(1 - R) + 1)\log(t + 1).$$

The right-hand side is clearly a linear function. For R equal to $1 - 1/t$ or $1 - 1/(t + 1)$, the right-hand side has the same values as the lower bounds we obtained for those two values of R. So we have obtained a lower bound for $\mu_g(R)$ which is continuous and piecewise linear.

We claim that this lower bound is also an upper bound. We used the graph $G(p, R, r)$ above. If we put $q = n = pt + r$, then $G(p, R, r)$ has the maximum number of cycles among those graphs with q edges which are obtained from a cycle of length p by duplicating edges. The graphs used to give the lower bound $f(q - 1, p)$ in Theorem 2.1.12 are also graphs of this type. Hence $G(p, R, r)$ has at least $f(q - 1, p)$ cycles. On the other hand, Theorem 2.1.12 says that any graph with p vertices and q edges has at most $qf(q - 1, p)$ cycles. So no graph with p vertices and q edges has more than q times as many cycles

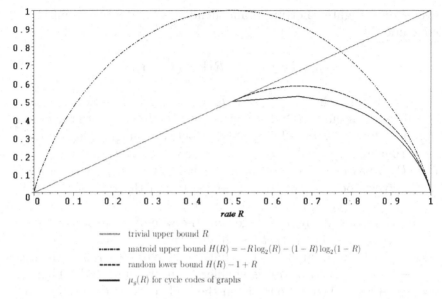

rate R

```
··········  trivial upper bound $R$
·—··—··—·  matroid upper bound $H(R) = -R \log_2(R) - (1 - R) \log_2(1 - R)$
— — — —  random lower bound $H(R) - 1 + R$
————————  $\mu_g(R)$ for cycle codes of graphs
```

Fig. 2.1. $\mu(R)$ versus R.

as $G(p, R, r)$. Hence the lower bound for $\mu_g(R)$ obtained from the graphs $G(p, R, r)$ is also an upper bound.   □

The function $\mu_g(R)$ is less than the matroid upper bound for all R and also less than the random upper bound for $R > 0.5$. The Agrell upper bound gives the same upper bound on μ as the trivial upper bound. Figure 2.1 shows these bounds.

2.1.3.   Minimum number of minimal codewords

Let $\mathbf{C}[n, k]$ denote the set of all $[n, k]$-codes with dual distance at least three (the motivation for the last condition is to avoid Corollary 2.1.20 which is met for direct sum of repetition codes). By analogy with the previous section, we define

$$m(n, k) = \min\{M(C) \,:\, C \in \mathbf{C}[n, k]\},$$

as the minimum of $M(C)$ over that set of codes. Similarly we define $m_g(n, k)$ by restricting the set of codes considered to be cycle codes of graphs.

2.1.3.1. Matroid bounds

In the sequel, we translate results from matroid to codes by considering the matroid of linear dependence of the columns of the parity-check matrix of the code. Thus, this matroid when attached to an $[n, k]$-code has n points and rank $n - k$. The circuits of the matroid correspond bijectively to the minimal codewords of the code. The matroid is called *simple* if it has no loops nor parallel elements. This is equivalent to the code having distance at least three. When the code is the cycle code of a connected graph on p vertices with q edges, the minimal codewords correspond to cycles and the parameters of the cycle code are $[q, q - p + 1]$ with dual distance the edge-connectivity of the graph. The following result was derived in [15].

Theorem 2.1.14 (Dosa, Szalkai, Laflamme). *Any matroid $\mathcal{M}$ of size μ and rank ν has at least $\mu - \nu$ circuits.*

By the above discussion the next result follows.

Corollary 2.1.15. *Any $[n, k]$-code C satisfies $M(C) \geq k$.*

We give a purely coding-theoretic proof of this fact.

Proof. By [5, Lemma 2.1], we know that the $M(C)$ minimal vectors span C, a vector space of dimension k. Therefore, elementary linear algebra entails that $M(C) \geq k$. □

This bound is met with equality for a direct sum of repetition codes.

The following result was also derived in [15].

Theorem 2.1.16 (Dosa, Szalkai, Laflamme). *Any loopless matroid $\mathcal{M}$ of size μ and rank ν has at least $b\binom{a+1}{2} + (\nu - b)\binom{a}{2}$ circuits, where a, b are the quotient and remainder of m by n.*

This translates as before into a result on linear codes.

Corollary 2.1.17. *Any $[n, k]$-code C of distance at least 2 satisfies*

$$M(C) \geq b\binom{a+1}{2} + (n - k - b)\binom{a}{2},$$

where a, b are the quotient and remainder of n by $n - k$.

Corollary 2.1.18. *Any 2-edge-connected graph with p vertices, q edges contains at least*

$$b\binom{a+1}{2} + (p-1-b)\binom{a}{2},$$

cycles where a, b are the quotient and remainder of q by $p-1$.

The bound in Corollary 2.1.18 is tight. Consider for example a tree on p vertices, where each edge is replaced by three edges. This graph has $q = 3(p-1)$ edges and contains $3(p-1)$ cycles. This graph satisfies Corollary 2.1.18 with equality where $a = 3$ and $b = 0$.

Dosa, Szalkai and Laflamme [15] suggested to sharpen the bounds of Theorems 2.1.14 and 2.1.16 for a loopless matroid without parallel elements. We first point out that a result by Kashyap [21] on codes can be extended to matroids. Then we consider graphic matroids.

Theorem 2.1.19. *Any loopless matroid $\mathcal{M}$ of size μ and rank ν without parallel elements has at least μ cocircuits.*

Proof.   Consider the lattice $L(\mathcal{M})$ of flats (maximal closed sets) of $\mathcal{M}$. Let W_r be the number of elements in $L(\mathcal{M})$ of rank r (Whitney number of the second kind).

Thus, the number of cocircuits of $\mathcal{M}$ is equal to $W_{\nu-1}$.

By the result of Greene [18] we have

$$W_{\nu-1} \geq W_1,$$

where W_1 is the number of elements in $L(\mathcal{M})$ of rank 1 (points of $L(\mathcal{M})$). Equivalently, it is the number of flats of $\mathcal{M}$ of rank 1. Since $\mathcal{M}$ is simple, then $W_1 = \mu$.   □

Corollary 2.1.20 (Kashyap [21]). *Any $[n, k]$-code C of dual distance at least 3 verifies $M(C) \geq n$.*

Note that our proof of Theorem 2.1.19 is purely combinatorial while Kashyap's arguments are geometric.

Corollary 2.1.21. *Any 3-edge-connected graph with q edges contains at least q cycles.*

The examples showing that Corollary 2.1.18 is best possible also show that Corollary 2.1.21 is best possible.

2.1.3.2. *Tables*

We have produced tables providing values for $m(n, k)$ and $m_g(n, k)$ for small values of n, k. By decreasing values of k we look at the values of $m(n, k)$. The quantity $m(n, k)$ becomes undefined when there are no codes of dual distance ≥ 3 for these values of n and k. The following proposition is helpful in our computations.

Proposition 2.1.22. *If $m(n, k) = n$, then for every integer T we have*

$$m(n + T, k + T) = n + T.$$

Proof. Let C be an $[n, k]$-code of dual distance at least 3 such that $M(C) = m(n, k) = n$. Take the direct sum with a universe code of length T. Specifically

$$D = C \oplus \mathbb{F}_2^T.$$

Thus D is an $[n + T, k + T]$-code. Then $M(D) = M(C) + T = n + T$. Thus $m(n + T, k + T) \leq M(D) = n + T$, and by Kashyap bound the result follows. □

The following values are immediate:

- $m(n, n)$ is undefined.
- $m(n, n - 1) = n$ since $M(C) = 3$ for $C = R_3^{\perp}$, where R_m denotes the repetition code of length m.
- $m(n, n - 2) = n$, for $n \geq 6$ since there is a $[6, 4]$ code C_6 with dual distance 3 and $M(C_6) = 6$, eg $C_6 = R_3^{\perp} \oplus R_3^{\perp}$.
- $m(n, k)$ is undefined for $k \leq 1$.

Tables 2.5 and 2.6 show values and bounds for $m(n, k)$ while Table 2.7 shows values for $m_g(n, k)$ for $1 \leq n \leq 15$. Lower bounds are given by the Kashyap bound while upper bounds are obtained by explicit codes. The values were computed using MAGMA [10]. We also used the graph generation program NAUTY of B. Mckay [23] in the computations for Table2.7. A blank entry means that $m(n, k)$ or $m_g(n, k)$ is undefined.

Table 2.5. $m(n, k)$ for $3 \leq n \leq 15, 1 \leq k \leq 9$.

n/k	1	2	3	4	5	6	7	8	9
3		3							
4			4						
5			5–6	5					
6			6–7	6	6				
7			7	7–8	7	7			
8				8	8–9	8	8		
9				9–12	9	9	9	9	
10				10–14	10	10	10	10	10
11				11–14	11–15	11	11	11	11
12				12–15	12–15	12–13	12	12	12
13				13–15	13–16	13–14	13	13	13
14				14–15	14–16	14	14–18	14	14
15				15	15–24	15–25	15	15–22	15

Table 2.6. $m(n, k)$ for $10 \leq n \leq 15, 10 \leq k \leq 15$.

n/k	10	11	12	13	14	15
10						
11	11					
12	12	12				
13	13	13	13			
14	14	14	14	14		
15	15	15	15	15	15	

Table 2.7. $m_g(n, k)$ for $3 \leq n \leq 15$.

n/k	1	2	3	4	5	6	7	8	9	10
3										
4										
5										
6			7							
7										
8				13						
9				14	22					
10					21	37				
11					22	30				
12					26	14	52			
13						30	39	85		
14						38	20	65	133	
15						46	21	29	103	197

2.2. Secret Sharing Schemes Based on Self-dual Codes

This section focuses on secret sharing schemes based on self-dual codes. First, we look at the access structure of the schemes constructed by Massey's method. The combinatorial properties of self-dual codes and invariant theory are used to describe the access structure. We then consider a generalization of the Massey scheme and describe the corresponding access structure.

2.2.1. Massey scheme and self-dual codes

We begin by exploring the class of divisible self-dual codes that is self-dual codes with Hamming weights multiple of a numerical constant $c > 1$. By the Gleason–Pierce–Turyn theorem [25, Theorem 1, p. 597], the only non-trivial possibilities for a finite field alphabet are $\mathbb{F}_2$ ($c = 1$ for Type I codes and $c = 2$ for Type II codes), $\mathbb{F}_3$ ($c = 3$ for Type III codes) and $\mathbb{F}_4$ ($c = 2$ for Type IV codes). Our motivations are threefold. First and foremost, the role of the dual code in such a scheme is important in characterizing access groups (Lemma 2.2.1). Next, these codes enjoy some design properties for codewords of given weight. We will see that 1-designs play an important role in our study when enumerating access structures by group size. Thirdly, their weight enumerators have strong invariance properties that allow us to use invariant theory to study them. In particular a class of weight enumerators introduced by Ozeki [29] under the name of Jacobi polynomials have proved useful in relation with designs [9] and coset weight enumeration [30, 31]. The various generating series of dimensions of spaces of invariants are best computed using a powerful computer algebra language like MAGMA [10].

2.2.1.1. *Preliminaries*

Here we recall some basic concepts about linear codes, designs and the Massey scheme for secret sharing.

Codes and designs: Let q be a prime power and denote the finite field of order q by $\mathbb{F}_q$. An $[n, k, d]$-linear *code* over $\mathbb{F}_q$ is a linear vector space in $\mathbb{F}_q^n$ with k denoting the dimension and d the minimum Hamming weight, where the *Hamming weight* of a vector is the number of non-zero coordinates of that vector. For a code C, the *Hamming weight enumerator* is given by $W_C(y) = \sum_{c \in C} y^{\text{wt}(c)}$, where $\text{wt}(c)$ is the Hamming weight of the vector c.

For any code $C \subseteq \mathbb{F}_q^n$, its orthogonal under the usual inner product is denoted by $C^\perp$. A code is said to be *self-orthogonal* if $C \subseteq C^\perp$ and *self-dual* if $C = C^\perp$. A binary self-dual code is said to be Type II if the Hamming weights of all its vectors are 0 (mod 4) and Type I otherwise. A ternary self-dual code is said to be Type III. It is immediate that in a Type III code all weights are a multiple of 3 since a ternary vector is self-orthogonal if and only if it has weight a multiple of 3. A self-dual code over $\mathbb{F}_4$ where all the weights are even is said to be Type IV. A matrix G is a generator matrix for a code C if the rows of G form a basis for C. For any undefined terms from coding theory see [20] or [25]. Throughout, we let $\mathbf{j}$ denote the all one vector.

A $t-(v, k, \lambda)$ *design* is a set of points $\mathcal{P}$, blocks $\mathcal{B}$, and an incidence relation between them such that $v = |\mathcal{P}|$, every block is incident with precisely k points, and every t distinct points are incident with λ blocks. With any design we denote by λ_s the number of blocks that are incident with a given s-tuple of points, for $s \leq t$. This parameter is easily computed by using the recursive formula $\lambda_s = \frac{(v-s)}{(k-s)}\lambda_{s+1}$ and using $\lambda_t = \lambda$.

2.2.1.2. *Massey scheme for secret sharing*

We let $s \in \mathbb{F}_q$ be the secret we wish to share. Let G be the generator matrix for a code C of length n and let G_i be the generic column of G, for $i = 0, \ldots, n - 1$. Let v be a vector such that $vG_0 = s$. The vector v is the information vector. We let $u = vG$. To each party corresponding to all coordinates except the first we assign u_i. Hence the number of parties concerned is $n - 1$. It is simple to compute the secret from this point. Assume that G_0 is a linear combination of the $n - 1$ columns $G_1, \ldots, G_{n-1}$. The secret s is then determined by the set of shares $\{u_{i_1}, u_{i_2}, \ldots, u_{i_m}\}$, if and only if G_0 is a linear combination $G_0 = \sum_{j=1}^m x_j G_{i_j}$ of the vectors $G_{i_1}, \ldots, G_{i_m}$, where $1 \leq i_1 < \cdots < i_m \leq n - 1$ and $m \leq n - 1$. So by solving this linear equation, we find x_j and from then on the secret by $s = vG_0 = \sum_{j=1}^m x_j vG_{i_j} = \sum_{j=1}^m x_j u_{i_j}$.

We use the following lemma throughout which appears in this form in [12]. See also [22, 26, 27] for descriptions of this technique.

Lemma 2.2.1. *Let G be a generator matrix of an $[n, k, d]$-code where $C^{\perp}$ has minimum weight higher than 1. In the secret-sharing scheme based on G, a set of m shares $\{u_{i_1}, u_{i_2}, \ldots, u_{i_m}\}$ determines the secret if and only if there is a codeword $(1, 0, \ldots, 0, c_{i_1}, 0, \ldots, 0, c_{i_m}, 0, \ldots, 0) \in C^{\perp}$, where $c_{i_j} \neq 0$ for at least one j, $1 \le i_1 \le \cdots < i_m \le n - 1$ and $1 \le m \le n - 1$.*

A scheme is said to be perfect if a group of shares either determines the secret or gives no information about the secret.

Let $\mathcal{P}$ be the set of parties involved in the secret-sharing. In this case $\mathcal{P}$ is the set of coordinates except for the first coordinate. The set Γ, called the *access structure* of the secret-sharing scheme, consists of subsets of $\mathcal{P}$ such that any element of Γ can uncover the secret. An element $A \in \Gamma$ is called a *minimum access group* if no element of Γ is a proper subset of A. Hence a set is a minimum access group if it can uncover the secret but no proper subset can uncover the secret. We let $\overline{\Gamma} = \{A \mid A \text{ is a minimum access group}\}$. We call $\overline{\Gamma}$ the minimum access structure. In general, determining the minimum access structure is a difficult problem.

2.2.1.3. *Access structure for self-dual codes*

We shall examine the access structure of codes that are self-dual. We begin with a theorem that holds for the access structure for any self-dual code.

Theorem 2.2.2. *In the access based on a self-dual code no two groups that can uncover the secret are disjoint.*

Proof. Two groups correspond to two vectors in the code that both have the first point in their supports. The two vectors are also orthogonal so they must have at least one other point in their supports. □

Let C be a self-dual code over $\mathbb{F}_q$ of length n with minimum distance d. We are interested in those self-dual codes such that the supports of the vectors of any weight hold a 1-design by the Assmus–Mattson theorem [25, Theorem 29, p. 177]. This consists of a rather large class of self-dual codes. In fact, extremal Type II codes of length a multiple of 24 will hold 5-designs for all weights.

In particular, we have the following lemma.

Lemma 2.2.3. *If C is a Type I or Type IV code of length n and minimum distance d, then the supports of all non-trivial weights hold a 1-design if $d \geq \frac{n+4}{4}$. If C is a Type II code of length n and minimum distance d, then the supports of all non-trivial weights hold a 1-design if $d \geq \frac{n+8}{6}$. If C is a Type III code of length n and minimum distance d, then the supports of all non-trivial weights hold a 1-design if $d \geq \frac{3}{4} \lfloor \frac{n+2}{3} \rfloor$.*

Proof. A Type I or Type IV code has $\frac{n-2}{2}$ possible non-trivial weights. Then $d - 2$ of these possible weights have no vectors where d is the minimum weight. Therefore, we need $d - 1 \geq \frac{n-2}{2} - (d - 2)$ for the Assmus–Mattson theorem to apply. This gives that $d \geq \frac{n+4}{4}$.

A Type II code has $\frac{n-4}{4}$ possible non-trivial weights. Then $\frac{d}{2} - 2$ of these possible weights have no vectors where d is the minimum weight. Therefore, we need $d - 1 \geq \frac{n-4}{4} - (\frac{d}{2} - 2)$ for the Assmus–Mattson theorem to apply. This gives that $d \geq \frac{n+8}{6}$.

A Type III code has $\lfloor \frac{n-1}{3} \rfloor$ possible non-trivial weights. Then $\frac{d}{3}$ of these possible weights have no vectors where d is the minimum weight. Therefore, we need $d - 1 \geq \lfloor \frac{n-1}{3} \rfloor - \frac{d}{3}$ for the Assmus–Mattson theorem to apply. This gives that $d \geq \frac{3}{4} \lfloor \frac{n+2}{3} \rfloor$.   □

Let G be the generator matrix of the code. In this scenario, we have that G generates both the code and its orthogonal. The weight enumerator of self-dual codes can be determined up to a few parameters by using Gleason's theorem and its many generalizations.

In this case, we have that $\mathcal{P}$ has $n - 1$ members corresponding to the coordinates of C which we denote by $r_1, \ldots, r_{n-1}$.

Throughout this section let $W_C(y) = \sum A_i y^i$. Let D_i denote the 1-design formed from the vectors of weight i and let $\lambda_s(D_i)$ denote the λ_s for that particular design.

Theorem 2.2.4. *The access structure of this secret-sharing scheme is given by*

$$\Gamma = \{A \mid A \text{ is the support of a vector } v \in C \text{ with } v_0 = 1\}. \quad (2.2.1)$$

The number of parties in the scheme is $n - 1$ and the access structure has the following properties:

- *Any group of size less than $d - 1$ cannot recover the secret.*
- *There are $\lambda_1(D_i)$ groups of size $i - 1$ that can recover the secret.*
- *It is perfect, which means that a group of shares either determines the secret or gives no information about the secret.*
- *When the parties come together $\lfloor \frac{d-1}{2} \rfloor$ cheaters can be found.*

Proof. The first three statements are immediate. The fact that there are $\lambda_1(D_i)$ groups of size $i-1$ that can recover the secret follows from the fact that there are exactly that many blocks through r_0 of weight i. Note also that any vectors that are scalar multiples of each other have the same support and it is the supports that form the design. The last statement follows from the fact that the minimum weight is d and deleting the first coordinate makes vectors of size $d - 1$ and hence that many errors can be corrected. $\square$

The following two results are immediate.

Proposition 2.2.5. *Let C be a binary self-dual code then the access structure consists of $C \setminus C_0$, where C_0 is the subcode of codimension 1 whose vectors are orthogonal to the vector $(1, 0, 0, \ldots, 0)$. There are precisely $2^{\frac{n}{2}-1}$ groups in the access structure.*

Corollary 2.2.6. *The groups in this secret-sharing scheme based on a self-dual code C have precisely the following size distribution generating function $\sum_i \lambda_1(D_i)y^{i-1}$.*

2.2.1.4. *Minimum access structure for binary self-dual codes*

We shall examine the minimum access structure for binary codes. Recall that it is a simple matter to determine possible weight enumerators of self-dual codes using Gleason's theorem [17]. Namely a Type I code is an element of $\mathbb{C}[(x^2 + y^2), (x^2y^2(x^2 - y^2)^2)]$ and a Type II code is an element of $\mathbb{C}[W_1(x, y) = x^8 + 14x^4y^4 + y^8, W_2(x, y) = x^4y^4(x^4 - y^4)^4]$.

Then we have the well-known Gleason's theorem first proven in [17].

Theorem 2.2.7 (Gleason). *The weight enumerator of a Type II self-dual code is a polynomial in $W_1(x, y)$ and $W_2(x, y)$, i.e. if C is a Type II code, then $W_C(x, y) \in \mathbb{C}[W_1(x, y), W_2(x, y)]$.*

For binary codes we can extend Corollary 2.2.6 a bit further since we know precisely the number of blocks in each design. Specifically, we get the following theorem.

Theorem 2.2.8. *Let C be a Type I code with $d \geq \frac{n+4}{4}$ or a Type II code with $d \geq \frac{n+8}{6}$. Set $W_C(y) = \sum A_i y^i$. The access structure contains exactly $\frac{iA_i}{n}$ groups of size $i - 1$.*

Proof. Under these conditions, the code has the property that all non-zero weights hold 1-designs. We use the formula $\lambda_s = \frac{v-s}{k-s}\lambda_{s+1}$ and the fact that $v = n$, $k = i$, and $\lambda_0 = A_i$ to compute $\lambda_1 = \frac{iA_i}{n}$ for the design of vectors of weight i. ☐

Theorem 2.2.9. *Let C be a binary self-dual code of length n with minimum weight d. Any vector corresponding to a group in the access structure with weight less than $2d$ is in the minimum access structure. The number of groups of size $r - 1$ plus the number of groups in the access structure of size $n - r - 1$ is the number of vectors of weight r in the code.*

Proof. The vectors of minimum weight that are in the access structure are all in the minimum access structure. If there were a vector with weight less than $2d$ in the access structure containing a vector of weight at least d then their sum would have weight less than d which is a contradiction. The second assertion follows from the well-known fact that the all one-vector j is always present in a binary self-dual code. Every vector v with weight r in the code has either a 1 or a 0 in the first coordinate. If it is a 1, then this vector gives a group of size $r - 1$. If v has a 0 in the first coordinate then $j - v$ has a 1 in the first coordinate and has weight $n - r$ giving a group of size $n - r - 1$. ☐

If the code is a Type I code, then there are an equal number of groups of size 1 (mod 4) and 3 (mod 4) and if the code is Type II, then all groups in the access structure are of size 3 (mod 4).

2.2.1.5.   *Example of a scheme based on the Golay Code*

We shall describe this secret-sharing scheme using the $[24, 12, 8]$-Golay code. The weight enumerator of the length 24 Golay code is:

$$1 + 759y^8 + 2576y^{12} + 759y^{16} + y^{24}. \qquad (2.2.2)$$

It is well known (see [25, Chapter 2]) that the supports of any non-zero weight form a 5-design. It is an easy computation to see that $\lambda_1(D_8) = 253$, $\lambda_1(D_{12}) = 1288$, and $\lambda_1(D_{16}) = 506$.

These groups together with the entire group comprise the 2048 elements of the access structure. Each of the 253 groups of size 8 must be in the minimum access structure. Additionally, each of the 1288 groups of size 12 must be in the access structure because if the support of a weight 8 vector were a subset of the support of a weight 12 vector, then the sum of these vectors would have weight 4 which is a contradiction. Clearly, the group of size 24 is not in the minimum access structure. We note that no weight 16 vector can have a support containing the support of weight 12 vector since it would produce a weight 4 vector in the code which is a contradiction. Notice that the 506 groups of size 16 correspond exactly to vectors of the form $\mathbf{j} + w$, where w is one of the 506 weight 8 vectors that do not have r_0 in their support. It is known that for a given vector of weight 8 there is exactly one other vector of weight 8 disjoint from it (see the intersection number triangle of the corresponding design [25, Chapter 2, Fig. 2.14]). Let v be a weight 8 vector with r_0 in its support and w the vector that is disjoint from it. Then $\mathbf{j} + w$ has r_0 in its support and contains the support of v. This gives that the support of each weight 8 vector is contained in the support of a unique weight 16 vector. Hence there are 253 weight 16 vectors whose support cannot be in the minimum access structure and 253 that are in the minimum access structure. This gives the following theorem.

Theorem 2.2.10. *In the secret-sharing scheme produced from the extended Golay code we have the following conditions:*

- *The access structure consists of 253 groups of size 7, 1288 groups of size 11, 506 groups of size 15 and 1 group of size 23.*
- *The minimum access structure consists of the 253 groups of size 7, the 1288 groups of size 11, and 253 groups of size 15.*
- *No group of size less than 7 can determine the secret.*

2.2.1.6. Examples of optimal Type I and Type II codes

We shall describe the access group by giving it as a polynomial $\sum B_i y^i$ where there are exactly B_i groups of size i that can uncover the secret. We give the structure for a Type II code of a given length and minimum distance d. We only describe the optimal codes which for these cases have unique weight enumerators:

- For $n = 8$ and minimum weight 4, the access structure is $7 y^3 + y^7$. For $n = 16$ and minimum weight 4, the access structure is $7 y^3 + 99 y^7 + 21 y^{11} + y^{15}$.
- For $n = 24$ and minimum weight 8, the access structure is $253 y^7 + 1288 y^{11} + 506 y^{15} + y^{23}$.
- For $n = 32$ and minimum weight 8, the access structure is $155 y^7 + 5208 y^{11} + 18259 y^{15} + 8680 y^{19} + 465 y^{23} + y^{31}$.
- For $n = 48$, $d = 12$ and minimum weight 12, the access structure is $4324 y^{11} + 178365 y^{15} + 1664740 y^{19} + 3840840 y^{23} + 2330636 y^{27} + 356730 y^{31} + 12972 y^{35} + y^{47}$.
- For the putative length $n = 72$ and minimum weight 16 code, the access structure would be: $55522 y^{15} + 5029640 y^{19} + 154320985 y^{23} + 1710077600 y^{27} + 7378984844 y^{31} + 12878360 560 y^{35} + 9223731055 y^{39} + 2687264800 y^{43} + 308641970 y^{47} + 13077064 y^{51} + 194327 y^{55} + y^{71}$.

We shall give the access structure for two interesting Type I codes. The first is $n = 22$ and $d = 6$, that is the baby Golay code. The code has access structure: $21 y^5 + 120 y^7 + 280 y^9 + 336 y^{11} + 210 y^{13} + 56 y^{15} + y^{21}$. The second is $n = 46$ and $d = 10$, that is the child of the quadratic residue code of length 48. The code has access structure: $220 y^9 + 2520 y^{11} + 17325 y^{13} + 81840 y^{15} + 263340 y^{17} + 582120 y^{19} + 898920 y^{21} + 980640 y^{23} + 756756 y^{25} + 409640 y^{27} + 153450 y^{29} + 39600 y^{31} + 7140 y^{33} + 792 y^{35} + y^{45}$.

2.2.1.7. Minimum access structure for Type III and Type IV codes

Unlike binary codes two vectors over other fields that are not multiples of each other can have the same support. For example, in the ternary Golay code there are 24 vectors of weight 12 but each of them have the same support and therefore correspond to a single group in the access structure. Then the number of groups in the access structure is not necessarily the size of a coset of a codimension 1 subcode.

We can say the following theorem.

Theorem 2.2.11. *The access structure formed from a Type III code has only groups of size 2 (mod 3) and contains at most $3^{\frac{n}{2}-1}$ groups. The access structure formed from a Type IV code has only groups of size 1 (mod 2) and contains at most $4^{\frac{n}{2}-1}$ groups.*

Proof. The weights in a Type III code are congruent to 0 (mod 3) and the weights in a Type IV code are congruent to 0 (mod 2). The first part of the statements follow. If C is a self-dual code, then C_0 is a subcode of codimension 1 orthogonal to the vector $(1, 0, 0, \ldots, 0)$. □

We give an example of the ternary Golay code, a Type III $[12, 6, 6]$ code with weight enumerator:

$$1 + 264y^6 + 440y^9 + 24y^{12}.$$

While there are different vectors that are not scalar multiples of each other of weight 12 in this code there are none of weight 6 nor 9. If two vectors in this self-dual code that were not scalar multiples of each other had the same support, then their sum would have to have weight 3 which is a contradiction since there are no vectors of that weight. If two vectors in this self-dual code that were not scalar multiples of each other had the same support, then their sum would have to have weight 6 or 3. If it were weight 3 it would be a contradiction and if it were weight 6 then their difference would have weight 3 which is a contradiction.

By the Assmus–Mattson theorem, the supports of the vectors of all non-trivial weights hold 5-designs. There are 132 blocks of size 6. Of these $64 = \lambda_1$ go through the point corresponding to the first coordinate. Hence there are 64 groups of size 5 in the access structure. Of course, all of these groups are in the minimum access structure as well. There are 220 blocks of size 9. There are $165 = \lambda_1$ blocks through the point corresponding to the first coordinate and hence there are 165 groups of size 8 in the access structure.

Consider a block of size 9 that has in its support the point p_1 corresponding to the first coordinate. There are three points q_1, q_2, q_3

that are not in the support of that vector. In the design formed from the vectors of weight 6, the value of λ_1^j, that is the number of blocks through 1 point and disjoint from 3, is 8. This means there are 8 blocks of size 6 through the point p_1 and disjoint from q_1, q_2 and q_3. Hence there must be a group of size 5 completely contained in the group of size 8 corresponding to this block. This gives that there are no groups of size 8 in the minimum access structure. It is immediate that there cannot be a group of size 11 in the minimum access structure.

2.2.1.8. *Joint weight enumerators and Jacobi polynomials*

The previous technique worked extremely well for binary codes holding 1-designs on all non-trivial weights. It was not as useful for ternary and quaternary codes. The next technique will work for codes over $\mathbb{F}_q$ with some straightforward computation. We shall focus on Type I, Type II, Type III and Type IV codes.

We begin with the definition of the joint weight enumerator with an unusual variable order.

Let A and B be codes. For $v \in A$, $w \in B$ define $i(v, w) := |\{i \mid v_i \neq 0 \text{ and } w_i = 0\}|$; $j(v, w) := |\{i \mid v_i \neq 0 \text{ and } w_i \neq 0\}|$; $k(v, w) := |\{i \mid v_i = 0 \text{ and } w_i = 0\}|$ and, $l(v, w) := |\{i \mid v_i = 0 \text{ and } w_i \neq 0\}|$.

The joint weight enumerator is given by

$$\mathcal{J}_{A,B} = \sum_{v \in A} \sum_{w \in B} a^{i(v,w)} b^{j(v,w)} c^{k(v,w)} d^{l(v,w)}.$$

Let T be a set of coordinate places, and $\mathbf{1}_T$ its indicator vector. The *Jacobi weight enumerator* of a self-dual code C can then be introduced as $J_{C,T} := \mathcal{J}_{\mathbf{1}_T, C}$. The reader can check for him/herself that, for all T, $J_{C,T}(x, y, x, y) = W_C(x, y)$ and that $J_{C,\emptyset}(w, z, x, y) = W_C(x, y)$. Jacobi weight enumerators were introduced by Ozeki by analogy with Jacobi modular forms [29]. The case of Type I codes is treated in [31] and Type II codes in [9]. Our definition is different for Type III codes of [30] but the philosophy is similar.

Theorem 2.2.12. *Keep notation as above. The weight enumerator in variables x, y of the supports of vectors that can uncover the secret in the scheme attached to C is the coefficient of $w^0 z^1$ in*

$J_{C,1}(w, z, x, y)$. *In particular, if C is homogeneous then this weight enumerator is $\frac{1}{n} \frac{\partial}{\partial y} W_C(x, y)$.*

Proof. A vector $v \in A$ can uncover the secret if and only if it is non-zero on the first coordinate. Since the vectors in D only have a non-zero element in the first coordinate then the only way the exponent of l can be non-zero is if the vector from A is non-zero on the first coordinate. The first statement is immediate by definition of the Jacobi polynomial. The second statement is a restatement in terms of generating functions of Prange's theorem [32, Theorem 80]. □

As an example, we let A be the binary Hamming $[8, 4, 4]$ code e_8 and $T = \{1\}$. Then the weight enumerator is $W_{e_8} = x^8 + 14x^4y^4 + y^8$. Then $\frac{\partial}{\partial y} W_{e_8}(x, y) = 56x^4y^3 + 8y^7$, hence the sought weight enumerator is $7x^4y^3 + y^7$.

2.2.1.9. *Invariants*

Throughout this section, we let C be a self-dual code and $T = \{1\}$ as described above. We shall describe the possible access structures for this situation using invariant theory. Suppose the weight enumerator of C is left invariant by a certain group G. Then the Jacobi weight enumerator of C is left invariant by every element of G acting simultaneously on every pair of variables (w, z) and (x, y). Such an invariant is called a *simultaneous invariant*. In fact, it is an invariant of the block matrix $\operatorname{diag}(g, g)$. The group consisting of all these block matrices are denoted by $G \oplus G$. In general, if C is self-dual over $\mathbb{F}_q$ with weights divisible by c the group $G = \langle M, N \rangle$, with

$$M = \frac{1}{\sqrt{q}} \begin{pmatrix} 1 & q-1 \\ 1 & -1 \end{pmatrix} \quad N = \begin{pmatrix} 1 & 0 \\ 0 & \omega \end{pmatrix}, \quad (2.2.3)$$

with ω a complex primitive root of one of order c. Define the block matrices

$$M_2 = \begin{pmatrix} M & 0 \\ 0 & M \end{pmatrix} \quad N_2 = \begin{pmatrix} N & 0 \\ 0 & N \end{pmatrix}. \quad (2.2.4)$$

With these notations, we see that $G \oplus G = \langle M_2, N_2 \rangle$. Polynomial invariants live in (complex) vector spaces graded by degree and bidegree. The vector space of invariants of total degree i under a group

G is denoted by $\mathbb{C}[w, z, x, y]_i^G$. To keep track of the degree in w, z and x, y separately we shall use the notation $\mathbb{C}[w, z, x, y]_{i,j}^G$. General results on Hilbert series assure us that the generating series for the dimensions of these spaces are rational. Molien theorems give us explicit expressions for these rational functions. The simple Molien series is then

$$\Phi_G(t) := \sum_{i=0}^{\infty} \dim(\mathbb{C}[w, z, x, y]_i^G)t^i = \frac{1}{|G|} \sum_{g \in G} \frac{1}{\det(I - tg)}.$$

The double Molien series is then

$$\Phi_G(t, s) := \sum_{i=0}^{\infty} \sum_{j=0}^{\infty} \dim(\mathbb{C}[w, z, x, y]_{i,j}^G)t^i s^j$$

$$= \frac{1}{|G|} \sum_{g \in G} \frac{1}{\det(I - tg)\det(I - sg)}.$$

For the problem at hand the quantity to control is $\dim(\mathbb{C}[w, z, x, y]_{1,j}^G)$ for $G = H \oplus H$, and H one of the four groups leaving one of the four types of codes invariant. Its generating function in the variable s is therefore $S_H(s) := \frac{\partial}{\partial t}\Phi_G(t, s)|_{t=0}$. In Table 2.8 we only give $S_H(s)$, as the double Molien series is too large for display. See [31, p. 549] for Type I.

2.2.2.   An extension of Massey scheme

We consider a generalization of the SSS based on linear codes proposed by Massey. Unlike in the classical case, there are only a few works on this general SSS. In the previous section, we saw that the design properties and joint weight enumerators of self-dual codes can be used in describing the access structure. Our main objective here

Table 2.8.   Dimension of space of invariants.

Type	$|H|$	$S_H(s)$
I	16	$\frac{s^7 + s}{s^{10} - s^8 - s^2 + 1}$
II	192	$\frac{s^{23} + s^7}{1 + s^{32} - s^{24} - s^8}$
III	48	$\frac{s^3 + s^{11}}{1 + s^{16} - s^{12} - s^4}$
IV	12	$\frac{s^5 + s}{s^8 - s^6 - s^2 + 1}$

is to extend the techniques and results to the case of general SSS based on linear codes.

2.2.2.1. General SSS based on linear codes

Let $\mathcal{P} = \{P_1, \ldots, P_n\}$ be the set of participants. The set of all possible secrets is $\mathcal{S} = \mathbb{F}_q^l$, where $l \geq 2$ and the set of all possible shares for P_i is $\mathcal{S}_i = \mathbb{F}_q$. Suppose we want to share the secret $s = (s_1, s_2, \ldots, s_l) \in \mathbb{F}_q^l$. Let $\mathcal{C}$ be an $[l + n, k, d]$ linear code over $\mathbb{F}_q$ with $d > l$. Consider a generator matrix

$$G = [G_1 \ G_2 \ \cdots \ G_l \ G_{l+1} \ \cdots \ G_{l+n}],$$

where g_i is the ith column. To generate the shares, the dealer picks randomly a vector $u \in \mathbb{F}_q^k$ such that

$$uG_i = s_i \quad \text{for } 1 \leq i \leq l.$$

The dealer then computes the corresponding codeword

$$c = (c_1, c_2, \ldots, c_l, c_{l+1}, \ldots, c_{l+n}) = uG,$$

where the first l coordinates are the components of the secret. Now the share of P_i is c_{l+i} for $i = 1, \ldots, l$. The information rate of the scheme is l. Thus, the scheme is non-perfect.

We note that when $l = 1$ then we have the classic Massey scheme. This construction is not new as it was already considered in [22, 28] for threshold schemes and in [8] for the general case. It is also related to the generalized vector space construction in [35].

In [8], Blakley and Kabatianskii proved the following theorem that gives a characterization of the amount of information that can be obtained by a subset of participants.

Theorem 2.2.13. *Let* $B = \{P_{i_1}, P_{i_2}, \ldots, P_{i_m}\} \subseteq \mathcal{P}$ *and define*

$$J = \text{span}\{G_1, G_2, \ldots, G_l\} \cap \text{span}\{G_{i_1}, G_{i_2}, \ldots, G_{i_m}\}.$$

(i) *B can uniquely determine the secret, i.e. $B \in \Gamma$, if and only if* $J = \text{span}\{G_1, G_2, \ldots, G_l\}$.

(ii) *B cannot obtain any information about the secret if and only if* $J = \{0\}$.

(iii) *B can obtain partial information about the secret if and only if* $\{0\} \subset J \subset \text{span}\{G_1, G_2, \ldots, G_l\}$.

2.2.2.2. Access structure

We study in this section the access structure of the general SSS based on linear codes. We start by giving a characterization of the authorized groups using the dual code that generalizes Lemma 2.2.1.

Proposition 2.2.14. *Let C be an $[l+n, k, d]$-linear code over $\mathbb{F}_q$ and let B be a subset of $\mathcal{P}$ such that $B = \{P_{i_1}, \ldots, P_{i_m}\}$. In the general SSS based on C the participants in B can determine the secret s if and only if there exist codewords $v_j \in C^\perp$, $1 \leq j \leq l$, satisfying the following conditions:*

(i) *The subvector of v_j consisting of its first l coordinates is equal to the jth unit vector e_j in $\mathbb{F}_q^l$.*

(ii) $\operatorname{supp}(v_j) \subseteq \{j, i_1, \ldots, i_m\}$.

Proof. Suppose there exist codewords $v_j \in C^\perp$, $1 \leq j \leq l$, satisfying conditions (i) and (ii). For $j = 1, \ldots, l$, we have

$$s \cdot v_j = c_j + \sum_{r=1}^m \alpha_{jr} c_{i_r} = 0$$

for some constants $\alpha_{jr}, 1 \leq r \leq m$, which are not all zero. Hence, the secret s can be determined as a linear combination of the shares of participants in B.

Suppose the participants in B can determine the secret. Then for each $j = 1, \ldots, l$, we have an equation of the form

$$c_j = \sum_{r=1}^m \beta_{jr} c_{i_r}$$

for some constants $\beta_{jr}, 1 \leq r \leq m$, which are not all zero. The equation can be rewritten as

$$(c_1, c_2, \ldots, c_l, c_{l+1}, \ldots, c_{l+n}) \cdot (e_j, 0, \ldots, -\beta_{j1}, \ldots, -\beta_{jm}, 0, \ldots, 0) = 0.$$

Now the codewords $(e_j, 0, \ldots, -\beta_{j1}, \ldots, -\beta_{jm}, 0, \ldots, 0)$ are in $C^\perp$ and satisfy conditions (i) and (ii). $\square$

Example 2.2.15. Let $\mathcal{C}_1$ be the $[8,3,4]$-linear code over $\mathbb{F}_3$ with generator matrix

$$G = \begin{bmatrix} 1 & 0 & 0 & 0 & 2 & 2 & 1 & 1 \\ 0 & 1 & 0 & 1 & 2 & 1 & 2 & 1 \\ 0 & 0 & 1 & 2 & 0 & 1 & 0 & 2 \end{bmatrix}.$$

We consider the scheme based on the dual of $\mathcal{C}_1$ with $l = 2$ (so we have six participants). Applying the proposition, we can verify that the access structure consists of 4 groups of size 5 and 1 group of size 6.

Example 2.2.16. Consider the scheme based on the $[8,4,4]$ extended binary Hamming code with $l = 3$. In this case, we have a total of five participants. There are 4 groups of size 4 and 1 group of size 5 in the access structure.

In [11], it was shown that any group of size at most $d^\perp - l - 1$ has no information about the secret and any group of size at least $n + l - d + 1$ can recover the secret. Here we show that no group of size at most $d_l^\perp - l - 1$ is in the access structure, where $d_l^\perp$ is the lth generalized Hamming weight of $\mathcal{C}$.

Corollary 2.2.17. *Any group of $d_l^\perp - l - 1$ or less participants is not in the access structure, where $d_l^\perp$ is the lth generalized Hamming weight of $\mathcal{C}^\perp$.*

Proof. The lth generalized Hamming weight of a linear code is the minimum support of its subcodes of dimension l. A minimal access group $B = \{P_{i_1}, \ldots, P_{i_m}\}$ corresponds to an $[l + n, l]$ subcode $\mathcal{D}$ of $\mathcal{C}^\perp$ such that $\mathrm{supp}(\mathcal{D}) = \{1, \ldots, l, i_1, \ldots, i_m\}$. Hence, $m \geq d_l^\perp - l$. $\square$

In general, it is not easy to determine $d_l^\perp$ for $l \geq 2$. In the case of binary linear codes, we can show that the size of an access group is at least $\frac{3}{2}(d^\perp - l)$, where $d^\perp$ is the minimum weight of $\mathcal{C}^\perp$. This bound is weaker than the one given by $d_l^\perp$, but easier to calculate.

Corollary 2.2.18. *Consider the general SSS based on a binary linear code $\mathcal{C}$. If $l \geq 2$, then any group of $\frac{3}{2}(d^\perp - l) - 1$ or less participants is not in the access structure.*

Proof. As in the proof of Corollary 2.2.17, a minimal access group of size m corresponds to an $[l + n, l]$ subcode $\mathcal{D}$ of $\mathcal{C}^\perp$ whose support has size $l + m$. Moreover, deleting the first l coordinates of $\mathcal{D}$ as well as those coordinates which are not in its support yields a binary $[m, l]$-code of minimum weight at least $d^\perp - l$. Recall that $A_2(n, d)$ is the maximum size of a (not necessarily linear) binary code of length n and minimum weight at least d. The above yields $A_2(m, d^\perp - l) \geq 2^l > 2$. On the other hand, it is well known that $A_2(n, d) \leq 2$ whenever $n \leq \frac{3}{2}d - 1$. This yields $m \geq \frac{3}{2}(d^\perp - l)$. $\qquad\square$

Proposition 2.2.19. *When all participants come together and attempt to determine the secret, at most $\lfloor (d - 1)/2 \rfloor$ invalid shares can be identified and corrected.*

Proof. The secret and shares form a codeword of a linear code $\mathcal{C}$ with minimum distance d. Hence, at most $\lfloor (d - 1)/2 \rfloor$ errors can be corrected. $\qquad\square$

2.2.2.3.   Relation between access structure and joint weight enumerator

We describe the connection between the g-fold joint weight enumerator and the access structure. The following definition is taken from [13].

Definition 2.2.20. Let $A_1, A_2, \ldots, A_g$ be codes of length n over $\mathbb{F}_q$. The *g-fold joint weight enumerator* of $A_1, A_2, \ldots, A_g$ is defined as follows:

$$J_{A_1, A_2, \ldots, A_g}(x_a; a \in \mathbb{F}_2^g) = \sum_{c_1 \in A_1, \ldots, c_g \in A_g} \prod_{a \in \mathbb{F}_2^g} x_a^{n_a(c_1, \ldots, c_g)},$$

where $c_j = (c_{j1}, \ldots, c_{jn})$, $n_a(c_1, \ldots, c_g) = |\{i | a = (\overline{c_{1i}}, \ldots, \overline{c_{gi}})\}|$, and $\overline{c_{ji}} = 1$ if $c_{ji} \neq 0$ and $\overline{c_{ji}} = 0$ if $c_{ji} = 0$. Here $(x_a; a \in \mathbb{F}_2^g)$ is a 2^g-tuple of variables with $\mathbb{F}_2^g$, that is, $(x_{00\ldots0}, x_{00\ldots1}, \ldots, x_{11\ldots1})$.

When $g = 2$ then we have the joint weight enumerator [24]. The joint weight enumerator of a code with itself is called the *biweight enumerator*. The joint weight enumerator is a generalization of the weight enumerator.

From this point onwards, we only deal with general secret sharing schemes based on binary linear codes. First we consider the case

$l = 2$, i.e. the secret $s = (s_1, s_2)$. For simplicity, we use the corresponding decimal representation of the subscripts of the variables in the g-fold joint weight enumerator. Let $T_1 = \{1\}$ and $T_2 = \{2\}$ with indicator vectors 1_{T_1} and 1_{T_2} respectively. Consider the 4-fold joint weight enumerator $\mathcal{J}_{1_{T_1}, 1_{T_2}, \mathcal{C}^\perp, \mathcal{C}^\perp}(x_a)$, where $a \in \mathbb{F}_2^4$. We are interested in the coefficient of $x_{10} x_5$. The coefficient is a polynomial in $x_0 x_1 x_2 x_3$ and it gives information on the number and supports of pairs of codewords $u, v \in \mathcal{C}^\perp$ whose first two coordinates are $(u_1, 0)$ and $(0, v_2)$ respectively, where u_1 and v_2 are both non-zero. In general, for secrets of length l we use the $2l$-fold joint weight enumerator $\mathcal{J}_{1_{T_1}, \ldots, 1_{T_l}, \mathcal{C}^\perp, \ldots, \mathcal{C}^\perp}(x_a; a \in \mathbb{F}_2^{2l})$, where $a \in \mathbb{F}_2^{2l}$. The following theorem generalizes a result in [14] where Jacobi polynomials were used.

Theorem 2.2.21. *Let X_1 be the subset of $\mathbb{F}_2^{2l}$ consisting of all vectors whose first l coordinates are zero and let*

$$X_2 := \{(e_j, e_j) \mid j \in \{1, \ldots, l\}\},$$

where $e_j \in \mathbb{F}_2^l$ is the jth unit vector. Then the coefficient of $\prod_{a \in X_2} x_a$ in

$$\mathcal{J}_{1_{T_1}, \ldots, 1_{T_l}, \mathcal{C}^\perp, \ldots, \mathcal{C}^\perp}(x_a; a \in \mathbb{F}_2^{2l})$$

is a polynomial $p(x_a; a \in X_1)$. Identify X_1 with $\{0, \ldots, 2^l - 1\}$ via the binary number representation and write

$$p = \sum_{\mu \in \mathbb{N}_0^{2l}} c_\mu \prod_{a \in X_1} x_a^{\mu_a}.$$

Then the number $M_{\mathcal{C}}(m)$ of groups of size m in the access structure of the scheme based on $\mathcal{C}$ satisfies

$$M_{\mathcal{C}}(m) \le \sum_\mu c_\mu,$$

where the sum is over all μ with $\sum_{i=1}^{2^l - 1} \mu_i = m$. Moreover, if $m < \frac{3}{2} d^\perp - 1$ then equality holds.

Proof. The sum of the coefficients c_μ, where $\sum_{i=1}^{2^l - 1} \mu_i = m$, equals the number of tuples $(v_1, \ldots, v_l)$ of elements of $\mathcal{C}^\perp$ such that the projection of v_j onto the first l coordinates is the jth unit vector in $\mathbb{F}_2^l$, and

$$\left| \cup_{j=1}^l \operatorname{supp}(v_j) \cap \{l+1, \ldots, l+n\} \right| = m.$$

Hence due to Proposition 2.2.14, every such tuple determines a group in the access structure of the scheme based on $\mathcal{C}$, and every minimal access group occurs as a union of supports of such a tuple. However, in general there may be different tuples of codewords that correspond to the same access group. In this situation, there exists a tuple $(v_1, \ldots, v_l)$ as above and an element $c \in \mathcal{C}^\perp$ such that

$$\operatorname{supp}(c) \subseteq \cup_{j=1}^l \operatorname{supp}(v_j) \cap \{l+1, \ldots, l+n\}.$$

Then for any $j \in \{1, \ldots, l\}$,

$$|\operatorname{supp}(c) \cap \operatorname{supp}(v_j) \cap \{l+1, \ldots, l+n\}| \geq \operatorname{wt}(c) + \operatorname{wt}(v_j) - 1 - m$$

and hence

$$d^\perp \leq \operatorname{wt}(c + v_j)$$
$$\leq 1 + m - (\operatorname{wt}(c) + \operatorname{wt}(v_j) - 1 - m)$$
$$\leq 2m + 2 - 2d^\perp,$$

which yields $m \geq \frac{3}{2}d^\perp - 1$. Hence if $m < \frac{3}{2}d^\perp - 1$, then the sum of the coefficients c_μ with $\sum_{i=1}^{2^l-1} \mu_i = m$ equals the number of access groups of size m. $\qquad\qquad\square$

If $\mathcal{C}$ is self-orthogonal, then there exists a weaker condition than the one in Theorem 2.2.21 under which the number of access groups of size m can be read off from the $2l$-fold joint weight enumerator. To state this condition, we need the notion of the *code extension enumerator* below.

Definition 2.2.22. Let $\mathcal{D}$ be a linear self-orthogonal $[n, k, d]$-code. For a vector c not in $\mathcal{D}$, we denote by $\langle c, \mathcal{D} \rangle$ the code generated by c and $\mathcal{D}$. The code extension enumerator is the complex polynomial

$$P_\mathcal{D}(t) = \sum_c t^{d(\langle c, \mathcal{D} \rangle)},$$

where the sum is over a system of representatives of $\mathcal{D}^\perp / \mathcal{D}$.

Clearly $\deg(P_{\mathcal{D}}) \leq d$, and a summand $t^{d'}$ in $P_{\mathcal{D}}(t)$ gives rise to a linear self-orthogonal $[n, k + 1, d']$-code.

Now consider the general SSS based on a binary self-orthogonal linear code $\mathcal{C}$ and let $(v_1, \ldots, v_l)$ be a tuple of elements of $\mathcal{C}^{\perp}$ giving rise to an access group of size m, as in Proposition 2.2.14. Let $\mathcal{D}$ be the linear code generated by all the v_j, where the columns where all the v_j are zero are deleted. Then $\mathcal{D}$ is a self-orthogonal $[l + m, l]$ code of minimum distance at least $d^{\perp}$.

Assume that there exists another tuple of elements of $\mathcal{C}^{\perp}$ leading to the same access group, i.e. in Theorem 2.2.21, we have strict inequality for $M_{\mathcal{C}}(m)$. Then there exists a non-zero element $c \in \mathcal{C}^{\perp}$ with

$$\mathrm{supp}(c) \subseteq \bigcup_{j=1}^{l} \mathrm{supp}(v_j) \cap \{l + 1, \ldots, l + n\}.$$

Let $c' \in \mathbb{F}_2^{l+m}$ be obtained from c by deleting the coordinates where all the v_j are zero. Then $\langle c', \mathcal{D} \rangle$ has minimum weight at least $d^{\perp}$, hence gives rise to a summand $t^{d(\langle c', \mathcal{D} \rangle)}$ in $P_{\mathcal{D}}(t)$, where $d(\langle c', \mathcal{D} \rangle) \geq d^{\perp}$.

Corollary 2.2.23. *Consider the general SSS based on a binary self-orthogonal linear code $\mathcal{C}$ and let $\mathcal{T}$ be the set of all tuples in $\mathcal{C}^{\perp}$ that give rise to an access group of size m (cf. Proposition 2.2.14). For a tuple $(v_1, \ldots, v_l) \in \mathcal{T}$, let $\mathcal{D}(v_1, \ldots, v_l)$ be the code generated by all the v_j, in which the columns where all the v_j are zero are deleted. If for all such tuples, all monomials in $P_{\mathcal{D}(v_1,\ldots,v_l)}(t)$ (except for the monomial corresponding to $0 \in \mathcal{D}^{\perp}/\mathcal{D}$) have degree less than $d^{\perp}$ then equality holds in Theorem 2.2.21, i.e. the number of groups of size m in the access structure of the scheme based on $\mathcal{C}$ can be read off from $\mathcal{J}_{1_{T_1}, \ldots, 1_{T_l}, \mathcal{C}^{\perp}, \ldots, \mathcal{C}^{\perp}}$.*

2.2.2.4. *Binary self-dual codes*

In this section, we focus on schemes based on binary self-dual codes and the case $l = 2$. The *automorphism group* of a binary code $\mathcal{C}$ is the set of all permutations of coordinates which map the code to itself. The automorphism group is said to be *t-transitive* if for each pair of subsets (of coordinates) E_1, E_2 with t elements, there is a permutation in the group which maps E_1 to E_2. When $t = 1$, we use the term *transitive automorphism group*.

Based on the previous section, we use $\mathcal{J}_{1_{T_1}, 1_{T_2}, \mathcal{C}, \mathcal{C}}(x_0, \dots, x_{15})$ and determine the coefficient of $x_{10}x_5$. Let us denote this coefficient by Z. Under some conditions, we can determine Z using the biweight enumerator of $\mathcal{C}$.

Proposition 2.2.24. *Let $\mathcal{C}$ be an $[n, k, d]$ binary self-dual code. If $\mathcal{C}$ has a 2-transitive automorphism group, then*

$$Z = \frac{1}{n(n-1)} \frac{\partial^2}{\partial x_2 \partial x_3} \mathcal{J}_{\mathcal{C}, \mathcal{C}}(x_0, x_1, x_2, x_3)$$

$$= \frac{1}{n(n-1)} \frac{\partial^2}{\partial x_3 \partial x_2} \mathcal{J}_{\mathcal{C}, \mathcal{C}}(x_0, x_1, x_2, x_3).$$

Proof. The first part of the proof is taken from [19]. We can write the biweight enumerator as

$$\mathcal{J}_{\mathcal{C}, \mathcal{C}}(x_0, x_1, x_2, x_3) = \sum A_{i,j,k,l} x_0^i x_1^j x_2^k x_3^l,$$

where $A_{i,j,k,l}$ is the number of pairs of codewords with $n_{00} = i, n_{01} = j, n_{10} = k, n_{11} = l$. For a given coefficient $A_{i,j,k,l}$ and coordinate position h, let $N_h(i, j, k, l)$ be the set of all pairs of codewords in $\mathcal{C}$ which contribute to $A_{i,j,k,l}$ and with 01 pattern at h. It follows that

$$\sum_{h=1}^{n} |N_h(i, j, k, l)| = j A_{i,j,k,l}$$

since any pair in N_h has j positions with the 01 pattern. Since the automorphism group is transitive, then $|N_h(i, j, k, l)|$ is independent of h. Thus,

$$|N_h(i, j, k, l)| = \frac{j}{n} A_{i,j,k,l}$$

and in particular,

$$|N_2(i, j, k, l)| = \frac{j}{n} A_{i,j,k,l}.$$

Let $N'_h(i, j, k, l)$ be the set of all pairs of codewords in $N_2(i, j, k, l)$ with 10 pattern at position h. Using the arguments above and since the automorphism group is 2-transitive, then $|N'_h(i,j,k,l)|$ is independent of h and

$$|N'_h(i,j,k,l)| = \frac{k}{n-1}|N_2(i,j,k,l)|$$

$$= \frac{kj}{n(n-1)}A_{i,j,k,l}.$$

The proposition now follows. □

Since the following examples deal with self-dual codes, we shall remark the following proposition.

Proposition 2.2.25. *In the general SSS with $l = 2$ based on a binary self-dual code C, the size of every minimal group in the access structure is even.*

Proof. A minimal access group of size m in the access structure corresponds to a pair (v_1, v_2) of words in $C^{\perp} = C$ such that $v_1 = (1, 0, \ldots)$ and $v_2 = (0, 1, \ldots)$ and

$$m = |(\mathrm{supp}(v_1) \cup \mathrm{supp}(v_2)) - \{1, 2\}|.$$

The latter equals

$$\mathrm{wt}(v_1) - 1 + \mathrm{wt}(v_2) - 1 - |\mathrm{supp}(v_1) \cap \mathrm{supp}(v_2)|.$$

Since C is self-dual, the weight of every word in C is even. Moreover, the parity of $|\mathrm{supp}(v_1) \cap \mathrm{supp}(v_2)|$ equals the inner product of v_1 with v_2, hence is zero as well. Hence m is even. □

Example 2.2.26. The automorphism group of the $[8, 4, 4]$ extended Hamming code is 2-transitive and its biweight enumerator is

$$\mathcal{J}_{C,C}(x_0, x_1, x_2, x_3) = x_3^8 + 14x_2^4x_3^4 + x_2^8 + 14x_3^4x_1^4$$
$$+ 14x_2^4x_1^4 + x_1^8 + 168x_0^2x_1^2x_2^2x_3^2$$
$$+ 14x_3^4x_0^4 + 14x_2^4x_0^4 + 14x_1^4x_0^4 + x_0^8.$$

We obtain $Z = 4x_1^3x_2^3 + 12x_0^2x_1x_2x_3^2$. When $l = 2$, the total number of participants is 6. Since $\frac{3}{2}d^{\perp} - 1 = 5$, we can read off the number of access groups of size 4 as 12. The only other access group is the one formed by all participants.

Example 2.2.27. The biweight enumerator of the $[24, 12, 8]$ Golay code g_{24} was computed in [24] and it is known that the automorphism group of this code is 5-transitive. Applying the proposition above, we obtain

$$
\begin{aligned}
Z = {} & 6160x_0^{12}x_1^3x_2^3x_3^4 + 22176x_0^{10}x_1^5x_2^5x_3^2 + 7392x_0^{10}x_1^5x_2x_3^6 \\
& + 7392x_0^{10}x_1x_2^5x_3^6 + 2640x_0^8x_1^7x_2^7 + 73920x_0^8x_1^7x_2^3x_3^4 \\
& + 73920x_0^8x_1^3x_2^7x_3^4 + 36960x_0^8x_1^3x_2^3x_3^8 + 36960x_0^6x_1^9x_2^5x_3^2 \\
& + 12320x_0^6x_1^9x_2x_3^6 + 36960x_0^6x_1^5x_2^9x_3^2 + 266112x_0^6x_1^5x_2^5x_3^6 \\
& + 7392x_0^6x_1^5x_2x_3^{10} + 12320x_0^6x_1x_2^9x_3^6 + 7392x_0^6x_1x_2^5x_3^{10} \\
& + 18480x_0^4x_1^{11}x_2^3x_3^4 + 147840x_0^4x_1^7x_2^7x_3^4 + 73920x_0^4x_1^7x_2^3x_3^8 \\
& + 18480x_0^4x_1^3x_2^{11}x_3^4 + 73920x_0^4x_1^3x_2^7x_3^8 + 6160x_0^4x_1^3x_2^3x_3^{12} \\
& + 36960x_0^2x_1^9x_2^5x_3^6 + 36960x_0^2x_1^5x_2^9x_3^6 + 22176x_0^2x_1^5x_2^5x_3^{10} \\
& + 176x_1^{15}x_2^7 + 672x_1^{11}x_2^{11} + 176x_1^7x_2^{15} + 2640x_1^7x_2^7x_3^8.
\end{aligned}
$$

For the general SSS based on g_{24} with secret length $l = 2$, the number of groups in the access structure of size $m = 10$ can be read off from Z as 6160 due to Theorem 2.2.21, since $10 < \frac{3}{2}d^{\perp} - 1 = 11$. For every tuple (v_1, v_2) giving rise to an access group of size $m = 12$, we can compute $P_{D(v_1, v_2)}(t)$ explicitly, using the information on the pairs of codewords that is given by Z. It turns out that in all the cases, all monomials have degree less than 8, hence due to Corollary 2.2.23, the number of access groups of size 12 equals 36960.

2.2.2.5. *Invariant theory*

Suppose $\mathcal{C}$ is an $[n, k, d]$ binary self-dual code. We shall apply invariant theory in describing the access structure. We consider the case $l = 2$. Thus, we shall look at the 4-fold joint weight enumerator $\mathcal{J}_{1_{T_1}, 1_{T_2}, \mathcal{C}, \mathcal{C}}(x_a)$, where $a \in \mathbb{F}_2^4$.

If all the codewords of $\mathcal{C}$ have weights divisible by 4, then we have a Type II code. Otherwise, we have a Type I code. In [24], it was shown that the biweight enumerator of a Type I code is invariant under the group G_1 generated by all permutation matrices, all 16 matrices diag($\pm 1, \pm 1, \pm 1, \pm 1$), and

$$T_1 = \frac{1}{\sqrt{2}} \begin{bmatrix} 1 & 1 & 0 & 0 \\ 1 & -1 & 0 & 0 \\ 0 & 0 & 1 & 1 \\ 0 & 0 & 1 & -1 \end{bmatrix}.$$

The biweight enumerator of a Type II code is invariant under the group G_2 generated by G_1 and $T_2 = \text{diag}(1, i, 1, i)$ [19].

Let G stand for G_1 or G_2 depending on the type of code we are dealing with. Following the arguments in [19] and [24, Section III], and using the MacWilliams theorem in [13], we can verify that $\mathcal{J}_{1_{T_1}, 1_{T_2}, C, C}(x_a)$ is left invariant by every element of G acting simultaneously on the following sets of variables:

$$V_1 = \{x_0, x_1, x_2, x_3\}, V_2 = \{x_4, x_5, x_6, x_7\},$$

$$V_3 = \{x_8, x_9, x_{10}, x_{11}\}, V_4 = \{x_{12}, x_{13}, x_{14}, x_{15}\}.$$

Hence, $\mathcal{J}_{1_{T_1}, 1_{T_2}, C, C}(x_a)$ is a simultaneous invariant for the diagonal action of G. As a consequence, we can extend the results in [14] regarding the Molien series. Note that the exponents of the variables in V_4 are always zero, hence we can just consider the remaining three sets. The vector space of invariants that we are going to use is $\mathbb{C}[x_a]_{i,j,k}^G$ where $x_a \in \mathbb{F}_2^4 \setminus V_4$ and i, j, k are the total degrees of the variables in V_1, V_2, V_3 respectively. The corresponding generalized Molien series [34] is given by

$$\Phi_G(r, s, t) = \sum_{i=0}^{\infty} \sum_{j=0}^{\infty} \sum_{k=0}^{\infty} \dim(\mathbb{C}[x_a]_{i,j,k}^G)$$

$$= \frac{1}{|G|} \sum_{g \in G} \frac{1}{\det(I - rg)\det(I - sg)\det(I - tg)}.$$

Based on the previous section, we are interested in $\dim(\mathbb{C}[x_a]_{r,1,1}^G)$. Its generating function in the variable r is given by

$$F_G(r) = \frac{\partial}{\partial s \partial t} \Phi_G(r, s, t) \Big|_{(s,t)=(0,0)}.$$

Using MAGMA [10], we obtain the following for Type I:

$$F_G(r) = (r^{20} + r^{16} - 2r^{14} + 2r^{12} + r^{10} + r^8 - r^6 + 1)$$
$$/(r^{32} - 2r^{30} + 2r^{28} - 4r^{26} + 5r^{24} - 4r^{22} + 6r^{20} - 6r^{18}$$
$$+ 4r^{16} - 6r^{14} + 6r^{12} - 4r^{10} + 5r^8 - 4r^6 + 2r^4 - 2r^2 + 1).$$

For Type II we have

$$F_G(r) = (4r^{62} + 4r^{54} + 5r^{46} + 6r^{38} + 7r^{30} + 3r^{22} + 2r^{14} + r^6)$$
$$/(r^{96} - r^{88} - 2r^{72} + 2r^{64} - r^{56} + 2r^{48} - r^{40}$$
$$+ 2r^{32} - 2r^{24} - r^8 + 1).$$

References

[1] E. Agrell. On the voronoi neighbor ratio for binary linear codes. *IEEE Trans. Inf. Theory*, 44(7):3064–3072, 1998.

[2] A. Alahmadi, R.E.L. Aldred, R. dela Cruz, S. Ok, P. Solé and C. Thomassen. The minimum number of minimal codewords in an [n, k]-code and in graphic codes. *Discrete Appl. Math.*, 184:32–39, 2015.

[3] A. Alamadhi, R.E.L. Aldred, R. dela Cruz, P. Solé and C. Thomassen. The maximum number of minimal codewords in an [n, k]-code. *Discrete Mathematics*, 313(15):1569–1574, 2013.

[4] A. Alamadhi, R.E.L. Aldred, R. dela Cruz, P. Solé and C. Thomassen. The maximum number of minimal codewords in long codes. *Discrete App. Math.*, 161(3):424–429, 2013.

[5] A. Ashikhmin and A. Barg. Minimal vectors in linear codes. *IEEE Trans. Inf. Theory*, 44(5):2010–2017, 1998.

[6] A. Ashikhmin, A. Barg, G. Cohen and L. Huguet. Variations on minimal codewords in linear codes. In *Proc. 11th Int. Symp. Applied Algebra, Algebraic Algorithms and Error-Correcting Codes*, AAECC-11, pp. 96–105. Springer-Verlag, 1995.

[7] A. Betten. Distance optimal indecomposable codes over *GF*(2). Available online at http://www.math.colostate.edu/~betten/research/cod es/GF2/codes_GF2.html.

[8] G. Blakley and G. Kabatianskii. Linear algebra approach to secret sharing schemes. In *Error Control, Cryptology, and Speech Compression*, Lecture Notes in Computer Science, Vol. 829, pp. 33–40. Springer, Berlin, 1994.

[9] A. Bonnecaze, B. Mourrain and P. Solé. Jacobi polynomials, type II codes, and designs. *Designs, Codes Cryptography*, 16:215–234, 1999.

[10] W. Bosma, J. Cannon and C. Playoust. The Magma Algebra System I: The User Language. *J. Symbolic Comput*, 24:235–265, 1997.

[11] H. Chen, R. Cramer, S. Goldwasser, R. de Haan and V. Vaikuntanathan. Secure Computation from Random Error Correcting Codes. In *Advances in Cryptology — EUROCRYPT 2007*, Lecture Notes in Computer Science, Vol. 4515, pp. 329–346. Springer-Verlag, 2007.

[12] C. Ding, D. Kohel and S. Ling. Secret-sharing with a class of ternary codes. *Theoret. Comput. Sci.*, 246:285–298, 2000.

[13] S. Dougherty, Masaaki Harada and Manabu Oura. Note on g-fold joint weight enumerators of self-dual codes over $\mathbb{Z}_k$. *Appl. Algebra Eng. Commun. Comput.*, 11:437–445, 2001.

[14] S. Dougherty, S. Mesnager and P. Solé. Secret-sharing schemes based on self-dual codes. In *Proc. IEEE Information Theory Workshop, ITW 2008*, Porto, Portugal, 2008.

[15] G. Dósa, I. Szalkai and C. Laflamme. The maximum and minimum number of circuits and bases of matroids. *Pure Math. Appl.*, 15(4):383–392, 2004.

[16] R.C. Entringer and P.J. Slater. On the maximum number of cycles in a graph. *Ars Combinatoria*, 11:289–294, 1981.

[17] A.M. Gleason. Weight polynomials of self-dual codes and the macwilliams identities. In *Actes, Congrés International de Mathématiques (Nice, 1970)*, Vol. 3, pp. 211–215, Paris, 1971. Gauthiers-Villars.

[18] C. Greene. A rank inequality for finite geometric lattices. *J. Combin. Theory*, 9(4):357–364, 1970.

[19] W. Huffman. The biweight enumerator of self-orthogonal binary codes. *Discrete Math.*, 26:129–143, 1979.

[20] W.C. Huffman and V. Pless. *Fundamentals of Error-Correcting Codes*. Cambridge University Press, 2003.

[21] N. Kashyap. On the convex geometry of binary linear codes. Available online at http://http://ita.ucsd.edu/workshop/06/papers/82.pdf.

[22] E. Karnin, J. Greene and M. Hellman. On secret sharing systems. *IEEE Trans. Inf. Theory*, 29(1):35–41, 1983.

[23] B. McKay. Nauty — program for computing automorphism groups of graphs and digraphs. Available online at http://cs.anu.edu.au/~bdm/nauty/.

[24] F. MacWilliams, C. Mallows and N. Sloane. Generalizations of Gleason's theorem on weight enumerators of self-dual codes. *IEEE Trans. Inf. Theory*, 18:794–805, 1972.

[25] F.J. MacWilliams and N.J.A. Sloane. *The Theory of Error-correcting Codes.* North-Holland, Amsterdam, 1977.

[26] J.L. Massey. Minimal codewords and secret sharing. In *Proc. 6th Joint Swedish-Russian Workshop Inf. Theory*, pp. 276–279, Molle, Sweden, 1993.

[27] J.L. Massey. Some applications of coding theory in cryptography. In P.G Farrell, editor, *Codes and Ciphers, Cryptography and Coding IV*, pp. 33–47, Esses, UK, 1995. Formara Ltd.

[28] R. McEliece and D. Sarwate. On sharing secrets and reed-solomon codes. *Commun. ACM*, 24:583–584, 1981.

[29] M. Ozeki. On the notion of jacobi polynomials for codes. *Math. Proc. Cambridge Philos. Soc.*, 121(1):15–30, 1997.

[30] M. Ozeki. On the covering radius problem for ternary self-dual codes. *Theoret. Comput. Sci.*, 263(1):311–332, 2001.

[31] M. Ozeki. Jacobi polynomials for singly even self-dual codes and the covering radius problem. *IEEE Trans. Inf. Theory*, 48:547–557, 2002.

[32] V. Pless. *Introduction to the Theory of Error-Correcting Codes.* John Wiley & Sons, Inc., New York, 2nd edition, 1989.

[33] N.J.A. Sloane. Covering arrays and intersecting codes. *J. Combin. Designs*, 1(1):51–63, 1993.

[34] R. Stanley. Invariants of finite groups and their applications to combinatorics. *Bull. Amer. Math. Soc.*, 3:475–497, 1979.

[35] M. van Dijk. A linear construction of secret sharing schemes. *Designs, Codes Cryptography*, 12:161–201, 1997.

Chapter 3

Blakley Secret-Sharing Scheme

Blakley is one of the first founders of secret-sharing schemes. Blakley's scheme [4] is a (k, n)-threshold secret-sharing scheme. In a (k, n)-threshold secret-sharing scheme, the secret is divided into n shares and each share is distributed to one of n parties called shareholders. Only k or more shareholders combining their shares together can recover the secret while $k - 1$ or less shareholders cannot obtain any information about the secret.

Blakley's method is based on finite geometry. In this scheme, hyperplane geometry is used to solve the secret-sharing problem [12]. To generate a (k, n)-threshold scheme, each of the n participants is given an hyperplane equation in a k-dimensional space over a finite field. In some cases, each hyperplane passes through a certain point. The secret is the intersection point of the hyperplanes. Once colluding together, a set of k participants can reconstruct the secret by solving a system of linear equations [5].

Multisecret-sharing scheme is one of the important secret-sharing schemes. Some of them are constructed by [7, 13, 16, 18, 25, 30].

3.1. Linear Codes

Denote the finite field of order q by $\mathbb{F}_q$, where q is a prime power. An $[n, k]$-code C over $\mathbb{F}_q$ of length n, and dimension k is a subspace in $\mathbb{F}_q^n$ of dimension k over $\mathbb{F}_q$. The dual code of C consists of all vectors in $\mathbb{F}_q^n$ that are orthogonal to every codeword of C. This code is denoted by $C^\perp$ and is an $[n, n - k]$-code. One of the important invariants of a linear code C is the generator matrix G. G is a $k \times n$ matrix the rows of which form a basis of C. A generator matrix for the dual code $C^\perp$ is a parity-check matrix H.

The hull of a code is the intersection of C with $C^\perp$. If the hull of a code is trivial, this code is linear complementary dual (LCD).

3.1.1. LCD codes

A linear code with complementary code (LCD) is a linear code C satisfying $C \cap C^\perp = \{0\}$. Any code over a field is equivalent to a code generated by a matrix of the form $(I_k|A)$, where I_k denotes the $k \times k$ identity matrix [11].

3.2. Ramp Secret-Sharing Schemes

Another family of secret-sharing schemes is the ramp secret-sharing scheme. In this scheme, first a secret s is splitted into multiple shares $y_1, y_2, \ldots, y_N$. Then only authorized subsets of the pieces can recover s. The encoding rule is as follows. Each secret s corresponds a set of possible share vectors

$$Y = (y_1, y_2, \ldots, y_N).$$

Ramp secret-sharing schemes strike a balance between coding efficiency and security. For example, in the (K, N, n)-threshold ramp secret-sharing scheme, we can reconstruct s from randomly K or more pieces, but no information on s can be obtained from $K - n$ or fewer pieces. Moreover, any $K - \ell$ pieces can recover s for $\ell = 1, 2, \ldots, n - 1$. If $n = 1$, then this (K, N, n)-threshold secret-sharing scheme means the usual (K, N)-ramp secret-sharing scheme. If a ramp secret-sharing scheme does not recover any part of a secret from any randomly chosen $K - \ell$ shares (for $\ell = 1, 2, \ldots, n$), then this scheme is called a strong ramp secret-sharing scheme.

A linear ramp secret-sharing scheme is called t-privacy if the set of size t has no information about the secret, but a set of size at least $t + 1$ has some information about it.

3.3. Multisecret-Sharing Schemes Based on Linear Codes

3.3.1. Scheme description

In this part, we propose a new system to construct the multisecret-sharing schemes based on linear codes. We use Blakley's method to explain our approach [1].

We need an $[n, k]$-code C over $\mathbb{F}_q$ with generator matrix G.

3.3.2. Secret distribution

Let $\mathbb{F}_q^n$ be the secret space and let a given codeword be the secret $S = (s_1, s_2, \ldots, s_n)$. The rows of a generator matrix G are minimal access elements, and all of elements of C are participants in this scheme. The dealer, knowing the secret S, computes the share y of the user with attached codeword c, by taking the scalar product of that codeword with the secret. Thus

$$y = \langle c, s \rangle = c.S^T,$$

where ^{T} denotes transposition.

3.3.3. Secret recovery

Consider again the system with private secret S and the coalition corresponding to the rows of G. By the preceding subsection, we have

$$G.S^T = Y^T,$$

where $Y = (y_1, y_2, \ldots, y_k)$, and y_i is the share attached to the row i of G. The set of solutions of this system forms an affine space with associated vector space $C^\perp$. In other words, if S is a special solution then $S + d$ with $d \in C^\perp$, is also a solution and every solution is of that form. Since we assume that C is LCD or, in other words, that $C \cap C^\perp = \{0\}$, we see that the system admits a unique solution in C. Moreover C is LCD if $\left(\frac{G}{H} \right)$ is invertible [23]. Note that the condition that $S \in C$ can be expressed matricially as $HS^T = 0$. The secret can then be computed in practice by solving the following linear system of n equations and n unknowns:

$$G.S^T = Y^T,$$

$$H.S^T = 0.$$

Note that the LCD condition implies that the matrix of this system in S, namely the square matrix $\left(\frac{G}{H}\right)$, is of full rank n. This gives another proof of unicity of S, by inversion of $\left(\frac{G}{H}\right)$.

The following properties of the scheme are immediate but important.

Theorem 3.3.1. *We obtain the following informations in this multisecret-sharing scheme.*

(1) *The access structure forms the k-tuple of codewords that are linearly independent.*
(2) *The number of elements recovering the secret is at least k.*

Proof.

(1) The secret is reconstructed by a full rank matrix G whose set of rows is the said k-tuple.
(2) The number of rows of G cannot be less than k by definition. So only k elements can reach the secret, but no set of elements of size less than k can do it.   □

Corollary 3.3.2. *This new scheme is also a (k, q^k, k)-ramp secret-sharing scheme with $k - 1$ privacy.*

Proof. The number of participants recovering the secret is k and the number of participants who are all of elements of C is q^k. The k-tuples of codewords of participants that are linearly independent can reach the secret together. But some k-tuples, (those that are linearly dependent) cannot. Moreover the secret S is splitted into multiple shares $(s_1, s_2, \ldots, s_n)$.   □

3.4. Statistics on Coalitions

Theorem 3.4.1. *Let C be an $[n, k]$-code over $\mathbb{F}_q$ with generator matrix G. In a multisecret-sharing scheme based on C the number of* *minimal coalitions is*

$$\frac{q^k(q^k - 1)(q^k - q) \cdots (q^k - q^{k-1})}{k!}.$$

Proof. A minimal coalition is a set of participants, whose attached codewords form a basis of C. The number of bases of $\mathbb{F}_q$-vector space of dimension k is given by the said formula. □

Remark 3.4.2. Note that this number is strictly less than $\binom{q^k}{k}$.

Example 3.4.3. We consider a LCD $[7, 4]$-code C over $\mathbb{F}_2$ found by a random search in MAGMA [20]. A generator matrix G can be given as follows:

$$G = \begin{pmatrix} 1 & 0 & 0 & 0 & 1 & 1 & 0 \\ 0 & 1 & 0 & 0 & 1 & 1 & 1 \\ 0 & 0 & 1 & 0 & 1 & 1 & 1 \\ 0 & 0 & 0 & 1 & 1 & 1 & 0 \end{pmatrix} = \begin{pmatrix} g_1 \\ g_2 \\ g_3 \\ g_4 \end{pmatrix}.$$

The parity-check matrix H of this code is

$$H = \begin{pmatrix} 1 & 1 & 1 & 1 & 1 & 0 & 0 \\ 1 & 1 & 1 & 1 & 0 & 1 & 0 \\ 0 & 1 & 1 & 0 & 0 & 0 & 1 \end{pmatrix} = \begin{pmatrix} h_1 \\ h_2 \\ h_3 \end{pmatrix}.$$

There are $2^4 = 16$ codewords in the code C. These codewords are

$$\{(0000000), (1000110), (1100001), (0100111),$$
$$(0110000), (1110110), (1010001), (0010111),$$
$$(0011001), (1011111), (1111000), (0111110),$$
$$(0101001), (1101111), (1001000), (0001110)\}.$$

Now we examine a multisecret-sharing scheme based on C. Let the secret vector be $S = (1101111)$. We calculate the shares as follows:

$$y_1^T = g_1 S^T = \langle (1000110), (1101111) \rangle = 1,$$
$$y_2^T = g_2 S^T = \langle (0100111), (1101111) \rangle = 0,$$
$$y_3^T = g_3 S^T = \langle (0010111), (1101111) \rangle = 1,$$
$$y_4^T = g_4 S^T = \langle (0001110), (1101111) \rangle = 1.$$

Moreover,

$$h_1 S^T = \langle (1111100), (1101111) \rangle = 0,$$
$$h_2 S^T = \langle (1111010), (1101111) \rangle = 0,$$
$$h_3 S^T = \langle (0110001), (1101111) \rangle = 0.$$

Therefore, we should solve the following linear system to recover the secret:

$$\begin{pmatrix} G \\ H \end{pmatrix} S^T = \begin{pmatrix} Y^T \\ 0 \end{pmatrix}.$$

$$\begin{pmatrix} 1 & 0 & 0 & 0 & 1 & 1 & 0 \\ 0 & 1 & 0 & 0 & 1 & 1 & 1 \\ 0 & 0 & 1 & 0 & 1 & 1 & 1 \\ 0 & 0 & 0 & 1 & 1 & 1 & 0 \\ 1 & 1 & 1 & 1 & 1 & 0 & 0 \\ 1 & 1 & 1 & 1 & 0 & 1 & 0 \\ 0 & 1 & 1 & 0 & 0 & 0 & 1 \end{pmatrix} \cdot \begin{pmatrix} s_1 \\ s_2 \\ s_3 \\ s_4 \\ s_5 \\ s_6 \\ s_7 \end{pmatrix} = \begin{pmatrix} 1 \\ 0 \\ 1 \\ 1 \\ 0 \\ 0 \\ 0 \end{pmatrix}.$$

Conversely, it can be seen that the secret is $S = (1100101)$ by solving the above linear system.

Example 3.4.4. We consider a LCD $[3, 2]$-code C over $\mathbb{F}_2$. Its generator matrix G and parity-check matrix H are

$$G = \begin{pmatrix} 1 & 1 & 0 \\ 1 & 0 & 1 \end{pmatrix} = \begin{pmatrix} g_1 \\ g_2 \end{pmatrix},$$
$$H = \begin{pmatrix} 1 & 1 & 1 \end{pmatrix} = \begin{pmatrix} h_1 \end{pmatrix}.$$

It is clear that the number of codewords of C is $2^2 = 4$. These are

$$C = \{(000), (110), (101), (011)\}.$$

We try to construct a multisecret-sharing scheme based on C. Let the secret vector be $S = (011)$. We calculate the shares as follows:

$$y_1^T = g_1 S^T = \langle (110), (011) \rangle = 1,$$
$$y_2^T = g_2 S^T = \langle (101), (011) \rangle = 1.$$

Moreover,

$$h_1 S^T = \langle (111), (011) \rangle = 0.$$

If we solve the following linear system, then we reach the secret:

$$\binom{G}{H} S^T = \binom{Y^T}{0}.$$

$$\begin{pmatrix} 1 & 1 & 0 \\ 1 & 0 & 1 \\ 1 & 1 & 1 \end{pmatrix} \cdot \begin{pmatrix} s_1 \\ s_2 \\ s_3 \end{pmatrix} = \begin{pmatrix} 1 \\ 1 \\ 0 \end{pmatrix}.$$

It is seen that the secret is $S = (011)$.

Example 3.4.5. We consider a LCD $[7,2]$-code over $\mathbb{F}_2$ whose generator matrix G and parity-check matrix H are given by

$$G = \begin{pmatrix} 1 & 0 & 1 & 1 & 1 & 0 & 0 \\ 0 & 1 & 0 & 1 & 0 & 1 & 1 \end{pmatrix} = \begin{pmatrix} g_1 \\ g_2 \end{pmatrix},$$

$$H = \begin{pmatrix} 1 & 0 & 1 & 0 & 0 & 0 & 0 \\ 1 & 1 & 0 & 1 & 0 & 0 & 0 \\ 1 & 0 & 0 & 0 & 1 & 0 & 0 \\ 0 & 1 & 0 & 0 & 0 & 1 & 0 \\ 0 & 1 & 0 & 0 & 0 & 0 & 1 \end{pmatrix} = \begin{pmatrix} h_1 \\ h_2 \\ h_3 \\ h_4 \\ h_5 \end{pmatrix}.$$

C has $2^2 = 4$ codewords:

$$C = \{(0000000), (1011100), (0101011), (1110111)\}.$$

We examine a multisecret-sharing scheme based on C. Let the secret vector be $S = (0101011)$. We calculate the shares as follows:

$$y_1^T = g_1 S^T = \langle (1011100), (0101011) \rangle = 1,$$
$$y_2^T = g_2 S^T = \langle (0101011), (0101011) \rangle = 0.$$

Moreover,

$$h_1 S^T = \langle (1010000), (0101011) \rangle = 0,$$
$$h_2 S^T = \langle (1101000), (0101011) \rangle = 0,$$
$$h_3 S^T = \langle (1000100), (0101011) \rangle = 0,$$
$$h_4 S^T = \langle (0100010), (0101011) \rangle = 0,$$
$$h_2 S^T = \langle (0100001), (0101011) \rangle = 0.$$

Now we need to solve the following linear system to obtain the secret:

$$\begin{pmatrix} G \\ H \end{pmatrix} S^T = \begin{pmatrix} Y^T \\ 0 \end{pmatrix}.$$

$$\begin{pmatrix} 1 & 0 & 1 & 1 & 1 & 0 & 0 \\ 0 & 1 & 0 & 1 & 0 & 1 & 1 \\ 1 & 0 & 1 & 0 & 0 & 0 & 0 \\ 1 & 1 & 0 & 1 & 0 & 0 & 0 \\ 1 & 0 & 0 & 0 & 1 & 0 & 0 \\ 0 & 1 & 0 & 0 & 0 & 1 & 0 \\ 0 & 1 & 0 & 0 & 0 & 0 & 1 \end{pmatrix} \cdot \begin{pmatrix} s_1 \\ s_2 \\ s_3 \\ s_4 \\ s_5 \\ s_6 \\ s_7 \end{pmatrix} = \begin{pmatrix} 1 \\ 0 \\ 0 \\ 0 \\ 0 \\ 0 \\ 0 \end{pmatrix}.$$

By solving this system, it can be seen that the secret is $S = (0101011)$.

3.4.1. Security analysis

Assume that t users with $t < k$ with corresponding t codewords being linearly independent collude together to try to guess the secret. Let V_t be the span of these t codewords. They can find a complementary subspace W_t of V_t into C so that $C = V_t \oplus W_t$. Thus, the dimensions of V_t and W_t are t and $k - t$, respectively. By using Theorem 3.4.1 twice, double counting shows that the number of times any basis of V_t can be extended into a basis of C is equal to

$$X(k,t) = \frac{\prod_{i=0}^{k-1}(q^k - q^i)}{(k-t)! \prod_{i=0}^{t-1}(q^t - q^i)}.$$

Given a basis of W_t there are q^{n-t} choices for shares of the codewords of this basis.

The probability of success of such an attack is thus

$$q^{-(k-t)} \frac{1}{X(k,t)}.$$

For instance if $k = t + 1$, we see that for large k the quantity $X(k,t)$ is of the order of q^k. Thus, the security of the system requires k to be large. Having a large q is also beneficial to security but might be costly in term of arithmetic implementation.

3.4.2.   Information theoretic efficiency

The information rate ρ of the scheme is one of the other basic parameters in secret sharing [24]. It is the ratio of the size (in q-digits) of the secret to the maximum size of the pieces given to the participants. Since the secret is a codeword of a code of dimension k, its size is k. If we regard a share as the ordered pair of a scalar y_i and a codeword, then we see that the size is $k + 1$. Thus, the information rate of the SSS is

$$\rho = \frac{k}{k+1}.$$

If the information rate of a secret-sharing scheme is equal to one, which is the maximum possible value, then this scheme is called to be ideal. So the information rate of our scheme is close to one for $k \to \infty$.

3.4.3.   Comparison with other schemes

In this section, we compare our scheme with other code-based secret-sharing schemes by means of, respectively, the number of participants, the size of a secret, and the number of coalitions for an $[n, k]$-code over $\mathbb{F}_q$. We denote by A, B, and C these three quantities in the following table. In the fourth column, the symbol t denotes the error-correcting capacity of code.

It transpires that the length of the code does not enter directly into the parameters of the new scheme. For codes of similar alphabets and dimensions, the new scheme allows exponentially more participants and more coalitions, compared to the other schemes, for a secret size of the same order of magnitude.

Moreover, Massey scheme is a single secret-sharing system in contrast with the other three schemes. All the schemes in the table are ideal in the sense that the size of each secret equals the size of any shares. In Ding scheme, the reconstruction algorithm is based on linear algebra while the one in Çalkavur *et al.* scheme is based on decoding. We use Blakley's method to explain the reconstruction algorithm and obtain a linear equation system for our scheme. The advantage of our new system is the fact that it has a unique solution since it consists of n independent equations and n unknowns. So the secret will be recovered definitely:

System	[22]	[10]	[7]	This section
A	$n-1$	n	n	q^k
B	q	q^k	q^k	q^n
C	$\binom{n}{k}$	$\binom{n}{k}$	$\geq \binom{n}{d-t}$	$\frac{\prod_{i=0}^{k-1}(q^k-q^i)}{k!}$
ρ	1	$\frac{k}{k-1}$	1	$\frac{k}{k+1}$

In addition to our scheme is also a (k, n, q^k)-ramp secret-sharing scheme. It is clear that this scheme does not get out any part of a secret from any randomly chosen $k - \ell$ shares (for $\ell = 1, 2, \ldots, n$). Otherwise, this contradicts that the rows of generator matrix are linear independent. So this new scheme is a strong ramp secret-sharing scheme.

3.4.4. Conclusion and open problems

In this section, we have presented a new multisecret-sharing scheme based on LCD codes.

We have used Blakley's method to explain the reconstruction algorithm. We have determined the access structure and have calculated the information rate of this scheme. Regarding security, we can say that this system stands well, for codes of a reasonably high dimension. Compared to other secret-sharing schemes which are based on codes, it displays for codes of same order of magnitude of parameters more users and more coalitions at the price of shorter secret sizes.

Surprisingly, our scheme does not use the error correcting properties of the LCD codes employed. It would be nice to use them for cheater detection for instance.

3.5.   A New Approach to Construct a Secret-Sharing Scheme Based on Blakley's Method

In this section, we propose a new approach to construct Blakley's scheme by using finite fields [6].

Let the number of elements of finite field be $q = p^m$, where p is a prime number and $m \in \mathbb{Z}^+$.

We choose the secret and IDs of participants from the following set:

$$M_q = \{a : 0 \le a \le q - 1, a \in \mathbb{Z}\}.$$

We transform the selected integers to the polynomials of $\mathbb{F}_q[x]$ by Algorithm 1.

Algorithm 1

---

input: $a \in M_q$
output: $b \in \mathbb{F}_q$

1. Step 1. a is transformed into a vector of length m with respect to the base p.
2. Step 2. these vectors are written as a polynomial in $\mathbb{F}_q[x]$.

Example 3.5.1. Consider $4 \in M_8 \Rightarrow 4 = (100)_2 = \theta^2 \in \mathbb{F}_8$, where θ is a primitive element of $\mathbb{F}_8$.

We transform the obtained polynomials to the integers by Algorithm 2.

Algorithm 2

---

input: $b \in \mathbb{F}_q$
output: $a \in M_q$

1. Step 1. b is transformed into a vector of length m with respect to the base p.
2. Step 2. these vectors are written with respect to base 10.

Example 3.5.2. Consider $\theta^2 \in \mathbb{F}_8 \Rightarrow \theta^2 = (100)_2 = 4 \in M_8$.

3.5.1. Proposed scheme

We regard the finite field $\mathbb{F}_q$ as the secret space. We aim to construct a (k, n)-threshold scheme based on Blakley's method. ($n \le q$, the size of k participants is m) We choose any vector $x = (x_1, x_2, \ldots, x_m) \in M_q$ whose first coordinate is the secret. Since the scheme will be a

(k, n)-threshold scheme, at least k participants out of n will recover the secret. Consider n vectors of length m to find the secret shares for all n participants. Let these be $A_{u_1}, A_{u_2}, \ldots, A_{u_n}$. Then calculate the secret shares for each n participants such that

$$
\begin{aligned}
y_{u_1} &= A_{u_1} \cdot x^T \\
y_{u_2} &= A_{u_2} \cdot x^T \\
&\;\;\vdots \qquad \vdots \\
y_{u_n} &= A_{u_n} \cdot x^T
\end{aligned}
$$

These values of y_{u_i} $(1 \leq i \leq n)$ transform to the elements of $\mathbb{F}_q$.

Assume that $u_1, u_2, \ldots, u_k$ participants can recover the secret. In this case, it is constructed the following linear equation system. $A \cdot x^T = y$,

$$
\begin{pmatrix} A_{u_1} \\ A_{u_2} \\ \vdots \\ A_{u_k} \end{pmatrix}_{k \times k} \cdot \begin{pmatrix} x_1 \\ x_2 \\ \vdots \\ x_k \end{pmatrix}_{k \times 1} = \begin{pmatrix} y_{u_1} \\ y_{u_2} \\ \vdots \\ y_{u_k} \end{pmatrix}_{k \times 1}.
$$

The secret can be reached by solving the above system of equations.

If the matrix A is non-singular, then the secret can be recovered. Otherwise, it cannot be reached.

Example 3.5.3. Assume that $\mathbb{F}_8$ is the secret space. Let the number of participants be $n = 5$, the threshold value be $k = 3$ and the secret be $s = 4$. We construct a secret-sharing scheme based on $\mathbb{F}_8$ with these parameters by using Blakley's method.

Consider the polynomial $f(x) = x^3 + x^2 + 1$ which is irreducible over $\mathbb{F}_2$. Let θ be a root of f. We know that if $f \in \mathbb{F}_2[x]$ is an irreducible polynomial over $\mathbb{F}_2$ degree d, then by adjoining a root of f to $\mathbb{F}_2$, we get a finite field with 2^d elements.

Let θ be a root of $f(x)$. So the elements of $\mathbb{F}_8$ are as follows:

$$\mathbb{F}_8 = \{0,\ 1,\ \theta,\ \theta + 1,\ \theta^2,\ \theta^2 + 1,\ \theta^2 + \theta,\ \theta^2 + \theta + 1\},$$

$$\theta^1 = \theta,$$

$$\theta^2 = \theta^2,$$

$$\theta^3 = \theta^2 + 1,$$

$$\theta^4 = \theta^2 + \theta + 1,$$
$$\theta^5 = \theta + 1,$$
$$\theta^6 = \theta^2 + \theta,$$
$$\theta^7 = 1.$$

The transformation between M_8 and $\mathbb{F}_8$ is as follows.

$$0 \longleftrightarrow 0,$$
$$1 \longleftrightarrow 1,$$
$$2 \longleftrightarrow \theta,$$
$$3 \longleftrightarrow \theta + 1,$$
$$4 \longleftrightarrow \theta^2,$$
$$5 \longleftrightarrow \theta^2 + 1,$$
$$6 \longleftrightarrow \theta^2 + \theta,$$
$$7 \longleftrightarrow \theta^2 + \theta + 1.$$

We choose the vector $x = (6, 3, 4) \in M_8$ whose first coordinate is the secret.

Since the scheme will be $(3, 5)$-threshold scheme, we consider the five vectors as the participants.

Let these vectors be

$$A_{u_1} = (0, 2, 2),$$
$$A_{u_2} = (1, 3, 3),$$
$$A_{u_3} = (1, 5, 5),$$
$$A_{u_4} = (0, 3, 2),$$
$$A_{u_5} = (5, 2, 5).$$

These vectors correspond to the following vectors in $\mathbb{F}_8[x]$.

$$A'_{u_1} = (0, \theta, \theta),$$
$$A'_{u_2} = (1, \theta + 1, \theta + 1),$$
$$A'_{u_3} = (1, \theta^2 + 1, \theta^2 + 1),$$
$$A'_{u_4} = (0, \theta + 1, \theta),$$
$$A'_{u_5} = (\theta^2 + 1, \theta, \theta^2 + 1).$$

Now we calculate the secret pieces as below.

$$y_{u_1} = (0, \theta, \theta) \cdot (\theta^2 + \theta, \theta + 1, \theta^2)^T = \theta + 1 = \theta^5,$$

$$y_{u_2} = (1, \theta + 1, \theta + 1) \cdot (\theta^2 + \theta, \theta + 1, \theta^2)^T = \theta,$$

$$y_{u_3} = (1, \theta^2 + 1, \theta^2 + 1) \cdot (\theta^2 + \theta, \theta + 1, \theta^2)^T = \theta^2 + \theta + 1 = \theta^4,$$

$$y_{u_4} = (0, \theta + 1, \theta^2) \cdot (\theta^2 + \theta, \theta + 1, \theta^2)^T = 0,$$

$$y_{u_5} = (0, \theta + 1, \theta^2) \cdot (\theta^2 + \theta, \theta + 1, \theta^2)^T = 1.$$

The secret will be recovered when three participants combine their shares since the scheme is a $(3, 5)$-threshold scheme. Assume that the participants with number $2, 4, 5$ can recover the secret.

$$\left(\begin{array}{ccc|c} 1 & \theta^5 & \theta^5 & \theta \\ 0 & \theta^5 & \theta & 0 \\ \theta^3 & \theta & \theta^3 & 1 \end{array} \right) \begin{array}{l} l_2 \to \theta^2 l_2 \\ l_3 \to \theta^4 l_3 + l_1 \\ \hline \end{array} \longrightarrow,$$

$$\left(\begin{array}{ccc|c} 1 & \theta^5 & \theta^5 & \theta \\ 0 & 1 & \theta^3 & 0 \\ 0 & 0 & \theta & \theta^3 \end{array} \right) \begin{array}{l} l_3 \to \theta^6 l_3 \\ \hline \end{array} \longrightarrow,$$

$$\left(\begin{array}{ccc|c} 1 & \theta^5 & \theta^5 & \theta \\ 0 & 1 & \theta^3 & 0 \\ 0 & 0 & 1 & \theta^2 \end{array} \right) \begin{array}{l} l_2 \to l_2 + \theta^3 l_3 \\ \hline \end{array} \longrightarrow,$$

$$\left(\begin{array}{ccc|c} 1 & \theta^5 & \theta^5 & \theta \\ 0 & 1 & 0 & \theta^5 \\ 0 & 0 & 1 & \theta^2 \end{array} \right) \begin{array}{l} l_1 \to l_1 + \theta^5 l_2 + \theta^5 l_3 \\ \hline \end{array} \longrightarrow,$$

$$\left(\begin{array}{ccc|c} 1 & 0 & 0 & \theta^6 \\ 0 & 1 & 0 & \theta^5 \\ 0 & 0 & 1 & \theta^2 \end{array} \right),$$

$$x_3 = \theta^2 \Rightarrow x_3 = 4 \in M_8,$$

$$x_2 = \theta^5 = \theta + 1 \Rightarrow x_2 = 3 \in M_8,$$

$$x_1 = \theta^6 = \theta^2 + \theta \Rightarrow x_1 = 6 \in M_8,$$

$$x = (6, 3, 4).$$

It is seen that the secret $s = x_1 = 6$.

3.5.2. Security analysis

Finally, the security of the proposed approach is analyzed. In the proposed sharing algorithm, the secret is splitted into n shares and it is reconstructed by collecting k shares. The secret and shares are elements of a finite field. We know that these elements are uniquely determined. So the proposed approach is very reliable since there are no shadows of them.

3.5.3. Conclusion

This study presents the Blakley based secret-sharing approach. The security is increased thanks to the finite fields.

3.6. Some Multisecret-Sharing Schemes over Finite Fields

A cryptosystem is an implementation of cryptographic techniques providing information security services. Encryption is the process of scrambling a message and can provide a means of securing information. A secret-sharing scheme is an encryption method. The secret s is divided into n pieces called shares. The pieces alone have no information about the secret, but the secret can be reached by combining some pieces.

Multisecret-sharing schemes are one of the most important families of secret-sharing schemes, since the secret has been constructed as multiparty not single party. Thus, it is more difficult to reach the secret than for a single secret-sharing scheme. Some multisecret-sharing schemes are constructed in [7, 13, 16, 18, 25, 30]. In these schemes [2, 18, 25], there is a set of which consists of r secrets. The elements of this set can be shared and reconstructed at the same time or none of the r secrets can be retrieved. However, every (r, m, n)-multisecret-sharing scheme gives r single secret (m, n)-threshold schemes [10], especially, we presented in [7] a multisecret-sharing scheme based on error correcting codes. Moreover, in [1], we constructed a new multisecret-sharing scheme based on LCD codes. The reconstruction algorithm is given by using Blakley's method.

In cryptosystems, the secure storage of private keys is an important problem. Secret sharing satisfies the distribution of the private keys to the participants safely and does not trust a creature and central system. One type of such systems is blockchain systems. The private keys check the important seeds such as money and identities in this system. Their loss can have serious consequences. Thus, the distributed storage blockchain (DSB) scheme is introduced in [9, 27]. Krawczyk [17] consolidated the DSB scheme with Shamir's [28] secret-sharing scheme and private key encryption and information dispersal algorithm (IDA) [26]. The DSB scheme decreases the storage to a fraction of the original blockchain's burden.

Proactive secret sharing (PSS) was proposed by Herzberg *et al.* [15]. This is a stronger scheme by means of security. PSS is effective in the sharing of the shares to the participants when the secret s is kept. The participants get the new pieces of the secret s. These pieces are independent of the old ones and then the old pieces are removed. PSS protects the secret s from possible attacks.

Maram *et al.* [21] presented CHURP (CHUrn-Robust Proactive Secret Sharing). CHURP satisfies a secure secret sharing in dynamic setting. The collection of nodes keeps the secret changes in this scheme. It is also constructed for blockchains and has a simpler structure.

In the area of cryptocurrency, and blockchain design, secret-sharing schemes (SSS) are used extensively, in particular in electronic voting [3], data storage [27], and wallet management [14]. The most used of these schemes is the Shamir scheme [28]. In this note, we explore a variant of an alternative scheme, the Blakley scheme. We show that the Blakley scheme is not adapted to finite fields. We give a multisecret scheme which exploits similar ideas.

In a (t, n)-Blakley Scheme, the dealer selects a secret point $X = (x_1, x_2, \ldots, x_t)$ from $\mathbb{R}^t$. The secret key to be shared is the first coordinate of X. Other coordinates of X are random. For each participant $u \in P$, the dealer selects a random vector

$$A_u = (a_{u_1}, a_{u_2}, \ldots, a_{u_t}) \qquad (3.6.1)$$

from $\mathbb{R}^t$ and assigns the scalar

$$y_u = A_u X^T = \sum_{i=1}^{t} a_{u_i} x_i$$

as the secret share to user u.

In other words, the dealer assigns a hyperplane equation that is passing through X to each participant u. When a t-member coalition $W = \{u_1, u_2, \ldots, u_t\}$ is present, they have t-hyperplanes passing through X. The linear system formed by the shares of $u_i \in W$ is

$$\begin{pmatrix} A_{u_1} \\ A_{u_2} \\ \vdots \\ A_{u_t} \end{pmatrix} \cdot \begin{pmatrix} x_1 \\ x_2 \\ \vdots \\ x_t \end{pmatrix} = \begin{pmatrix} y_{u_1} \\ y_{u_2} \\ \vdots \\ y_{u_t} \end{pmatrix},$$

$$M_W X^T = Y_W^T,$$

(3.6.2)

where Y_W denotes the $1 \times t$ vector formed by the shares of participants included in W. Since all entries in M_W are generated randomly, M_W is non-singular with an overwhelming probability. Since M_W is non-singular, the subset W can find the secret by solving the linear system (2). When a coalition W' of size $t' < t$ is present, it only sees t' columns of A, yielding an underdetermined system to solve. Qualified coalitions find the secret and unqualified coalitions gain no information about the secret.

Remark 3.6.1. The Blakley scheme does not work well if we place $\mathbb{R}$ by a finite field, because the probabilistic argument for the non-singularity of M_w breaks down. Building a matrix of order n over the finite field $GF(q)$ by choosing its rows at random will not give a non-singular matrix with high probability, even large matrix order. The probability $P(n, q)$ of this event is

$$P(n, q) = |GL(n, q)| q^{-n^2} = \prod_{j=1}^{n} (1 - 1/q^j),$$

by $|GL(n, q)| = \prod_{j=1}^{n} (q^n - q^{n-j})$ [29]. Since the infinite product $\prod_{j=1}^{\infty} (1 - 1/q^j)$ converges, we see that

$$\lim_{n \to \infty} P(n, q) < 1.$$

For instance, for $q = 2$, we have the numerical approximation $P(n, 2) \sim 0.29$, for $n \to \infty$.

3.6.1. Notation

In this section, we consider a finite extension $\mathbb{F} = \mathbb{F}_q^m$ of the finite field $K = \mathbb{F}_q$ as a vector space over K. Then $\mathbb{F}$ has dimension m over K and if $\{\alpha_1, \ldots, \alpha_m\}$ is a basis of $\mathbb{F}$ over K, each element $\alpha \in \mathbb{F}$ can be uniquely represented in the form

$$\alpha = c_1 \alpha_1 + \cdots + c_m \alpha_m$$

with $c_j \in K$ for $1 \leq j \leq m$.

3.6.2. Scheme description

In this subsection, we examine [8] a multisecret-sharing scheme over finite fields. To explain the reconstruction method, we use Blakley's algorithm.

- Let the vector space $\mathbb{F}_q^m$ be both the secret space, and the participants set.
- Let any vector of $\mathbb{F}_q^m$ be the secret.

The m secrets are the m coordinates of a vector $X \in \mathbb{F}_q^m$. Let P denote an m-subset of participants. For each participant $u \in P$, the dealer selects a random vector

$$A_u = (a_{u_1}, a_{u_2}, \ldots, a_{u_t}) \tag{3.6.3}$$

from $\mathbb{F}_q^m$ and assigns the scalar

$$y_u = A_u X^T = \sum_{i=1}^{t} a_{u_i} x_i$$

as the secret share to user u. The linear system formed by the shares of $u_i \in W$ is

$$\begin{pmatrix} A_{u_1} \\ A_{u_2} \\ \vdots \\ A_{u_t} \end{pmatrix} \cdot \begin{pmatrix} x_1 \\ x_2 \\ \vdots \\ x_t \end{pmatrix} = \begin{pmatrix} y_{u_1} \\ y_{u_2} \\ \vdots \\ y_{u_t} \end{pmatrix},$$

$$M_W X^T = Y_W^T. \tag{3.6.4}$$

So we obtain a linear equation system in X and the secret can be retrieved by solving this system, provided M_W is non-singular, or, equivalently the family $(A_u)_{u \in W}$ is free.

Theorem 3.6.2. *This multisecret-sharing scheme has the following properties:*

(1) *The access structure consists of sets of m elements.*
(2) *No subset of size less than m can be used in recovering the secret.*

Proof. The following facts are immediate by basic linear algebra.

(1) Any basis of $\mathbb{F}_q^m$ can recover the secret by combining their shares, as the matrix of the system in non-singular in that case.
(2) The above system is undetermined in that case, because the matrix of the system is not square. □

Corollary 3.6.3. *This multisecret-sharing scheme is a (m, m)-threshold secret-sharing scheme.*

Proof. The secret is recovered thanks to the basis elements of $\mathbb{F}_q^m$ in this scheme. Thus, each minimal access set consists of m elements. The size of secret is m, since it is any vector of $\mathbb{F}_q^m$. That is, in this scheme, all m secrets of X can be determined together. Therefore, the new scheme is a (m, m)-threshold scheme. □

Corollary 3.6.4. *The multisecret-sharing scheme satisfying of the above theorem is also a ramp secret-sharing scheme with $m - 1$ privacy.*

Proof. The number of participants retrieving the secret is m. This means that the size of minimal access subsets is m. So this scheme is also a ramp secret-sharing scheme with $m - 1$ privacy by definition of a ramp secret-sharing scheme. It is clear that the size of minimal access subsets is m. □

3.6.3. Statistics on coalitions

Theorem 3.6.5. *Let $\mathbb{F}_q^m$ be the finite extension over the finite field $\mathbb{F}_q$. In a multisecret-sharing scheme over $\mathbb{F}_q$ the number of minimal* *coalitions is*

$$\frac{|GL(m,q)|}{m!} = \prod_{j=1}^{m}(q^m - q^{m-j}).$$

Proof. Recall that in our scheme, the secret space is the finite extension $\mathbb{F}_q^m$ and the minimal access sets consist of the bases. These m participants can recover the secret together. So the number of minimal coalitions is the number of rows of a non-singular matrix of order m over $\mathbb{F}_q$ up to ordering. $\qquad\qquad\square$

3.6.4. Security analysis

Assume that $t < m$ participants collude together and agree to pool their share to try and guess the secret. For the attack to be better than random choice we must assume that their corresponding vectors A_u are linearly independent. Assuming they correspond to a system of t linearly independent vectors they can be completed into a basis in $X(t, m, q)$ ways. In general, this quantity is a complicated combinatorial coefficient. Let us assume the most favorable case to the attackers that is $t = m - 1$. In that situation, the basis extension vector is any vector that is not in the linear span of the $m - 1$ vectors attached to the colluders. Thus $X(t, m, q) = q^m - q^{m-1}$. This vector being chosen there are q choices for its share.

Thus, the probability of success of the attack is $\frac{1}{(q-1)(q^m-q^{m-1})}$. To make this quantity small we should operate the system with a large m. Having a large q would increase the computational burden of the field arithmetic.

3.6.5. Information theoretic efficiency

The ratio of the size of the secret to the size of the participants gives the information rate [24] of the secret-sharing scheme. In this scheme, the secret is a vector of dimension m and its size is m. The sharings are the sets of basis elements and their size is m. Thus, the information rate is

$$\rho = \frac{m}{m} = 1.$$

This scheme is **ideal**, since $\rho = 1$.

3.6.6. Comparison with other schemes

In this section, we compare our scheme with other secret-sharing schemes in the literature by means of, in order, the number of participants, the size of a secret, and the number of coalitions for an arithmetic over $\mathbb{F}_q$. We denote by A, B, and C these three quantities in the following table. In the fourth column, the symbol t denotes the error-correcting capacity of code. As a basis of comparison, in columns 2–4, we consider an $[n, k, d \geq 2t + 1]$-code over $\mathrm{GF}(q)$. For codes of similar alphabets and dimensions, the new scheme allows exponentially more participants and more coalitions, compared to the other schemes, for a secret size of the same order of magnitude.

Massey's scheme has a single secret sharing system, not a multisecret-sharing. To recover the secret, the linear algebra in Ding's scheme is used. The reconstruction algorithm is based on the decoding in Çalkavur *et al.* scheme [7]. In our new system, to recover the secret, we use Blakley's method. However, the secret will be retrieved safely since the system has m independent equations and m unknowns. This means there exists a unique solution in the system.

System	[22]	[10]	[7]	This paper
A	$n - 1$	n	n	q^m
B	q	q^k	q^k	q
C	$\binom{n}{k}$	$\binom{n}{k}$	$\geq \binom{n}{d-t}$	$\frac{\prod_{i=0}^{m-1}(q^m - q^i)}{m!}$
ρ	1	$\frac{k}{k-1}$	1	1

3.6.7. Conclusions

In this work, we construct a multisecret-sharing scheme over finite fields. We use Blakley's algorithm to explain the recovering method of a secret. We determine the access structure, examine the statistics on coalitions and show the ideality and perfectness of our scheme. Attack analysis indicates that the important security parameter is the dimension m of the vector space we consider.

Compared to other schemes based on finite fields, our scheme displays for the same order of magnitude of parameters more users and more coalitions. It is also a multisecret scheme.

References

[1] A. Alahmadi, A. Altassan, A. AlKenani, S. Çalkavur, H. Shoaib and P. Solé. A multisecret-sharing scheme based on LCD codes. *Mathematics*, 8:272, 2020.

[2] L. Bai. A reliable (k, n)-image secret sharing scheme. In *Proc. 2006 2nd IEEE Int. Symp. Dependable, Autonomic and Secure Computing*, Indianapolis, IN, USA, pp. 1–6, 29 September–1 October 2006.

[3] S. Bartolucci, P. Bernat and D. Joseph. SHARVOT: secret SHARe-based VOTing on the blockchain, preprint, 2018, http://arxiv.org/pdf/1803.04861.pdf.

[4] G.R. Blakley. Safeguarding cryptographic keys. In *Proc. 1979 National Computer Conf.*, New York, Vol. 48, pp. 313–317, June 1979.

[5] I.N. Bozkurt, K. Kaya, A.A. Selçuk and A.M. Güloğlu. Threshold cryptography based on Blakley secret sharing. In *Proc. Information Security and Cryptology 2008*, Ankara, Turkey, December 2008.

[6] S. Çalkavur and F. Molla. The Blakley based secret sharing approach. *Sigma J. Eng. Natural Sci.*, 37(2):489–494, 2019.

[7] S. Çalkavur and P. Solé. Multisecret-sharing schemes and bounded distance decoding of linear codes. *Int. J. Comput. Math.*, 94(1):107–114, 2017.

[8] S. Çalkavur and P. Solé. Some multisecret-sharing schemes over finite fields. *Mathematics*, 8:654, 2020.

[9] K. Croman *et al.*, On scaling decentralized blockchains. In *Int. Conf. Financial Cryptography and Data Security*. Springer, Berlin/Heidelberg, Germany, pp. 106–125, 2016.

[10] C. Ding, T. Laihonen and A. Renvall. Linear multisecret-sharing schemes and error correcting codes. *J. Comput. Sci.*, 3(9):1023–1036, 1997.

[11] S.T. Dougherty, J.-L. Kim, B. Özkaya, L. Sok and P. Solé. The combinatorics of LCD codes: linear programming bound and orthogonal matrices. *Intern. J. Infor. Coding Theory*, 4(2/3):116–128, 2017.

[12] N. Al Ebri and C.Y. Yeun. Study on secret sharing schemes (SSS) and their applications. In *6th Int. Conf. Internet Technology and Secured Transactions*, Abu dhabi, United Arab Emirates, pp. 40–45, December 11–14, 2011.

[13] J. He and E. Dawson. Multistage secret sharing based on one-way function. *Electronic Lett.*, 30(19):1591–1592, 1994.

[14] S. He, Q. Wu, X. Lu, Z. Liang, D. Li, H. Feng, H. Zheng and Y. Li. A social-network-based cryptocurrency wallet-management scheme. *IEEE Access*, 6:7654–7663, 2018.

[15] A. Herzberg, S. Jarecki, H. Krawczyk and M. Yung. Proactive secret sharing or: How to cope with perpetual leakage. In *Annual Int. Cryptology Conf.* Springer, Berlin, Germany, 1995.

[16] E.D. Karnin, J.W. Greene and M.E. Hellman. On secret sharing systems. *IEEE Trans. Inf. Theory*, 29(1):35–41, 1983.

[17] H. Krawczyk. Secret sharing made short. In *Cryptology — CRYPTO '93, ser.* Lecture Notes in Computer Science, Vol. 773, Stinson, D.R., editor. Springer, Berlin, pp. 136–146, 1994.

[18] H.-X. Li, C.-T. Cheng and L.-J. Pang. A new (t, n)-threshold multisecret sharing scheme. In *Int. Conf. Computational and Information Science.* Springer, Berlin, *CIS 2005*, Vol. 3802, pp. 421–426, 2005.

[19] R. Lidl and H. Niederreiter. *Finite Fields*, G.-C. Rota, editor. Encyclopedia of Mathematics and Its Applications, Vol. 20, London, UK.

[20] MAGMA Computational Algebra System, Available online: http://magma.maths.usyd.edu.au/magma/, accessed on 2 December 2019.

[21] S.K.D. Maram, F. Zhang, L. Wang, A. Low, Y. Zhang, A. Juels and D. Song. CHURP: Dynamic-committee proactive secret sharing. In *Proc. 2019 ACM SIGSAC Conf. Computer and Communications Security*, Association for Computing Machinery: New York, NY, USA, pp. 2369–2386, 2019.

[22] J.L. Massey. Minimal codewords and secret sharing. In *Proc. 6th Joint Swedish–Russian Workshop on Information Theory*, Mölle, Sweden, pp. 276–279, 1993.

[23] X.T. Ngo, S. Bhasin, J.L. Danger, S. Guilley and Z. Najm. Linear complementary dual code improvement to strengthen encoded circuit against hardware trojan horses. In *2015 IEEE Int. Symp. Hardware Oriented Security and Trust (HOST)*, 5–7 May 2015, DOI: 10.1109/HST.2015.7140242.

[24] C. Padro. Robust vector space secret sharing schemes. *Inform. Process. Lett.* 68:107–111, 1998.

[25] L.J. Pang and Y.-M. Wong. A new (t, n)-multisecret sharing scheme based on Shamir's secret sharing. *Applied Math.*, 167(2):840–848, 2005.

[26] M.O. Rabin. Efficient dispersal of information for security, load balancing, and fault tolerance. *J. ACM*, 36:335–348, 1989.

[27] R.K. Raman and L.R. Varshney. Distributed storage meets secret sharing on the blockchain. In *ITA 2018*, http://ita.ucsd.edu/workshop/18/files/paper/paper_1714.pdf, February 2018.

[28] A. Shamir. How to share a secret. *Comm. ACM*, 22:612–613, 1979.

[29] D.E. Taylor. *The Geometry of the Classical Groups.* Sigma Series in Pure Mathematics, Vol. 9. Heldermann Verlag, Berlin, 1992.

[30] C.-C. Yang, T.-Y. Chang and M.-S. Hwang. A new (t, n)-multisecret-sharing scheme. *Appl. Math. Comput.*, 151(2):483–490, 2004.

Chapter 4

Alternative Schemes

This chapter collects some SSS, based on codes or finite fields arithmetic, that are still different from the classical schemes of Shamir, Blakley or Massey.

4.1. Codes and Coset Decoding

This section, in preparation for the next, recalls some prerequisite notions on Coding Theory, and can be skipped by experts in that domain. Let q be a prime power and denote the finite field of order q by $\mathbb{F}_q$. An $[n, k]$-code C over $\mathbb{F}_q$ is a subspace in $\mathbb{F}_q^n$, where n is length of the code C and k is dimension of C. The dual code of C is defined to be the set of those vectors $\mathbb{F}_q^n$ which are orthogonal to every codeword of C. It is denoted by $C^\perp$. The code $C^\perp$ is an $[n, n - k]$-code. A generator matrix G for a linear code C is a $k \times n$ matrix for which the rows are a basis of C. A parity-check matrix for a linear code C is a generator matrix for its dual code $C^\perp$. It is denoted by H.

Let C be an $[n, k]$-code over $\mathbb{F}_q$ with generator matrix G. C contains q^k codewords and can be used to communicate any one of q^k distinct messages.

We encode the message vector $x = x_1 x_2 \ldots x_k$ as the codeword xG.

If G is a generator matrix for C, then $C = \{uG | u \in \mathbb{F}_q^k\}$. The map $u \to uG$ maps the vector space q^k onto a k-dimensional subspace of $\mathbb{F}_q^n$.

4.1.1. Coset decoding

Suppose that C is an $[n, k]$-code over $\mathbb{F}_q$ and a is any vector in $\mathbb{F}_q^n$. Then the set $a + C$ defined by $a + C = \{a + x \mid x \in C\}$ is called a coset of C [18]. Suppose that a codeword x is sent, and that the vector y is received. Then the vector $e = y - x$ is called the error vector. The following result is an application of Lagrange theorem to elementary abelian groups [34].

Theorem 4.1.1. *Suppose C is an $[n, k]$-code over $\mathbb{F}_q$. Then,*

(i) *every vector of $\mathbb{F}_q^n$ is in some coset of C,*
(ii) *every coset contains exactly q^k vectors,*
(iii) *two cosets either are disjoint or coincide,*
(iv) *C contains exactly q^{n-k} cosets* [25].

4.1.2. Coset leader

The weight of a vector of $\mathbb{F}_q^n$ is the number of its non-zero components. The coset leader of a coset is an arbitrarily chosen vector of minimum weight in the coset.

4.2. Multisecret-Sharing Schemes and Error Correcting Codes

Error-correcting codes are used to correct errors when messages are transmitted through a noisy communication channel. Bounded distance decoding (i.e. decoding up to the error-correcting capacity) is a method of correcting errors that guarantees unique decoding. Secret sharing is a cryptographic protocol that allows a secret known from a person called the dealer to be distributed to n participants. No single participant knows the secret but some special subsets of participants called coalitions can. Karnin, Greene and Hellman examined the following situation [28]:

There are k secrets $s_1, s_2, \ldots, s_k$ to be shared. Such systems are called $[k, m, n]$ (multisecret-sharing) threshold schemes. Each $[k, m, n]$-threshold scheme for multisecret-sharing gives k single-secret (m, n)-threshold schemes [19].

4.2.1. Scheme description

In this section, we examine [9] a multisecret-sharing scheme based on error correcting codes with a known efficient bounded distance decoder [36]. Consider an $[n, k]$-code C over $\mathbb{F}_q$ which is a t-error correcting code. We construct now a multisecret-sharing scheme based on C.

Let $\mathbb{F}_q^k$ be the *secret space* and $\mathbb{F}_q^n$ be the *share space*. In the multisecret-sharing scheme, the dealer uses a share function $f : \mathbb{F}_q^k \to \mathbb{F}_q^n$ to compute the shares among the n participants. The sharing function is chosen as $f(s) = sG + h$, where $s = (s_1, \ldots, s_k) \in \mathbb{F}_q^k$ is the *secret* and G is a $k \times n$ matrix over $\mathbb{F}_q^n$ with rank k. Assume for convenience $s \neq 0$. Thus $c = sG$ is a non-zero codeword of the code C. The translation vector h is chosen by the leader to satisfy the following requirements:

(1) the weight of h is t;
(2) the support of h is included in the support of c.

Then the n participants recover the secret by combining their shares as follows:

- get $c + h$ by collecting its n coordinates (shares);
- get c from $c + h$ by decoding;
- get s from c by solving the linear system $sG = c$ of rank k.

The motivation for condition (2) above is the following proposition. Note first that we cannot allow any subset of participants indexed by the support of $c + h$ to recover the secret by shares pooling and decoding.

Proposition 4.2.1. *With the above notation, there is no h' of weight $< t$ such that the support of $c + h$ contains the support of $c + h'$ if and only if the support of h is included in the support of c.*

Proof. The condition is necessary for if there is any element x in the support of h outside the support of c then h' defined as $h'_x = 0$ and $h'_i = h_i$ for $i \neq x$ provides a contradiction. The condition is sufficient for, if true, in order to have an h' such that the support of $c + h$ contains the support of $c + h'$, the support of h' would need to contain the codesupport of h implying that h' would have larger weight than h. □

An immediate corollary is the following.

Corollary 4.2.2. *The multisecret-sharing scheme satisfied the hypothesis of the above theorems is also a $(d - t, n)$-threshold secret-sharing scheme, where d is the minimum distance and t the error-correcting capacity of C.*

Proof. In this scheme, the secret is recovered thanks to the minimal access sets. The minimal access sets consist of the vectors as $c + h$ with the support of h contained in the support of c and h of weight t. There are n participants in every set, as many as coordinates of C. The set of participants that is recovering the secret is also the support of these minimal access sets. The number of these participants in each of minimal access set is equal to the weight of $c + h$. So, the result follows. $\qquad\square$

Example 4.2.3. Let C be the binary $[5, 2]$-linear code with generator matrix

$$G = \begin{pmatrix} 1 & 0 & 1 & 0 & 1 \\ 0 & 1 & 0 & 1 & 1 \end{pmatrix}.$$

Since the minimum distance is 3, the code C corrects a single error. Now we construct a multisecret-sharing scheme based on C by using bounded distance decoding and examine some properties of this scheme.

First, we write the codewords of C:

$$C = \{00000, 10101, 01011, 11110\},$$

and the cosets of C are as follows:

$$00000 + C = \{00000, 10101, 01011, 11110\},$$
$$10000 + C = \{10000, 00101, 11011, 01110\},$$
$$01000 + C = \{01000, 11101, 00011, 10110\},$$
$$00100 + C = \{00100, 10001, 01111, 11010\},$$
$$00010 + C = \{00010, 10111, 01001, 11100\},$$
$$00001 + C = \{00001, 10100, 01010, 11111\},$$
$$11000 + C = \{11000, 01101, 10011, 00110\},$$
$$10010 + C = \{10010, 00111, 11001, 01100\}.$$

Let the message vector 10 be the secret s. So, the sharing function will be given by the formula

$$f(s) = sG + h = (10) \cdot \begin{pmatrix} 1 & 0 & 1 & 0 & 1 \\ 0 & 1 & 0 & 1 & 1 \end{pmatrix} + (10000)$$

$$= (10101) + (10000) = (00101).$$

We get $c = sG = (10101)$ from (00101) by decoding. Then we get the secret s from c by solving the linear system $sG = c$ of rank $k = 2$:

$$(s_1, s_2) \cdot \begin{pmatrix} 1 & 0 & 1 & 0 & 1 \\ 0 & 1 & 0 & 1 & 1 \end{pmatrix} = (10101).$$

Therefore, we recover the secret as $s = (10)$.

4.2.2. Statistics on coalitions

Denote the number of minimal coalitions of i participants by M_i, and let $M(z) = \sum_i M_i z^i$ be the generating function of these numbers.

Theorem 4.2.4. *Let C be a q-ary t-error correct code with weight enumerator $A(z)$. If $A^{(i)}(z)$ denotes the derivative of order i of $A(z)$, then*

$$M(z) = \frac{(q-1)^t A^{(t)}(z)}{t!}.$$

Proof. Recall that $A(z) = \sum_w A_w z^w$, where A_w denotes the number of codewords of C of weight w. Given a codeword c of weight w, the number of eligible h's is $\binom{w}{t}(q-1)^t$. The weight of $c + h$ is $w - t$. Differentiating t times $A(z)$ with respect to z the result follows. $\square$

Example 4.2.5. We continue with the above $[5, 2]$-binary code. Now we calculate the number of minimal access sets in the associated scheme. To get started, we need the weight enumerator of C:

$$A(z) = \sum_{i=1}^{5} A_i z^i = 1 + 2z^3 + z^4.$$

Since $t = 1$, we calculate the derivative of order 1 of $A(z)$.

$$A'(z) = 6z^2 + 4z^3$$

and

$$A'(1) = 10.$$

So, by Theorem 4.2.4 there are 10 minimal access sets, six of size 2 and four of size 3. For instance, $c = 10101$ yields half of those of size 2

$$c + h = 00101, 10001, 10100,$$

$c = 01011$ yields the other half of those of size 2

$$c + h = 00011, 01001, 01010$$

and $c = 11110$ yields all the size 3 access sets

$$c + h = 01110, 10110, 11010, 11100.$$

Example 4.2.6. Let $C = H_8$ be the extended binary Hamming code of parameters $[8, 4, 4]$. It is known that $A(z) = 1 + 14z^4 + z^8$. A direct calculation shows that $A'(z) = 56z^3 + 8z^7$. So this secret-sharing scheme admits 56 coalitions of size 3 and 8 coalitions of size 7.

In fact, the quantity $M(1)$ the total number of coalitions is a *binomial moment* of the weight distribution, a quantity known to enjoy a duality relationship.

Theorem 4.2.7. *Let C be a q-ary t-error correcting code, with dual weight distribution A'_i and with minimal coalition generator $M(z)$. We have*

$$M(1) = q^{k-t} \sum_{i=0}^{t} (-1)^i (q-1)^{t-i} \binom{n-i}{n-t} A'_i.$$

In particular if the dual distance of C is $> t$ we have

$$M(1) = q^{k-t}(q-1)^t \binom{n}{t}.$$

Proof. The first relation is an immediate consequence of the MacWilliams identities. See [44, (5.2.7), p. 226]. The second relation follows by letting $A'_0 = 1$, and $A'_i = 0$ for $i = 1, \ldots, t$. □

Example 4.2.6 (Continued). Let again $C = H_8$. The above calculations show that $A'(1) = 64$. It is well known that H_8 is self-dual, hence of dual distance 4. Theorem 4.2.7 with $t = 1$ shows then that $M(1) = 2^{4-1}1^1\binom{8}{1} = 64$, as it should.

4.2.3.   Democracy in secret-sharing

The following concept was introduced in [51].

Definition 4.2.8. A secret-sharing scheme is *democratic* of degree s if every group of s participants lies in the same number of minimal access sets, where $s \geq 1$.

If the code used in the SSS is very regular then so are the minimal coalitions. Recall that a code is s-homogeneous if the codewords of given weight hold an s-design. We shall prove a property very close to democracy.

Theorem 4.2.9. *If C is s-homogeneous, then the coalitions of given size are the blocks of an s-design.*

We shall require the following counting lemma of independent interest. Recall that λ_i is the number of blocks incidents with i given points. Thus, e.g. $\lambda_2 = 1$.

Lemma 4.2.10. *Let $\mathcal{B}$ be a $t - (v, k, \lambda)$ design and consider the set family S_r obtained from its blocks by removing r points in all possible ways, assuming $t + r < k$, and $\lambda_{k-r} = 1$. In this situation S_r is a $t - (v, k - r, \lambda\binom{k-t}{r})$ design with $b\binom{k}{r}$ blocks.*

Proof. Every t-tuple of points is contained in exactly λ blocks. Every such block contains outside the t-tuple $\binom{k-t}{r}$ r-tuples that can be removed to form an element of S_r. The elements so formed are pairwise distinct, since if not, the relevant blocks of $\mathcal{B}$ would be distinct and intersecting in at least $k - r$ points, which is ruled out by the condition $\lambda_{k-r} = 1$. □

We are now ready for the proof of the theorem.

Proof of Theorem 4.2.9. Follows by letting $t = s$ and $r = t$ in the notation of the lemma. □

Example 4.2.11. Let C be the binary $[23, 12, 7]$-linear code. Its packing radius is 3. Applying the above to the codewords of weight

3 which are known to hold a $4 - (23, 7, 1)$ Steiner system with 253 blocks we obtain a $4 - (23, 4, 1)$ design for the minimal coalitions; note that $\lambda = 1$ enforces $\lambda_4 = 1$. This is a complete design since $253\binom{7}{3} = \binom{23}{4}$. A less trivial design is obtained from codewords of weight 11 yielding a $4 - (23, 8, \binom{7}{3}))$ design with 45080 blocks when the total number of 8-tuples is $\binom{23}{8} = 490314$.

4.2.4. Comparison with other schemes

The basic secret-sharing scheme is Massey's secret-sharing scheme. Massey constructed a scheme based on an $[n, k]$ linear code using the generator matrix of this code. Let $s \in \mathbb{F}_q$ be the secret. Let G be the generator matrix for a code C of length n. In a secret-sharing scheme, a dealer has a secret.

The secret is created as follows:

Let u be any vector such that $ug_0 = s$, where g_0 is the first column vector of G. The vector u is the information vector. The dealer gives a share of the secret to each participant. There is a set P of subsets of the participants with the property that any subset of participants that is in P can determine the secret. This set is called minimal access set [7]. The access structure of a secret-sharing scheme is the set of all minimal access sets [37]. The secret s is shared to participants. The participants are recovered the secret by combining their shares.

One of the secret-sharing schemes is a (m, n)-threshold secret-sharing schemes. In a such scheme, the secret can be constructed from any m shares, but no subset of $m - 1$ shares reveals any information about the secret. A special class of a (m, n)-threshold secret-sharing scheme is a multisecret-sharing scheme. We recall some information about this scheme.

Let the secret spaces S_i $(1 \leq i \leq k)$ and the share spaces T_i $(1 \leq i \leq n)$ be vector spaces over a field $\mathbb{F}$. Then, the product spaces $S = S_1 \times \cdots \times S_k$ and $T = T_1 \times \cdots \times T_n$ are also vector spaces over $\mathbb{F}$. In a multisecret-sharing scheme a dealer uses a share function $f : S \to T$ to compute the shares among the n participants. Let $s = (s_1, \ldots, s_k)$ be the secret and $t = (t_1, \ldots, t_n) = f(s)$ be the share. If for all $a, a' \in \mathbb{F}$ and all $s, s' \in S$

$$f(as + a's') = af(s) + a'f(s')$$

then a multisecret sharing scheme is said to be linear.

Theorem 4.2.12. *A multisecret-sharing scheme defined over the above secret and share spaces is linear if and only if its share function is of the form*

$$f(s) = sG,$$

where $s = (s_1, \ldots, s_k) \in S$ *and* G *is a* $k \times n$ *matrix over* $\mathbb{F}$ *with rank* k [19].

We summarize the comparison with other code-based secret-sharing schemes in the following table, where we denote by P, S, C the number of participants, the size of a secret, the number of coalitions for an $[n, k]$-code over $\mathbb{F}_q$.

System	Massey	Ding *et al.*	This section
P	$n-1$	n	n
S	q	q^k	q^k
C	$\binom{n}{k}$	$\binom{n}{k}$	$\geq \binom{n}{d-t}$

Thus, Massey scheme is a single secret system in contrast with the other two schemes which are k-secret-sharing schemes. Both Ding scheme and our scheme are ideal in the sense that each secret is of the same size of a share [27], in these examples q. However, the reconstruction algorithm in Ding scheme is based on linear algebra, while the one in our scheme is based on decoding, a much harder problem, more resilient to algebraic attacks. Another advantage is the fact that the encoding is non-deterministic because of the choice of h left to the dealer.

4.2.5. Conclusion

In the present section, we have introduced a new multisecret-sharing scheme based on error correcting codes. The reconstruction algorithm is based on bounded distance decoding. The statistics of minimal coalitions are made by using weight enumerators and Pless power moment formula. The problem of democracy is tackled via block designs. In the comparison with known systems, the new system stands well, in particular in terms of security.

4.3. A New Secret-Sharing Scheme Based on Polynomials over Finite Fields

It is well known that monic polynomials play an important role in the development of the theory of algebraic structure of finite fields. Sun and Shieh [47] presented a polynomial-based secret-sharing scheme. They used Diffie-Hellman's principle to construct their scheme. Hwang and Chang [26] also employed polynomials to construct the secret-sharing scheme. In this paper, we present a secret-sharing scheme based on polynomials over GF(q), exploiting the structure of field extension of degree $d + 1$. For concreteness, we give some numerical examples. We prove that the scheme is both ideal and perfect. We give conditions on q and d to thwart passive attacks.

4.3.1. Polynomials over finite fields

Polynomials over finite fields form an important class of finite rings. There are numerous applications in this area. The polynomials we use should reflect the combinatorial properties of the point set. Certain special types of polynomials are monic polynomials. A monic polynomial is a single-variable polynomial in which the leading coefficients is equal to 1.

Definition 4.3.1. Let $f(x) = \sum_{i=0}^{n} a_i x^i$ be a polynomial over the ring R that is not the zero polynomial, so that we can suppose $a_n \neq 0$. Then a_n is called the *leading coefficient* of $f(x)$ and a_0 the *constant term*, while n is called the *degree* of $f(x)$, in symbols $n = \deg(f(x)) = \deg(f)$. By convention, we set $\deg(0) = -\infty$. Polynomials of degree ≤ 0 are called *constant polynomials*. If R has the identity 1 and if the leading coefficient of $f(x)$ is 1, then $f(x)$ is called a *monic polynomial* [32].

4.3.2. The scheme

In this section [10], we present a secret-sharing scheme based on operations in the field F. The secret space and the sharing space are both equal to GF(q^{d+1})*, the non-zero polynomials of degree d over GF(q). The secret, denoted s, is a polynomial of degree d over GF(q), and as a polynomial, it can also be denoted $s(x)$. The protocol uses a trusted dealer T to deliver the shares of the secret s to the m participants.

The setup is as follows:

(1) The shares, denoted $P_i(x)$, are randomly chosen by T.
(2) T chooses a primitive irreducible polynomial Q of degree $d+1$, then computes the product of the m shares modulo $Q(x)$:

$$P(x) = \prod_{i=1}^{m} P_i(x) \mod Q(x).$$

Thus $P(x)$ is of degree $\leq d$.
(3) T computes the polynomial $D(x)$ such that $D(x) = s(x) - P(x)$ and makes public $Q(x)$ and $D(x)$.
(4) The dealer sends the share $P_i(x)$, using a channel which preserves confidentiality, to user i for $(1 \leq i \leq m)$.

The reconstruction phase is as follows:
The m users pool their shares to compute $P(x) = \prod_{i=1}^{m} P_i(x)$ mod $Q(x)$ then $s(x) = D(x) + P(x)$.

Example 4.3.2. Suppose that $q = 2$, $d = 2$, $m = 3$, $Q(x) = x^3 + x + 1$, and $F = \mathrm{GF}(2)[x]/(Q(x))$. Take the shares as

$$P_1(x) = x^2 + 1, P_2(x) = x^2 + x + 1, P_3(x) = x^2 + x$$

and the secret as $s(x) = x^2 + x + 1$.
The dealer T calculates $P(x)$ in the field F.

$$P(x) = \prod_{i=1}^{3} P_i(x) = P_1(x) \cdot P_2(x) \cdot P_3(x)$$

$$= x^6 + x^4 + x^3 + x$$

$$= x.$$

Then T makes public $D(x) = s(x) + P(x)$. Note that the characteristic of the field is 2, hence subtraction and addition are the same. The calculation of $D(x)$ in this example gives

$$D(x) = (x^2 + x + 1) + (x),$$
$$D(x) = x^2 + 1.$$

The reconstruction phase is as follows. The m participants pool their shares to obtain $P(x)$, and then add the public value $D(x)$

$$s(x) = P(x) + D(x),$$

$$s(x) = x^2 + x + 1.$$

Example 4.3.3. Suppose that $q = 3$, $d = 3$, $m = 4$, $Q(x) = x^4 + 2 * x^3 + 2$, and $F = \mathrm{GF}(3)[x]/(Q(x))$. Take the shares as

$$P_1(x) = x^3 + 2x^2, \quad P_2(x) = x^3 + x + 1,$$

$$P_3(x) = x^3 + 2x, \quad P_4(x) = x^3 + x^2 + 2$$

and the secret $s(x) = x^3 + x^2 + 1$.

$$P(x) = \prod_{i=1}^{4} P_i(x) = P_1(x) \cdot P_2(x) \cdot P_3(x) \cdot P_4(x)$$

$$= x^{12} + 2x^{10} + x^7 + 2x^3 = 1.$$

The dealer makes public

$$D(x) = s(x) - P(x)$$

$$= (x^3 + x^2 + 1) - 1$$

$$= x^3 + x^2.$$

The reconstruction phase gives

$$s(x) = P(x) + D(x)$$

$$= x^3 + x^2 + 1.$$

4.3.3. Properties and security

In a secret sharing scheme, a large number of participants may increase the security. We can explain this situation using the information rate ρ [39]. This parameter is an important parameter determining the security and the efficiency of a secret-sharing scheme.

Proposition 4.3.4. *The size of the secret is* $\log_q(q^{d+1} - 1)$.

Proof. The secret space consists of the non-zero polynomials of degree d over $GF(q)$ and the number of these polynomials is $q^{d+1} - 1$. Therefore, the secret can be written using $d + 1$ elements of $\mathbb{F}_q$.

In our scheme, the size of a share is exactly equal to the size of the secret. The information rate is

$$\rho = \frac{\log_q(q^{d+1} - 1)}{\log_q(q^{d+1} - 1)} = 1.$$

We recall that if the size of the shares of all participants are less than or equal to the size of the secret, then the secret sharing scheme is said to be ideal [48]. Therefore, we have the following theorem.

Theorem 4.3.5. *The constructed scheme is ideal.*

For the property of perfect privacy, we have to show [3] that every rejected set cannot learn anything about the secret (in the information theoretic sense) from their shares. In terms of entropy function, it means that the entropy of the secret knowing the shares of any rejected set is equal to the entropy of the secret. In fact, the security of our scheme relies on the equation $s(x) = D(x) + P(x)$. Since $P(x)$ is a product of random polynomials, it can also be considered as random. Moreover s, D and P are of same size. This equation is therefore the same as the one of One Time Pad which has a perfect secrecy. It means that knowing D, an adversary cannot know any information about the secret. Moreover, an adversary who knows strictly less than m shares gets no information about the secret.

So this scheme has the property of perfect privacy [48] and it has a secure access structure. Moreover, the scheme is robust against passive adversaries. It means that if all the participants follow the protocol honestly, no attacker can retrieve the secret with a probability greater than $1/(q^{d+1} - 1)$. Indeed, suppose that $m - 1$ users collude, pool their shares, and try to guess the share of order m picking a random element of F^*. The probability of success of such an attack is $\frac{1}{(q^{d+1}-1)}$. More generally if r users with $r < m - 1$ try to mount an attack, having less information than $m - 1$ users, the probability of success of that attack will be strictly less than the above quantity.

Remark 4.3.6. This scheme is not an (m, m)-threshold secret-sharing scheme since the factorization in the field is not unique. Suppose, for example, that a share is equal to the product of all the shares. In this case, this share is theoretically able to recover the secret. This fact means that there is no predefined threshold to recover the secret from the shares, but it does not affect the security of the scheme.

It is also easy to see that the scheme is not monotone since the authorized coalition is unique.

4.3.4.　Conclusion

In this paper, we have studied a new secret-sharing scheme based on polynomial multiplications over $\mathrm{GF}(q)$. We have determined its access structure and computed its information rate. Our scheme is ideal and secure against passive attacks. Our scheme could be used in embedded systems because multiplications in a field are easily optimized and therefore the computational costs are lower than schemes using interpolation.

4.4.　Roots of Irreducible Polynomials

In this section, we remind some information about the set of roots of an irreducible polynomial over a finite field.

Lemma 4.4.1. *Let $f \in \mathbb{F}_q[x]$ be an irreducible polynomial over a finite field $\mathbb{F}_q$ and α be a root of f in extension field of $\mathbb{F}_q$. Then for a polynomial $h \in \mathbb{F}_q[x]$ we have $h(\alpha) = 0$ if and only if f divides h* [32].

Lemma 4.4.2. *Let $f \in \mathbb{F}_q[x]$ be an irreducible polynomial over $\mathbb{F}_q$ of degree m. Then $f(x)$ divides $x^{q^n} - x$ if and only if f divides h* [32].

Theorem 4.4.3. *If f is an irreducible polynomial in $\mathbb{F}_q[x]$ of degree m, then f has a root α in $\mathbb{F}_{q^m}$. Furthermore, all the roots of f are simple and are given by the m distinct elements $\alpha, \alpha^q, \alpha^{q^2}, \ldots, \alpha^{q^{m-1}}$ of $\mathbb{F}_{q^m}$* [32].

Corollary 4.4.4. *Let f be an irreducible polynomial in $\mathbb{F}_q[x]$ of degree m. Then the splitting field of f over $\mathbb{F}_q$ is given by $\mathbb{F}_{q^m}$ [32].*

Definition 4.4.5. Let $\mathbb{F}_{q^m}$ be an extension of $\mathbb{F}_q$ and let $\alpha \in \mathbb{F}_{q^m}$. Then the elements $\alpha, \alpha^q, \alpha^{q^2}, \dots, \alpha^{q^{m-1}}$ are called the conjugates of α with respect to $\mathbb{F}_q$ [32].

The conjugates of $\alpha \in \mathbb{F}_{q^m}$ with respect to $\mathbb{F}_q$ are distinct if and only if minimal polynomial of α over $\mathbb{F}_q$ has degree m. Otherwise, the degree d of this polynomial is a proper divisor of m and then the conjugates of α with respect to $\mathbb{F}_q$ are the distinct elements $\alpha, \alpha^q, \alpha^{q^2}, \dots, \alpha^{q^{d-1}}$ each repeated m/d times.

Theorem 4.4.6. *The conjugates of $\alpha \in \mathbb{F}_{q^*}$ with respect to any subfield of $\mathbb{F}_q$ have the same order in the group $\mathbb{F}_{q^*}$, where $\mathbb{F}_{q^*}$ is a cyclic group of non-zero elements of which consists of non-zero elements of $\mathbb{F}_q$ [32].*

Corollary 4.4.7. *If α is a primitive element of $\mathbb{F}_q$, then so are all its conjugates with respect to any subfield of $\mathbb{F}_q$ [32].*

4.4.1. Traces and norms

In this part, we consider the viewpoint of regarding a finite extension $F = \mathbb{F}_{q^m}$ of the finite field $K = \mathbb{F}_q$ as a vector space over K.

Definition 4.4.8. For $\alpha \in F = \mathbb{F}_{q^m}$ and $K = \mathbb{F}_q$, the trace $T_{r_{F/K}}(\alpha)$ of α over K is defined by

$$T_{r_{F/K}}(\alpha) = \alpha + \alpha^q + \alpha^{q^2} + \cdots + \alpha^{q^{m-1}}.$$

If K is the prime subfield of F, then $T_{r_{F/K}}(\alpha)$ is called the absolute trace of α and simply denoted by $T_{r_F}(\alpha)$ [32].

Definition of the trace may be obtained as follows.

Let $f \in K[x]$ be the minimal polynomial of α over K and its degree d is a divisor of m. Then $g(x) = f(x)^{m/d} \in K[x]$ is called the characteristic polynomial of α over K. By Theorem 4.4.6, the roots of f in F are given by $\alpha, \alpha^q, \alpha^{q^2}, \dots, \alpha^{q^{d-1}}$ and by Definition 4.4.5, the roots of g in F are precisely the conjugates of α with respect to K.

Hence

$$g(x) = x^m + a_{m-1}x^{m-1} + \cdots + a_0$$

$$= (x - \alpha) \cdot (x - \alpha^q) \cdot \ldots \cdot (x - \alpha^{q^{m-1}}) \qquad (4.4.1)$$

and a comparison of coefficients shows that

$$T_{r_{F/K}}(\alpha) = -a_{m-1}. \qquad (4.4.2)$$

$T_{r_{F/K}}(\alpha)$ is always an element of K [32].

Definition 4.4.9. For $\alpha \in F = \mathbb{F}_{q^m}$ and $K = \mathbb{F}_q$, the norm $N_{F/K}(\alpha)$ of α over K is defined by

$$N_{F/K}(\alpha) = \alpha \cdot \alpha^q \cdot \alpha^{q^2} \cdot \ldots \cdot \alpha^{q^{m-1}} = \alpha^{q^m-1}/(q-1).$$

Moreover, by comparing the constant term in (4.4.1), it can be written the following equation:

$$N_{F/K}(\alpha) = (-1)^m \cdot a_0.$$

Here, $N_{F/K}(\alpha)$ is also an element of K [32].

The number of distinct bases of F over K is too large, but there are two special types of bases. The first base is a polynomial basis $\{1, \alpha, \alpha^2, \ldots, \alpha^{m-1}\}$, made up of the powers of a defining element α of F over K, where α is taken to be a primitive element of F. Another type of basis is a normal basis.

Definition 4.4.10. Let $K = \mathbb{F}_q$ and $F = \mathbb{F}_{q^m}$. Then a basis of F over K of the form $\{\alpha, \alpha^q, \alpha^{q^2}, \ldots, \alpha^{q^{m-1}}\}$, consisting of a suitable element $\alpha \in F$ and its conjugates with respect to K, is called a normal basis of F over K [32].

4.4.2. Secret-sharing schemes

In this section, we should think about a case of some malicious behaviors lying among participants which are called cheaters. They modify their shares in order to cheat.

If a group of participants can recover the secret by combining their shares, then any group of participants containing this group can also recover the secret.

Definition 4.4.11. An access group is a subset of a set of participants that can recover the secret from its shares. A collection Γ of access groups of participants is called an access structure of the scheme. An element $A \in \Gamma$ is called a minimal access element. Hence a set is a minimal access group if it can recover the secret but no proper subset can recover the secret. Let $\bar{\Gamma}$ be the set of all minimal access elements.

We call $\bar{\Gamma}$ the minimal access structure [29].

Determining the minimal access structure is a hard problem [18].

Now let us consider the accessibility of an access structure of secret sharing scheme based on binary linear code. Let $P = \{P_1, P_2, \ldots, P_m\}$ be a set of m participants and let A_p be the set of all access elements on P.

Definition 4.4.12. The accessibility index on P is the map $\delta_p(\Gamma) : A_p \to \mathbb{R}$ given by

$$\delta_p(\Gamma) = \frac{|\Gamma|}{2^m}$$

for $\Gamma \in A_p$, where $m = |P|$. The number $\delta_p(\Gamma)$ will be called the accessibility degree of structure Γ [16].

4.4.3. The schemes

In this section, we present the new (t, n)-threshold schemes of [11] that combine Shamir scheme with our schemes.

4.4.4. First scheme

Let $\mathbb{F}_q$ be the secret space and $\mathbb{F}_{q^m}$ be the sharing space. We consider a finite extension of $\mathbb{F}_{q^m}$ of the finite field $\mathbb{F}_q$ as a vector space over $\mathbb{F}_q$, where m is the dimensional of $\mathbb{F}_{q^m}$ over $\mathbb{F}_q$. Assume a characteristic polynomial $g(x)$ of α, where $\alpha \in \mathbb{F}_{q^m}$ and the degree of $g(x)$ is m such that

$$g(x) = x^m + a_{m-1}x^{m-1} + \cdots + a_0.$$

- Let all of elements of $\mathbb{F}_{q^m}$, except 0, be the participants.
- The dealer picks the element $-a_{m-1} \in \mathbb{F}_q$ as the secret and distributes to m elements of $\mathbb{F}_{q^m}$ which are $\alpha, \alpha^q, \alpha^{q^2}, \ldots, \alpha^{q^{m-1}}$.

We know that these elements are also the normal basis elements of $\mathbb{F}_{q^m}$ and uniquely determined and each element of $\mathbb{F}_{q^m}$ can be written as the linear combination of basis elements. These m participants recover the secret while pooling their shares. In the first scheme, we need the trace function of α to recover the secret.

$$T_{r_{F/K}}(\alpha) = \alpha + \alpha^q + \alpha^{q^2} + \cdots + \alpha^{q^{m-1}}.$$

We also know that $T_{r_{F/K}}(\alpha)$ is also equal to $-a_{m-1}$, where $-a_{m-1}$ is the coefficient of x^{m-1} for the characteristic polynomial $g(x)$. So $\alpha, \alpha^q, \alpha^{q^2}, \ldots, \alpha^{q^{m-1}}$ elements can reach the secret together.

4.4.5.   Second scheme

Now we construct another scheme using the norm function. In this scheme the dealer picks the element $(-1)^m \cdot a_0 \in \mathbb{F}_q$ as the secret and distributes to the m elements of $\mathbb{F}_{q^m}$ which are $\alpha, \alpha^q, \alpha^{q^2}, \ldots, \alpha^{q^{m-1}}$. These m participants recover the secret while combining their shares as follows:

$$N_{F/K}(\alpha) = \alpha \cdot \alpha^q \cdot \alpha^{q^2} \cdot \ldots \cdot \alpha^{q^{m-1}}.$$

We know that $N_{F/K}(\alpha)$ is also equal to $(-1)^m a_0$. So $\alpha, \alpha^q, \alpha^{q^2}, \ldots,$ $\alpha^{q^{m-1}}$ elements can reach the secret together.

If $m - h$ say, with $1 \le h < m$, participants group together they can guess the secret with probability $\frac{1}{h+1} \le \frac{1}{2}$.

Another possible attack would be to isolate elements of $\mathbb{F}_{q^m}$ which are reached the secret. In our secret-sharing schemes, only the conjugates of α with respect to $\mathbb{F}_q$ can recover the secret. These elements are also the normal basis elements which are uniquely determined.

Theorem 4.4.13. *In these secret-sharing schemes based on extension fields we have the following properties:*

(i) *The access structure consists of the m elements.*
(ii) *No element of number less than m can be used in recovering the secret.*

Proof.   (i) The secret is recovered thanks to the normal basis elements and their number is m.

(ii) These m elements are uniquely determined. So there is no element which has this property. The proof is clear. □

Corollary 4.4.14. *With the above condition the extension field* $\mathbb{F}_{q^m}$ *determines* $(m, q^m - 1)$-*threshold scheme.*

Proof. It is clear that the number of non-zero elements of $\mathbb{F}_{q^m}$ is $q^m - 1$ and the number of normal basis elements is m. These m elements out of $q^m - 1$ can reach the secret together. □

Definition 4.4.15. The access structure of these secret-sharing schemes is given by

$$\Gamma = \{(\alpha^k, \beta) | k = 1, q, q^2, \ldots, q^{m-1}, \beta \in \mathbb{F}_{q^m}\}.$$

Theorem 4.4.16. *The number of parties in these secret-sharing schemes is* $q^m - 1$ *and the access structure has the following properties:*

(i) *Only m elements can be used to recover the secret but $(m - 1)$ cannot.*

(ii) *When the parties come together, up to $[\frac{m}{2}]$ cheaters can be found in each group. ("$[x]$" denotes the greatest integer less than or equal to x.)*

Proof. (i) It is seen that by Definition 4.4.15.
(ii) By definition of our scheme, $2 \leq m$ if and only if $1 \leq \frac{m}{2}$. □

The accessibility degree of the access structure for these secret-sharing schemes based on extension fields over finite fields can be defined as follows.

Definition 4.4.17. The accessibility index on P is the map $\delta_p(\Gamma)$: $A_p \to \mathbb{R}$ given by

$$\delta_p(\Gamma) = \frac{|\Gamma|}{q^m - 1},$$

for $\Gamma \in A_p$, where $m = |P|$ is the number of participants in the access structure. The number $\delta_p(\Gamma)$ will be called the accessibility degree of structure Γ.

Example 4.4.18. Let $\mathbb{F}_{2^3}$ be the secret-sharing space. This space is also m-dimensional vector space over $\mathbb{F}_2$. Consider the polynomial $f(x) = x^3 + x^2 + 1 \in \mathbb{F}_2[x]$. The coefficients of polynomial are $a_0 = 1, a_1 = 1, a_2 = 1$. So the secret is $-a_2 = -1 = 1$ and $m = 3, q = 2$. The normal basis elements of $\mathbb{F}_{q^m}$ are $\alpha, \alpha^2, \alpha^{2^{3-1}} = \alpha^4$. It is clear that

$$\alpha^0 = 1,$$
$$\alpha^1 = \alpha,$$
$$\alpha^2 = \alpha^2,$$
$$\alpha^3 = \alpha^2 + 1,$$
$$\alpha^4 = \alpha^3 + \alpha = \alpha^2 + \alpha + 1,$$
$$\alpha^5 = \alpha^3 + \alpha^2 + \alpha = \alpha + 1,$$
$$\alpha^6 = \alpha^2 + \alpha,$$
$$\alpha^7 = \alpha^3 + \alpha^2 = 1.$$

All the sharings are

$$K_1 = (\alpha^0, 1),$$
$$K_2 = (\alpha^1, \alpha),$$
$$K_3 = (\alpha^2, \alpha^2),$$
$$K_4 = (\alpha^3, \alpha^2 + 1),$$
$$K_5 = (\alpha^4, \alpha^2 + \alpha + 1),$$
$$K_6 = (\alpha^6, \alpha^2 + \alpha),$$
$$K_7 = (\alpha^7, 1).$$

K_2, K_3 and K_4 participants recover the secret while combining their shares by using the trace function of α as follows:

$$Tr_{F/K}(\alpha) = \alpha + \alpha^2 + \alpha^4 = \alpha + \alpha^2 + (\alpha^2 + \alpha + 1) = 1.$$

Now we assume that the secret is $(-1)^3 \cdot a_0 = (-1) \cdot 1 = -1 = 1$ and the same participants recover the secret calculating the norm of α as follows.

$$N_{F/K}(\alpha) = \alpha \cdot \alpha^2 \cdot \alpha^2 = \alpha^3 \cdot \alpha^4 = (\alpha^2 + 1) \cdot (\alpha^2 + \alpha + 1) = 1.$$

As it is seen that both of these schemes are the $(3, 7)$-threshold schemes. The accessibility degree of the access structure is $\frac{3}{2^3-1} = \frac{3}{7} = 0,42$.

4.4.6. Conclusion

In this section, we have constructed some (t, n)-threshold schemes using the trace and norm functions. These schemes are mainly based on finite extensions over finite fields. We introduced the access structure of these schemes. We defined the accessibility degree of the access structure. We obtained the new results. Possible attacks have been considered.

Our scheme has the same distributed as Shamir's scheme does. We send an element of $\mathbb{F}_q$ and the normal basis elements of $\mathbb{F}_{q^m}$ use the trace and norm functions to recover the secret.

The secret can be recovered only by the special participants which are uniquely determined. This means the access structure of these schemes is very strong and reliable.

4.5. Secret-Sharing Schemes and Syndrome Decoding

In this section, we examine [12] the relation between secret-sharing schemes based on a linear code which can correct a single error and syndrome decoding.

4.5.1. Syndrome decoding

For the syndrome decoding we need only two columns. They are syndromes and coset leaders. This table is called syndrome-decoding look-up table. We know that two vector x and y are in the same coset of C if and only if they have the same syndrome. We also know that there is one-to-one correspondence between cosets and syndromes. The procedure (for decoding) is

(i) if received vector is y, compute $S(y) = yH^T$,
(ii) locate $S(y)$ in the first column of the look-up table and determine the coset leader e which has the same syndrome with y,
(iii) decode y as $y - e$ [25].

Consider an $[n, k]$-code C over $\mathbb{F}_q$ which can correct a single error. Suppose that construct a secret-sharing scheme based on C. Let $\mathbb{F}_q^n$ be the secret space. There are participants and a dealer in this space. The dealer chooses randomly a codeword of $\mathbb{F}_q^k$ as a secret s. So, it can be chosen q^k secrets. The dealer distributes their shares to the participants. The participants recover the secret by combining their shares as follows:

The secret s is transmitted to a noisy channel. Since s is a code-word, will be as r by noisy. First we get the syndrome look-up table calculating syndromes of coset leaders via $S(r) = rH^T$. When a vector r is received, we calculate $S(r)$ and locate $S(r)$ in the first column of the look-up table and determine the coset leader e which has the same syndrome with r. Decode r as $r - e$. Hence the secret s is recovered.

Therefore we can write the following theorems:

Theorem 4.5.1. *Let C be an $[n, k]$-code over $\mathbb{F}_q$ which can correct a single error. Suppose that the secret s is transmitted and s will be as r. To determine the secret in the secret-sharing scheme based on C it should be $S(r) \neq 0$.*

Proof.   Suppose that $S(r) = 0$. Then $r \in C$. So, the secret s is not to distributed to participants. That is $s = r$. Thus, to determine the secret it should be $S(r) \neq 0$.   □

Theorem 4.5.2. *Let C be an $[n, k]$-code over $\mathbb{F}_q$ which can correct a single error. In the access structure of the secret-sharing scheme based on C there are $q^{n-k} - 1$ minimal access sets and n participants in each of minimal access set.*

Proof.   We know that there are q^{n-k} coset leaders in an $[n, k]$ linear code C over $\mathbb{F}_q$. Since $s \in \mathbb{F}_q^k$, there are exactly $q^{n-k} - 1$ non-zero coset leaders. Because the secret does not belong them. The coset leaders are also minimal access sets. Moreover, we know that the access structure of a secret-sharing scheme is the set of all minimal access sets. So, in the access structure of the secret sharing scheme based on C there are $q^{n-k} - 1$ minimal access sets. A minimal access set consists of vectors of length n. So that there are n participants in each of minimal access set. That is n participants recover the secret by combining their shares.   □

Theorem 4.5.3. *Let C be an $[n, k]$-code over $\mathbb{F}_q$ which can correct a single error. In the secret-sharing scheme based on C there are exactly $n(q^n - q^k)$ participants.*

Proof. The code C has q^{n-k} coset leaders and $q^{n-k} - 1$ non-zero coset leaders. These non-zero coset leaders are minimal access sets. There are q^k elements in every coset and each of these q^k elements consists of vectors of length n. So, there are nq^k participants in every coset. Hence the total number of elements in the non-zero coset leaders is $nq^k(q^{n-k} - 1) = n(q^n - q^k)$ which is the number of participants. $\square$

Example 4.5.4. Let C be the binary $[5, 2]$-code with generator matrix

$$G = \begin{pmatrix} 1 & 0 & 1 & 0 & 1 \\ 0 & 1 & 0 & 1 & 1 \end{pmatrix}.$$

The parity-check matrix H of C is

$$H = \begin{pmatrix} 1 & 0 & 1 & 0 & 0 \\ 0 & 1 & 0 & 1 & 0 \\ 1 & 1 & 0 & 0 & 1 \end{pmatrix}.$$

Since the minimum distance is 3, the code C corrects a single error. Now we construct a secret-sharing scheme based on C and examine some properties of this scheme.

First we write the codewords of C:

$$C = \{00000, 10101, 01011, 11110\}$$

and the cosets of C are

$$00000 + C = \{00000, 10101, 01011, 11110\},$$
$$10000 + C = \{10000, 00101, 11011, 01110\},$$
$$01000 + C = \{01000, 11101, 00011, 10110\},$$
$$00100 + C = \{00100, 10001, 01111, 11010\}$$
$$00010 + C = \{00010, 10111, 01001, 11100\},$$
$$00001 + C = \{00001, 10100, 01010, 11111\},$$
$$11000 + C = \{11000, 01101, 10011, 00110\},$$
$$10010 + C = \{10010, 00111, 11001, 01100\}.$$

It is seen that C has $q^{n-k} - 1 = 2^{5-2} - 1 = 7$ non-zero coset leaders. These are also the minimal access sets in the scheme based on C:

$$\{10000\}, \{01000\}, \{00100\}, \{00010\}, \{00001\}, \{11000\}, \{10010\}.$$

There are $n = 5$ participants in every minimal access set. In this scheme, the total number of participants is

$$n(q^n - q^k) = 5(2^5 - 2^2) = 140.$$

The coset leaders and syndromes of their are as follows:

Syndromes	Coset Leader
(000)	00000
(101)	10000
(011)	01000
(100)	00100
(010)	00010
(001)	00001
(110)	11000
(111)	10010

Let any element of C be the secret s. It will be shared to participants. Then the secret s is transmitted to channel. To determine the secret, it should be calculated from the received vector.

Let the secret s be 01011 and is transmitted to channel and received vector r be 01010. We calculate the syndrome of r:

$$S(r) = rH^T = (01010). \begin{pmatrix} 1 & 0 & 1 \\ 0 & 1 & 1 \\ 1 & 0 & 0 \\ 0 & 1 & 0 \\ 0 & 0 & 1 \end{pmatrix} = (001).$$

Here (001) belongs to (00001) coset leader. So, where the error vector is $e = (00001)$. Therefore

$$s = r - e$$

$$s = (01010) - (00001)$$

$$s = (01011)$$

is obtained.

Thus, the secret is recovered.

4.5.2. Why use syndrome decoding?

What is the advantage of using syndrome decoding in this scheme? The non-zero coset leaders are minimal access sets here. The components in every coset leader can recover the secret by combining their shares. Also the order of the components is crucial, because, if the position of any component is changed, then the secret cannot recover. This means that the access structure of this scheme is very strong and reliable.

4.5.3. Conclusion

In this section, we have explored the relation between secret-sharing schemes based on a linear code which can correct a single error and syndrome decoding. In this context, we have obtained the following results:

- in this scheme to determine the secret it should be $S(r) \neq 0$, where r is the received vector;
- there are $q^{n-k} - 1$ minimal access sets and n participants in every minimal access set;
- there are exactly $n(q^n - q^k)$ participants.

4.6. Secret Sharing, Zero Sum Sets, and Hamming Codes

In this section [14], we present a ramp secret-sharing scheme based on polynomial residue rings. It was shown in [24] that such schemes can be concatenated with a classical (t, n)-scheme. Thus, our scheme complements but does not compete with Shamir scheme for instance. We generalize and sometimes correct the results of [8]. To determine the residue rings where our scheme can be applied, we are led to characterize all finite commutative rings that are S_0. These are defined by the property that the sum of all their elements is zero. This result is of independent algebraic interest. When the residue ring is a finite field, to study the size distribution of admissible coalitions, we are led to study the weight distribution of a coset of shortened Hamming codes. The analysis employs the MacWilliams formula and the fact that Hamming codes are homogeneous.

4.6.1. Algebraic preliminaries

The aim of the first three subsections is to characterize commutative rings for which the sum of all elements is zero.

4.6.2. Integer residue rings

We begin with a lemma on integer residues.

Lemma 4.6.1. *If N is an odd integer, then $\sum_{i=1}^{N} i$ is an integer divisible by N.*

Proof. Summing an arithmetic series yields $\sum_{i=1}^{N} i = \frac{N(N+1)}{2}$. Since N is odd, the number $\frac{(N+1)}{2}$ is an integer.   □

Remark 4.6.2. Note that the result does not hold for even integers. For instance, $1 + 2 + 3 + 4 = 10$ is not a multiple of 4. In fact, the sum is congruent to $N/2$ modulo N.

We proceed to generalized the above result to polynomial residue rings. Let q be an arbitrary integer >1. Let f denote a polynomial of degree d in $\mathbb{Z}_q[x]$ and denote by $R(f)$ the quotient ring $\mathbb{Z}_q[x]/(f(x))$.

Theorem 4.6.3. *If q is odd and $d \geq 1$ or q is even and $d > 1$, then $\sum_{h \in R(f)} h = 0$.*

Proof. If $d = 1$ and q is odd, Lemma 4.6.1 applies with $N = q$. If $d > 1$, write the residue class representative h as

$$h = \sum_{i=0}^{d-1} h_i x^i.$$

We see that, for given i, any fixed value of h_i will appear q^{d-1} times when the h_j's with $j \neq i$ range over $\mathbb{Z}_q$. The result follows since then $d > 1$.   □

4.6.3. Zero-sum sets

We want to exhibit $R(f) = \mathbb{Z}_q[x]/(f(x))$ the sum of all elements of which is zero, but without smaller size zero-sum sets. The next result shows that composite q's should be avoided.

Lemma 4.6.4. *Assume* $d > 1$. *If* m *divides* q, *then* $R(f)$ *has a zero-sum set of size* m^d.

Proof. Writing $q = ms$, and $g = f \pmod{m}$, we see that $R(g)$ embeds additively into $R(f)$ by the map $h \mapsto sg$. Thus, $R(f)$ by Theorem 4.6.3 applied to $R(g)$ has a zero sum-set of size m^d. $\quad\square$

Next, we show that composite f's should be avoided.

Lemma 4.6.5. *Assume* $d > 1$. *If* h *of degree* $d > s > 1$ *divides* f, *then* $R(f)$ *has a zero-sum set of size* q^s.

Proof. Writing $f = hr$, and we see that $R(h)$ embeds additively into $R(f)$ by the map $g \mapsto rg$. Thus, $R(f)$ by Theorem 4.6.3 applied to $R(h)$ has a zero-sum set of size q^s. $\quad\square$

Eventually, $p^d - 1$ should not be composite.

Lemma 4.6.6. *Assume* $R(f) = \mathrm{GF}(p^d)$ *and that* $d > 1$. *If* s *divides* $p^d - 1$, *then* $R(f)$ *has a zero-sum set of size* s.

Proof. In that case, the multiplicative group of $R(f)$ contains s roots of unity of order s, which add up to zero. $\quad\square$

4.6.3.1. *Generalization to rings*

Definition 4.6.7. A ring R is S_0 if and only if

$$\sum_{x \in R} x = 0.$$

Proposition 4.6.8. *If the ring* R *contains a unit* u *such that* $1 - u$ *is also a unit, then* R *is* S_0.

Proof. Let $S = \sum_{x \in R} x$. Since u is invertible, then the map $x \mapsto ux$ permutes R. Thus, $uS = S$, and so $(1 - u)S = 0$. $\quad\square$

Remark 4.6.9. The condition is sufficient but not necessary as the ring $\mathbb{F}_2 \times \mathbb{F}_2$ is S_0 and contains only one unit $u = (1,1)$. Thus, $(1,1) - u = (0,0)$, which is not a unit.

The following result is well-known.

Corollary 4.6.10. *Every finite field $\mathbb{F}_q$ except $\mathbb{F}_2$ is S_0.*

Proof.   If $q > 2$, any non-zero element $u \neq 1$ is such that $1 - u$ is invertible.   □

The following result shows that many rings are S_0.

Corollary 4.6.11. *Every ring of odd characteristic is S_0.*

Proof.   If the characteristic is odd, then $u = 2$ is a unit and also $1 - u = -1$.   □

We are still far from a characterization as there are many even characteristic S_0 rings, like e.g., the direct product $\mathbb{F}_2 \times \mathbb{F}_2$. A complete characterization was given in [45]. To be self-contained, we sketch a proof here.

Theorem 4.6.12. *A commutative ring is not S_0 if and only if its additive group contains only one summand of even size in its decomposition as a direct sum of cyclic groups.*

Proof.   The sum of all the elements of a finite abelian group G is equal to the sum of elements of order 2. Call $\mathcal{N}$ the set consisting of 0 and the elements of order 2. The set $\mathcal{N}$ is an abelian group, or, equivalently, a vector space over $\mathbb{F}_2$, of dimension k, say. Thus, the set of all elements of $\mathcal{N}$ is zero if and only if it is the case for $\mathbb{F}_{2^k}$. By Corollary 4.6.1, this happens if and only if $k = 1$, if and only if $|\mathcal{N}| = 2$. Thus, G contains exactly one element of order 2. This happens if and only if it contains only one summand of even size in its fundamental decomposition as a direct sum of cyclic groups.   □

4.6.4.   Secret-sharing schemes

Definition 4.6.13 (Minimal Access Set). A subset of participants is called a minimal access set, if the participants in the subsets can recover the secret by combining their shares, but any subset of these cannot do so [37].

Definition 4.6.14 (Access Structure). The access structure of a secret-sharing scheme is the set of all minimal access sets [37].

Definition 4.6.15 (Ramp Secret-Sharing Scheme). Ramp secret-sharing scheme (RSS) is a relaxation of secret-sharing scheme. In a RSS of parameters (m, t, n) with $m < t < n$, all t-subsets can reconstruct the secret, no j-subsets with $j < m$ can reconstruct the secret, and some j-subsets with $m \leq j < t$ can reconstruct the subset. There is a lot of work on the ramp secret-sharing scheme. Some of them are given in [1, 13]. Alahmadi *et al.* [1] explain a multisecret-sharing scheme based on LCD codes. They use Blakley's method to construct their scheme. Çalkavur and Solé [13] introduce some multisecret-sharing schemes over finite fields. In their work, they claim that the Blakley scheme does not work well if they replace $\mathbb{R}$ with a finite field. These two schemes are also the ramp secret-sharing schemes.

4.6.5. The scheme

Assume a polynomial residue ring $R(f) = \mathrm{GF}(2^d)$ that satisfies the hypothesis of Theorem 4.6.3 and construct a threshold scheme based on this ring. Put $n = 2^d$, with $d > 2$. We construct a $(3, n-1, n-1)$-ramp scheme. The motivation for this special choice of $R(f)$ is as follows. From Lemmas 4.6.4–4.6.6, the recommended values of $R(f)$ in the notation of Section 4.6.2 are

(1) $q = 2$,
(2) f irreducible,
(3) $2^d - 1$ prime,
(4) $d > 4$.

The primes of the form $2^d - 1$ are called Mersenne primes. The first few admissible d's are $2, 3, 5, 7$. The largest known in April 2020 was for $d = 82{,}589{,}933$ [23]. For that value of d, the quantity $2^d - 1$ is the largest known prime today.

The share dealing protocol proceeds as follows:

- All of the elements of $\mathrm{GF}(2^d)$ are written as binary vectors of length d.
- The dealer picks any element of $\mathrm{GF}(2^d)$ as the secret.
- He distributes the remaining $n - 1$ elements of $R(f)$ to the $n - 1$ users.

The recovery phase is as follows. The set of all $n-1$ users pool their shares together, and add them up obtaining a sum Σ. Thus, the secret is then computed as $s = -\Sigma$. We summarize the discussion in the following proposition.

Proposition 4.6.16. *With the above conditions, the finite field* $\mathrm{GF}(2^d)$ *determines a* $(3, 2^d - 1, 2^d - 1)$*-ramp secret-sharing scheme.*

Proof. By Corollary 4.6.10, the finite field $\mathrm{GF}(2^d)$ is S_0. Anticipating the next section, we see that the zero sum sets of $\mathrm{GF}(2^d)$ are in bijection with the codewords of the Hamming code of parameters $[2^d - 1, 2^d - 1 - d, 3]$. This means, in the scheme, there are $2^d - 1$ participants, and the secret is split in $2^d - 1$ pieces and there are zero-sum set of size 3 corresponding to weight 3 codewords in Hamming scheme. The results follow. □

4.6.6. Coding interpretation

The following result is elementary but essential. A coalition is any zero-sum set containing the secret, minus the secret itself.

Proposition 4.6.17. *There is a bijective correspondence between coalitions of size* w *and codewords of weight* $w + 1$ *in the Hamming code* $\mathcal{H}_d$ *of parameters* $[n - 1, n - 1 - d, 3]$.

Proof. Let H be the matrix with columns all the $2^d - 1$ non-zero binary vectors of length d. As is well-known [34], this matrix is a parity-check matrix for the said Hamming code $\mathcal{H}_d$. Let C be a coalition, and let χ_C be the characteristic vector of $C' = C \cup s$, where s denotes the secret. Since C' is a zero-set, we know that $H\chi_C = 0$, implying $\chi_C \in \mathcal{H}_d$. Furthermore, $|C'| = |C| + 1$ equals the Hamming weight of χ_C. □

4.6.7. Random choice attack

An obvious attack is to suppose a coalition with a zero-set containing the secret minus the secret, and let the members of the coalition add up their shares. The following result is immediate by the coding interpretation of Proposition 4.6.17. Denote by $\mathcal{H}_d^-$ the code obtained from $\mathcal{H}_d$ by puncturing in an arbitrary position, and only retaining the codewords which were equal to one in that position. In other words, it is the coset of the shortened code into the punctured code at the same position.

Proposition 4.6.18. *The probability that a random set of* $[1, \ldots, n-2]$ *size* w *is a coalition is* $\frac{A_w}{\binom{n-2}{w}}$, *where* A_w *is the number of codewords of weight* w *in* $\mathcal{H}_d^-$.

Proof. By Proposition 4.6.17, the characteristic vector of a coalition is a codeword of $\mathcal{H}_d^-$, where the puncture has been done at the coordinate place determined by the secret. $\qquad\square$

The A_w's can be computed by the generating function:

$$\sum_{w=0}^{n-2} A_w x^{n-1-w} y^w = \frac{1}{n-1} \frac{\partial}{\partial y} W(x,y),$$

(coming from [6, Theorem 3]), where $W(x,y)$, the weight enumerator of $\mathcal{H}_d$, is easily computed by MacWilliams transform:

$$W(x,y) = \frac{1}{2^d} \big((x+y)^{n-1} + (n-1)(x+y)^{n-1-n/2} (x-y)^{n/2} \big),$$

using the fact that the dual of the Hamming code, the so-called Simplex code is a one-weight code [34, Chapter 5, Problem 3].

Example 4.6.19. For small values of d, a direct computation in MAGMA [33] yields the following data. The weight distribution is described as a list

$$[\langle 0,1 \rangle, \ldots, \langle i, A_i \rangle, \ldots].$$

We consider $d = 3$, when $\mathcal{H}_3$ is a $[7,4,3]$-code.

- The weight distribution of $\mathcal{H}_3$, punctured at coordinate 1 is $[\langle 0,1 \rangle, \langle 2,3 \rangle, \langle 3,8 \rangle, \langle 4,3 \rangle, \langle 6,1 \rangle]$.
- The weight distribution of $\mathcal{H}_3$, shortened at coordinate 1 is $[\langle 0,1 \rangle, \langle 3,4 \rangle, \langle 4,3 \rangle]$.
- On the contrary, we see that the weight distribution of $\mathcal{H}_3^-$, is $[\langle 0,1 \rangle, \langle 2,3 \rangle, \langle 3,4 \rangle]$.

Higher values of d (say e.g. $d = 7$) are feasible but lead to longer formulas.

To be concrete, we give a special case.

Proposition 4.6.20. *In this scheme, there are $\frac{n}{2} - 1$ coalitions of size 2.*

Proof. By Proposition 4.6.17, such an access set is of the form $\{x, x+s\}$, where s is the secret and x is an arbitrary non-zero vector different from s. Replacing x by $x+s$ gives the same set. $\quad\square$

These calculations show that the value of n should be large for the scheme to be secure.

4.6.8. Information rate

Another important parameter in secret sharing is the information rate ρ of the scheme. It is equal to the ratio of the size of the secret to the maximum size of the pieces of participants [39]. Since the secret is an element of length d in $\mathrm{GF}(2^d)$, its size is d. Thus, the information rate is 1.

If the information rate is equal to one, then this scheme is called the ideal. Thus, our new scheme is an ideal secret-sharing scheme.

4.6.9. Comparison with other schemes

Let $\mathbb{F}_{q^n}$ denote the finite extension of degree n of the finite field $\mathbb{F}_q$. Now, we compare our scheme with other ramp type schemes in the following table. The number of participants, the size of a secret, and the number of coalitions for an $[n, k]$-code over $\mathbb{F}_q$ are denoted by T, R, S, respectively. Moreover, consider a polynomial residue ring $R(f) = \mathrm{GF}(2^d)$.

System	[1]	[13]	This section
T	q^k	q^n	$2^d - 1$
R	q^n	q	2^d
S	$\dfrac{\displaystyle\prod_{i=0}^{k-1}(q^k - q^i)}{k!}$	$\dfrac{\displaystyle\prod_{i=0}^{n-1}(q^n - q^i)}{n!}$	$\geq \dfrac{2^d - 1}{2} - 1$
ρ	$\dfrac{k}{k+1}$	1	1

4.6.10.   Combination with Shamir's scheme

The advantage of using a secret with values in a finite field is that it can be used in conjunction with Shamir's scheme which is based on polynomial interpolation over a finite field.

4.6.11.   Conclusions

In the present section, we have generalized the work [8] to a wider class of quotient rings. Possible attacks have been considered. Secure values of f, n, d have been recommended. Even in the recommended values of the parameters, there are still zero sum-sets of size 2^{d-1}. Moreover, our scheme has the same distributed secret as Shamir's scheme does. We send the residue classes in disguise over open channels and then participants use properties of zero-sum sets to recover the secret. The combined scheme has the following useful advantages over Shamir's original scheme:

- The shares are elements of a polynomial residue ring that can be sent over open channels and then participants use ring-theoretic methods to recover the secret.
- Once the long-term private information (the share) is distributed, several different secrets can be distributed without updating the long-term private information.
- While recovering the secret, if participants do not want to, they do not have to reveal their shares to each other.

On the combinatorial side, it would be interesting to derive an upper bound on the size of nontrivial zero-sum sets in $R(f)$. Characterizing the distribution of zero-sum sets in general commutative rings seems to be a challenging problem in ring theory, as it cannot use the standard decomposition theorems, like CRT and so on.

4.7.   The Least Squares Solutions in Code-Based Multisecret-Sharing Scheme

The theory of generalized inverses of matrices has been applied in many areas since 1950. Some of them are Markov chains, robotics differential equations, etc. Especially, the applications over finite fields of this theory have an important role in cryptography and coding theory. In this section, we are closely following [38] to study a new multisecret-sharing scheme by using the generalized inverses of matrices and least-squares solutions in linear codes. We determine the access structure. Its security improves on that of multisecret-sharing schemes.

4.7.1.   Introduction

Secret-sharing scheme is an important cryptographic protocol. We need a secret space to construct a secret sharing scheme. There exist some participants and a dealer in this space. The dealer has a secret and allocates it the other shareholders. In a minimal t-subset of participants reach the secret together. These subsets are also minimal access sets. The access structure consists of all of minimal access sets in a secret-sharing scheme. One of the secret-sharing schemes is a (t, m)-threshold secret-sharing scheme. In such a scheme, the secret can be constructed from any t shares, but no subset of $t - 1$ shares finds out any clue about the secret.

Secret-sharing schemes were invented by Blakley [5] and Shamir [46] in 1979. Shamir's scheme is a threshold secret-sharing scheme and based on polynomial interpolation. Blakley's scheme is based on finite geometry [2]. More clearly, this scheme uses hyperplane geometry as a solution of the secret-sharing problem. Blakley's scheme is also a threshold secret-sharing scheme.

Coding theory is another approach to the construction of secret-sharing scheme. Several authors have examined to obtain the secret-sharing schemes using linear error correcting codes [18, 28, 35, 36, 43, 53]. Massey used linear codes to construct a secret sharing scheme and explained the relationship between the access structure and the minimal codewords of the dual code of the main code [35, 53]. Multisecret-sharing scheme is a special class of (t, n)-threshold secret-sharing scheme. Some of kinds of this scheme were worked in [9, 21, 22, 31, 42, 50].

The theory of generalized inverses of matrices has been used in special branches of mathematics. There are several applications in this area [4]. One of them is seen in linear codes [17, 30]. Özel *et al.* [38] studied about generalized inverses of matrices and least-squares solutions in linear codes. In this work, we apply for the results in [38] to cryptography. In this context, we construct a new multisecret-sharing scheme and obtain the original results. Moreover, the existence of the Moore–Penrose inverse over real or complex field is a very interesting topic for generalized inverses. In this chapter, we use the conditions of existence of the Moore–Penrose inverse over finite fields [20, 41, 49] to construct our new cryptosystem.

We organize the work as follows. In Section 4.7.2, we give some basics of linear codes, secret-sharing schemes and the generalized inverses of matrices. A new multisecret-sharing scheme and the explanatory examples in order to show this scheme are given in Section 4.7.3. In this section, the security analysis of the scheme is also studied. In Section 4.7.4 we compare our scheme with other code-based schemes in the literature. Section 4.7.5 concludes the paper.

4.7.2. Preliminaries

In this section, we remind some necessary mathematical information used in this work.

4.7.2.1. *Linear codes*

A linear code C of length n over $\mathbb{F}_q$ is a k-dimensional subspace of an $\mathbb{F}_q$-vector space $\mathbb{F}_q^n$, where $\mathbb{F}_q$ is a finite field of q elements. The Hamming distance $d(x, y)$ between two vectors x and y in $\mathbb{F}_q^n$ is the number of entries in which they differ in C. The weight of a codeword is the number of its non-zero positions. A linear code of length n, dimension k and minimum distance d is represented by $[n, k, d]$-code. The elements of a linear code are called codewords. If a codeword is sent throughout a channel and an error occurs meaning that the sent vector is disrupted, then if there exists a codeword which is the closest to the received codeword, then the decoding process is completed by choosing the closest codeword. This decoding technique is known as the majority decoding method.

The codewords of dual code of C are orthogonal to every codeword of C. The dual code is an $[n, n - k]$-code and denoted by $C^\perp$. The basis elements of C consists of the rows of a matrix G. This matrix is called the generator matrix of a linear code C and it is a $k \times n$ matrix. The generator matrix of the dual code $C^\perp$ is called the parity-check matrix of C and it is a $(n - k) \times n$ matrix, denoted by H.

4.7.2.2. *Multisecret-sharing schemes*

A multisecret-sharing scheme is a method to share more than secret among a group of participants in such a way that:

- any authorized subset of participants is able to recover all the secrets,
- any non-authorized subset of participants obtains no information about any of the secrets [40].

4.7.2.3. *Ramp secret-sharing schemes*

Ramp secret sharing scheme is a class of multisecret-sharing schemes. The secret s is broken into multiple shares $s_1, s_2, \ldots, s_N$. Only eligible subsets of the shares can retrieve s. Each secret s is showed by a share vector

$$S = (s_1, s_2, \ldots, s_N).$$

A linear ramp secret-sharing scheme is called t-privacy if the set of size t has no information about the secret, but at least the set of size $t + 1$ has some information about it.

4.7.2.4. *Symmetric matrices*

In the following sections, we have to remind the valuable informations in [38].

Definition 4.7.1. Let A be a square matrix of order n over a finite field $\mathbb{F}_q$. Then A is said to be symmetric if $\forall x, y \in \mathbb{F}_q^n$, then $\langle Ax, y \rangle = \langle x, Ay \rangle$.

Definition 4.7.2. Let A be a square matrix. The smallest positive integer k satisfying $R(A^k) = R(A^{k+1})$ is called index of A and it is denoted by $\operatorname{Ind} A$.

Lemma 4.7.3. *Let A be a square matrix of order n over a finite field $\mathbb{F}_q$ such that $A^2 = A$. Then A is symmetric if and only if*

$$\mathbb{F}_q^n = R(A) \oplus (R(A))^\perp. \tag{4.7.1}$$

4.7.2.5. *Generalized inverses of matrices over a finite field*

Definition 4.7.4. Let A be an $m \times n$ matrix over a finite field $\mathbb{F}_q$. The Moore–Penrose inverse of A is an $n \times m$ matrix X over $\mathbb{F}_q$ satisfying the following equations:

(1) $AXA = A$,
(2) $XAX = X$,
(3) $(AX)^T = AX$,
(4) $(XA)^T = XA$,

and it is denoted by A^+. Let $A^{\{i, i \in \{1,2,3,4\}\}}$ designate any matrix X satisfying ith equation of the previous system and then it is called i-inverse of A. By a generalized inverse, we mean a type of i-inverse of A, for $i \in \{1, 2, 3, 4\}$.

Lemma 4.7.5. *Let A be an $m \times n$ matrix over an arbitrary field $\mathbb{F}_q$ and let X be a $\{1, 2\}$-inverse of A. Then we have*

(1) $(AX)^2 = AX$ *and* $(XA)^2 = XA$,
(2) $R(AX) = R(A), N(AX) = N(X)$,
(3) $\mathbb{F}_q^n = R(X) \oplus N(A)$,
(4) $\mathbb{F}_q^m = R(A) \oplus N(X)$.

The existence of the $\{1, 2\}$-inverses of a matrix over a finite field is proved in [20, 41]. From Lemmas 4.7.3 and 4.7.5, we have the following corollary.

Corollary 4.7.6. *Let A be a $m \times n$ matrix over a finite field $\mathbb{F}_q$. Then $A^{\{1,2,3\}}$ exists if and only if $\mathbb{F}_q^m = R(A) \oplus (R(A))^\perp$.*

4.7.2.6. *Least squares solutions*

The equation $Ax = b$ is consistent if and only if $b \in R(A)$. Otherwise, the residual vector $r = b - Ax$ is non-zero for all x. It may be desired to find an approximate solution x which makes r closest to zero. That is minimizing some norm of r. In other words, finding x which makes b the nearest to $R(A)$. This solution is called the least squares solution. In $\mathbb{C}^n$, the nearest to a set is its orthogonal projection on this set (the orthogonal is for the Euclidean norm), which means that $\mathbb{C}^n$ is decomposed in the orthogonal direct sum. In [4] it has been showed that the general solutions are given by

$$x = A^{\{1\}}b + (I - A^{\{1\}}A)y, y \in \mathbb{C}^n.$$

Also, it has shown that r is minimized if and only if $x = A^{\{1,3\}}b$ for any $\{1,3\}$-inverses of A [4]. Consequently, there is one-to-one correspondence between the least squares solutions of the equation $Ax = b$ and the $\{1,3\}$-inverses of A. It will be noted that if A is of full column rank, then the least squares solution is unique. In fact, $A^{\{1,3\}}$ is one of the left inverses of A. So $I - A^{\{1,3\}}A = 0$ and $(A^{\{1,3\}}A)^* = I^* = I$ and $r(A^{\{1,3\}}) = r(A)$. Hence $A^{\{1,3\}}$ becomes $A^{\{1,2,3,4\}} = A^+$ [52]. Then $x = A^+b$.

4.7.3. Multisecret-sharing schemes and least-squares solutions in linear codes

In this section, we work on a new multisecret-sharing scheme. We use the generalized inverses of matrices and least-squares solutions in linear codes [15]. Actually, we benefit the working principle of [38].

Consider an $[n, k]$-code C over $\mathbb{F}_q$ with generator matrix G and parity-check matrix H. We know that $r(G) = k$, where $r(G)$ is denoted to the rank of G. So G^T, the transpose of G is a $n \times k$ matrix of full column rank k. From the previous subsection, if $(G^T)^{\{1,3\}}$ exists, then it is a left inverse of G^T. This inverse is represented by $(G^T)^+$. Therefore we obtain

$$\mathbb{F}_q^n = R(G^T) \oplus N((G^T)^+) \tag{4.7.2}$$

or equivalently

$$r(G) = r(GG^T) = r(G^TG) \text{ (see [49])}.$$

Since $R(G^T) = C, N((G^T)^+)$ is the orthogonal code $C^\perp = R(H^T)$. From equation (4.7.2),

$$\mathbb{F}_q^n = R(G^T) \oplus R(H^T) \tag{4.7.3}$$

is obtained.

We can write the following statement for $s \in \mathbb{F}_q^n$,

$$s = (G^T((G^T))^+ s. \tag{4.7.4}$$

We have $G^T \cdot x = s \in C$ for a message $x \in \mathbb{F}_q^k$. If a received message is not in C, this means $s \notin R(G^T)$. In this case, $G^T \cdot x = s$ is contradictory, so it will be attractive to obtain the codeword the closest to s. From equation (4.7.4), we have

$$s - G^T \cdot x = ((G^T)((G^T))^+ s - G^T x) + H^T \cdot s'. \tag{4.7.5}$$

Since we have the orthogonal direct sum, equation (4.7.5) gives the following statement.

$$w_H(s - G^T \cdot x) = w_H((G^T)((G^T))^+ s - G^T x) + w_H(H^T s') \tag{4.7.6}$$

$$\geq d + w_H(H^T s'), \tag{4.7.7}$$

where w_H and d are the weight and minimum Hamming distance, respectively. The minimizing of $s - G^T \cdot x$ for d in equation (4.7.7) is equivalent that x is a solution of the consistent equation

$$G^T \cdot x = (G^T)((G^T))^+ s = (G^+ G)s, \tag{4.7.8}$$

that is $w_H((G^T)((G^T))^+ s - G^T x) = 0$.

Then $x = ((G^T))^+ \cdot s$ is the unique least squares solution of $G^T x = s$. When equation (4.7.3) is satisfied, the code and the dual code are complementary or equivalently

$$r(G) = r(GG^T) = r(G^T G).$$

In this situation, a received word will be decoded correctly to a word of the code.

Theorem 4.7.7 ([38]). *Let G be a generator matrix of an $[n, k]$-code C over $\mathbb{F}_q$. Then there is the unique word $x \in \mathbb{F}_q^k$ approaching a received word s near the codewords of C if and only if equation (4.7.3) (or equivalently $r(G) = r(GG^T) = r(G^T G)$) is satisfied. In this case, $x = ((G^T))^+ \cdot s$.*

It will be noted that $G^+ = G^T(GG^T)^{-1}$. So the calculation of the Moore–Penrose inverse of a matrix of full rank is within reach.

4.7.3.1. *Scheme description*

Now we construct a new multisecret-sharing scheme by using the above algorithm. In this scheme, the dealer uses a share function $f : \mathbb{F}_q^n \backslash \mathbb{F}_q^k \to \mathbb{F}_q^n$ to compute the shares among the n participants. The sharing function is chosen as $f(s) = s - G^T \cdot x$, where $s = (s_1, s_2, \ldots, s_n)$ is the secret, G is a $k \times n$ matrix over $\mathbb{F}_q$ with rank k, $x = ((G^T))^+ \cdot s$ and $G^+ = G^T(GG^T)^{-1}$.

- the participants are elements of $\mathbb{F}_q^n$,
- let $\mathbb{F}_q^n \backslash \mathbb{F}_q^k$ be the secret space,
- let the secret be $s = (s_1, s_2, \ldots, s_n) \in \mathbb{F}_q^n \backslash \mathbb{F}_q^k$ and $s = G^T x$, where $x \in \mathbb{F}_q^k$,
- calculate $G^T \cdot G$.
- if $r(G) = r(GG^T) = r(G^TG)$, then there exists the unique x. This means the secret s will be recovered,
- $x = ((G^T))^+ \cdot s$, where $G^+ = G^T(GG^T)^{-1}$,
- $f(s) = s - G^T \cdot x = r$, where r is the share,
- get s by solving the equation system $(s_1, s_2, \ldots, s_n) - G^T \cdot x = r$,
- finally the secret is reached.

Example 4.7.8. Let C be the $[3, 2]$-code over $\mathbb{F}_3$ with generator matrix

$$G = \begin{pmatrix} 1 & 2 & 0 \\ 1 & 1 & 0 \end{pmatrix}.$$

We construct a multisecret-sharing scheme based on C by using the generalized inverses over finite fields to the least-squares solutions in linear codes. The elements of $(\mathbb{F}_3)^3$ are as follows:

$$\{000, 120, 110, 210, 220, 200, 020, 010, 100, 001, 002, 012, 021, 101, 102,$$
$$201, 202, 112, 211, 111, 222, 121, 212, 011, 022, 221, 122\}.$$

The codewords of C are

$$\{000, 120, 110, 210, 220, 200, 020, 010, 100\}.$$

Let the secret be $s = (111) \notin C$. This means the equality $s = G^T \cdot x$ is inconsistent.

(i)

$$G^T \cdot G = \begin{pmatrix} 1 & 1 \\ 2 & 1 \\ 0 & 0 \end{pmatrix} \cdot \begin{pmatrix} 1 & 2 & 0 \\ 1 & 1 & 0 \end{pmatrix} = \begin{pmatrix} 2 & 0 & 0 \\ 0 & 2 & 0 \\ 0 & 0 & 0 \end{pmatrix}.$$

Since $r(G) = r(G^T G) = r(GG^T) = 2$, there exists the unique x. That is, the secret can be recovered.

(ii) We have $G^+ = G^T (GG^T)^{-1}$.

$$G \cdot G^T = \begin{pmatrix} 1 & 2 & 0 \\ 1 & 1 & 0 \end{pmatrix} \cdot \begin{pmatrix} 1 & 1 \\ 2 & 1 \\ 0 & 0 \end{pmatrix} = \begin{pmatrix} 2 & 0 \\ 0 & 2 \end{pmatrix}.$$

It is clear that

$$(G \cdot G^T)^{-1} = \begin{pmatrix} 2 & 0 \\ 0 & 2 \end{pmatrix}$$

and

$$G^+ = \begin{pmatrix} 1 & 1 \\ 2 & 1 \\ 0 & 0 \end{pmatrix} \cdot \begin{pmatrix} 2 & 0 \\ 0 & 2 \end{pmatrix} = \begin{pmatrix} 2 & 2 \\ 1 & 2 \\ 0 & 0 \end{pmatrix}.$$

(iii)

$$x = (G^+)^T \cdot s = \begin{pmatrix} 2 & 1 & 0 \\ 2 & 2 & 0 \end{pmatrix} \cdot \begin{pmatrix} 1 \\ 1 \\ 1 \end{pmatrix} = \begin{pmatrix} 0 \\ 1 \end{pmatrix}.$$

Let the message vector (111) be the secret. So the sharing function will be as

$$f(s) = s - G^T \cdot x = r = \begin{pmatrix} 1 \\ 1 \\ 1 \end{pmatrix} - \begin{pmatrix} 1 \\ 1 \\ 0 \end{pmatrix} = \begin{pmatrix} 0 \\ 0 \\ 1 \end{pmatrix}.$$

Then we get the secret s by solving the following equation:

$$\begin{pmatrix} s_1 \\ s_2 \\ s_3 \end{pmatrix} - \begin{pmatrix} 1 \\ 1 \\ 0 \end{pmatrix} = \begin{pmatrix} 0 \\ 0 \\ 1 \end{pmatrix}.$$

So the secret is

$$\begin{pmatrix} s_1 \\ s_2 \\ s_3 \end{pmatrix} = \begin{pmatrix} 1 \\ 1 \\ 1 \end{pmatrix}.$$

Proposition 4.7.9. *In our scheme, determines the secret if and only if $r(G) = r(GG^T) = r(G^T G)$ is satisfied.*

Proof. By Theorem 4.7.7, there is the unique word $x \in \mathbb{F}_q^k$ approaching a received word s near the codewords of C if and only if $r(G) = r(GG^T) = r(G^T G)$ is satisfied. □

Example 4.7.10. Consider the $[3, 1]$-code C over $\mathbb{F}_3$ with generator matrix $G = (1, 2, 1)$. In this case,

$$C = \{000, 121, 212\}.$$

We try to construct a multisecret-sharing scheme based on C by using the same method.

Let the secret be $s = (011) \notin C$. So the equality $s = G^T \cdot x$ is inconsistent. There are two words of the code $c_1 = (121)$ and $c_2 = (212)$ such that

$$w_H(s - c_1) = w_H(s - c_2) = 2 \le 3 = d,$$

so the secret s will be decoded to c_1 or to c_2.

Now if we look for the conditions of the existence of the least squares solutions and the existence the Moore–Penrose inverse of G, we find that

$$r(G) = 1 = r(G^T \cdot G) = r \begin{pmatrix} 1 & 2 & 1 \\ 2 & 1 & 2 \\ 1 & 2 & 1 \end{pmatrix} \ne 0 = r(G \cdot G^T).$$

That is, the least squares solution exists but not unique. However, it cannot be constructed a multisecret-sharing scheme based on this code.

Proposition 4.7.11. *The size of a secret is $q^n - q^k$ in the multisecret-sharing scheme satisfied the hypothesis of the above conditions.*

Proof. The secret space is $\mathbb{F}_q^n \backslash \mathbb{F}_q^k$ in this scheme. So it is clear that the size of a secret is $q^n - q^k$. □

Theorem 4.7.12. *The new cryptosystem is a $(n - w_H(r), n)$-threshold scheme, where $w_H(r)$ is the weight of $(s - G^T \cdot x)$.*

Proof. In the scheme, the secret is recovered by the vectors of length n in $\mathbb{F}_q^n$. These vectors consist of minimal access sets. There are n participants in every set, as many as coordinates of C. The number of participants recovering the secret is equal to $n - w_H(r)$. Because $w_H(r)$ determines the position of a secret vector. □

Corollary 4.7.13. *This scheme is also a ramp secret sharing scheme with* $n - w_H(r) - 1$ *privacy.*

Proof. By Theorem 4.7.12, $n - w_H(r)$ participants can recover the secret, but $n - w_H(r) - 1$ cannot. So the proof is clear. □

4.7.3.2. *Statistics on coalitions*

Denote the number of minimal coalitions of j participants by X_j, and let $X(z) = \sum_j X_j z^j$ be the generating function of these numbers.

Theorem 4.7.14. *Let C be a q-ary code with minimum distance d and weight enumerator $A(z)$. If $A^{(j)}(z)$ denotes the derivative of order j of $A(z)$, then*

$$X(z) = \frac{(q-1)^d A^{(d)}(z)}{d!}.$$

Proof. Recall that $A(z) = \sum_w A_w z^w$, where A_w denotes the number of codewords of C of weight w. Given a codeword c of weight w, the number of suitable r's is $\binom{w}{d}(q-1)^d$. The weight of r is $w - d$. Differentiating d times $A(z)$ with respect to z the result follows. □

Example 4.7.15. We continue with the above $[3,2]$-code over $\mathbb{F}_3$. The minimum distance of this code is $d = 1$. We calculate the number of minimal coalitions. First we should compute the weight enumerator of C:

$$A(z) = \sum_{j=1}^{3} A_j z^j = 1 + 4z + 4z^2.$$

Since $d = 1$, we calculate the derivative of order 1 of $A(z)$.

$$A'(z) = 4 + 8z$$

and

$$A'(1) = 12.$$

So, by Theorem 4.7.14 there are 12 minimal access sets and each set has weight of 2 since $n - w_H(r) = 3 - 1 = 2$. These are {120, 110, 210, 220, 012, 021, 101, 102, 201, 202, 011, 022}. Actually, the quantity $X(1)$ the total number of coalitions is a binomial moment of the weight distribution.

Theorem 4.7.16. *Let C be an $[n, k, d]$-code over $\mathbb{F}_q$ with dual weight distribution A'_j and with minimal coalition generator $X(z)$. We have*

$$X(1) = q^{k-d} \sum_{j=0}^{d} (-1)^j (q-1)^{d-j} \binom{n - w_H(r) - j}{n - w_H(r) - d} A'_j.$$

Especially, if the dual distance of C is $> d$, then we have

$$X(1) = q^{k-d}(q-1)^d \binom{n - w_H(r)}{d}.$$

Proof. The first relation is a result of the MacWilliams identities [44]. The second relation is obtained by letting $A'_0 = 1$, and $A'_j = 0$ for $j = 1, \ldots, d$. $\qquad\square$

4.7.3.3. *Security analysis*

In single-secret sharing schemes some participants may present a falsified share for cheating. This problem is the same as for single-secret sharing in multisecret-sharing. Possible attacks should be guessed beforehand. The size of a secret and the shares given to the participants are assigned the security of a system. If the size of pieces of participants is large, then the memory require for the participants will be too powerful. At this point, it is needed to compute the information rate of the scheme. The information rate [8] is an important parameter to explain the security of system. It is the ratio of the length (in q-digits) of the secret to the maximum length of the pieces given to the participants. So this rate is

$$\rho = \frac{n - k}{n}$$

for our scheme.

Moreover, we use the generalized inverses of matrices and least-squares solutions in linear codes [38] to build this multisecret-sharing scheme. We need as a word $x \in \mathbb{F}_q^k$ to reach the secret and this codeword is the unique when $r(G) = r(GG^T) = r(G^T G)$ is satisfied. So any word, except x, cannot be reached the secret. Thus, it is seen that the new system is reliable by means of security.

4.7.4. Comparison with other schemes

In this section, we conclude the comparison our scheme with other code-based secret-sharing schemes in terms of, respectively, the number of participants, the size of a secret, and the number of coalitions for an $[n, k]$-code over $\mathbb{F}_q$. We denote by S, C, O these schemes in the following table:

System	[35]	[19]	[9]	This paper
S	$n-1$	n	n	n
C	q	q^k	q^k	$q^n - q^k$
O	$\binom{n}{k}$	$\binom{n}{k}$	$\geq \binom{n}{d-t}$	$\geq \binom{n}{n-w_H(r)}$
ρ	1	$\frac{k}{k-1}$	1	$\frac{n-k}{n}$

4.7.5. Conclusion and open problems

In this chapter, we have constructed a new multisecret-sharing scheme by using the generalized inverses of matrices and least-squares solutions in linear codes [38]. In fact, we have applied for the results in [38] to obtain a cryptosystem.

We have determined the general structure and minimal access structure of the scheme. We have explained the statistics on coalitions in detail. Analyzed the security and compared with the other secret-sharing schemes which are based on codes.

Since the Moore–Penrose inverse of a matrix of full rank is not required and is not expensive, this new system is too useful among the other cryptosystems.

At the moment, our scheme does not use the generalized inverse of the product (sum) of two or three matrices. Because these forms are some of open questions about generalized inverses of matrices. It would be nice to use them to construct a cryptosystem [15, 38].

References

[1] A. Alahmadi, A. Altassan, A. AlKenani, S. Çalkavur, H. Shoaib and P. Solé. A multisecret-sharing scheme based on LCD codes. *Mathematics*, 8:272, 2020.

[2] N. Al Ebri and C.Y. Yeun. Study on secret sharing schemes (SSS) and their applications. In *6th Int. Conf. Internet Technology and Secured Transactions*, 11–14 December 2011, Abu Dhabi, United Arab Emirates, pp. 40–45, 2011.

[3] A. Beimel. Secret-sharing schemes: a survey. In *Int. Conf. Coding and Cryptology*, pp. 11–46. Springer, Berlin, 2011.

[4] A. Ben-Israel and T.N.E. Greville. *Generalized Inverses, Theory and Applications*. Springer-Verlag, New York, 2003.

[5] G.R. Blakley. Safeguarding cryptographic keys. In *Proc. 1979 National Computer Conf.*, New York, June 1979, pp. 313–317, 1979.

[6] A. Bonnecaze, B. Mourrain and P. Solé. Jacobi polynomials, type II codes, and designs. *Des. Codes Cryptogr.*, 16:215–234, 1999.

[7] E.F. Brickell. Some ideal secret sharing schemes. In *Advances in Cryptology-EUROCRYPT '89*, Lecture Notes in Computer Science, Vol. 434, pp. 468–475. Springer, 1990.

[8] S. Çalkavur. A secret sharing scheme based on residue class rings. *Appl. Math. Inf. Sci.*, 9:1–3, 2015.

[9] S. Çalkavur and P. Solé. Multisecret-sharing schemes and bounded distance decoding of linear codes. *Int. J. Comput. Math.*, 94(1):107–114, 2017.

[10] S. Çalkavur, P. Solé and A. Bonnecaze. A new secret sharing scheme based on polynomials over finite fields. *Mathematics*, 8(8), 2020.

[11] S. Çalkavur. Secret sharing schemes based on extension fields. *European J. Pure Appl. Math.*, 11(2):410–416, 2018.

[12] S. Çalkavur. Secret sharing schemes and syndrome decoding. *J. Math. Statist. Sci.*, 2016:741–750, 2016.

[13] S. Çalkavur and P. Solé. Some multisecret-sharing schemes over finite fields. *Mathematics*, 8:654, 2020.

[14] S. Çalkavur and P. Solé. Secret sharing, zero sum sets, and Hamming codes. *Mathematics*, 8:1644, 2020.

[15] S. Çalkavur, S.K. Nauman, C. Özel, and H. Zekraoui. The least-squares solutions in linear codes based on multisecret-sharing approach. *International Journal of Information and Coding Theory*, 5(3):290–302, 2020.

[16] F. Carreras, A. Magana and C. Munuera. The accessibility of an access structure. *RAIRO-Theoretical Inform. Appl.*, 40(04):559–567, 2006.

[17] E. Dawson and C.K. Wu. Generalized inverse in public key cryptosystem design. *IEEE Proc. Comput. Digit. Tech.*, 145(5):321–326, 1998.

[18] C. Ding, D. Kohel and S. Ling. Secret sharing with a class of ternary codes. *Theor. Comp. Sci.*, 246:285–298, 2000.

[19] C. Ding, T. Laihonen and A. Renvall. Linear multisecret-sharing schemes and error correcting codes. *J. Comput. Sci.*, 3(9):1023–1036, 1997.

[20] J.D. Fulton. Generalized inverse of matrices over finite field. *Discrete Math.*, 21:23–29, 1978.

[21] J. He and E. Dawson. Multistage secret sharing based on one-way function. *Electronic Lett.*, 30(19):1591–1592, 1994.

[22] L. Horn. Comment: Multistage secret sharing based on one-way function. *Electronic Lett.*, 31(4):262, 1995.

[23] GIMPS Webpage; Available online: https://www.mersenne.org/primes/?press= (accessed on 28 April 2020).

[24] M. Habeeb, D. Kahrobaei and V. Shpilrain. A secret sharing scheme based on group presentations and the word problem. *Contemp. Math. Am. Math. Soc.*, 582:143–150, 2012.

[25] R. Hill. *A First Course in Coding Theory*. Oxford University, Oxford, 1986.

[26] S. Hwang and C. Chang. A dynamic secret sharing scheme with cheater detection. In *ACISP'96*, Lecture Notes in Computer Science, Vol. 1172, pp. 136–146. Springer-Verlag, Berlin, 1993.

[27] W.-A. Jackson, K.M. Martin and C. O'Keefe. Ideal secret sharing schemes with multiple secrets. *J. Cryptology* 9:223–250, 1996.

[28] E.D. Karnin, J.W. Greene and M.E. Hellman. On secret sharing systems. *IEEE Trans. Inf. Theory*, IT-29(1):35–41, 1983.

[29] J.L. Kim and N. Lee. Secret sharing schemes based on additive codes over GF(4). *Appl. Algebra Eng. Commun. Comput.*, 1–19, 2016.

[30] D. Lee, H. Yoon, P. Kim, J. Park, N.Y. Kim and N. Park. SNR enhancement of OTDR using biorthogonal codes and generalized inverses. *IEEE Photonics Technol. Lett.*, 17(1):163–165, 2005.

[31] H.-X. Li, C.-T. Cheng and L.-J. Pang. A new (t, n)-threshold multisecret sharing scheme. In *CIS 2005*, 3802:421–426, 2005.

[32] R. Lidl and H. Niederreiter. *Finite Fields*, Encyclopedia of Mathematics and Its Applications, Vol. 20, University of London, London, 1996.

[33] Magma Website. Available online: http://magma.maths.usyd.edu.au/magma/ (Accessed on 1 March 2020).

[34] F.J. MacWilliams and N.J.A. Sloane. *The Theory of Error-Correcting Codes*. North-Holland, Amsterdam, 1977.

[35] J.L. Massey. Minimal codewords and secret sharing. In *Proc. 6th Joint Swedish-Russian on Information Theory*, Mölle, Sweden, pp. 276–279, 1993.

[36] K. Okada and K. Kurosawa. MDS secret sharing scheme secure against cheaters. *IEEE Trans. Inf. Theory*, 46(3):1078–1081, 1997.

[37] H. Özadam, F. Özbudak and Z. Saygı. Secret sharing schemes and linear codes. In *Proc. Inform. Security Cryptology Conf. Int. Participation*, Seoul, Korea, 4–6 December 2007, pp. 101–106.

[38] C. Özel, M. Güllüsaç and H. Zekraoui. Generalized inverses of matrices and least-squares solutions in linear codes. In *CITCEP*, Krakow, 2015.

[39] C. Padro. Robust vector space secret sharing schemes. *Inform. Process. Lett.*, 68:107–111, 1998.

[40] N. Pakniat, M. Noroozi and Z. Eslami. Reducing multi-secret sharing problem to sharing a single-secret based on cellular automata. *IACR Cryptol. ePrint Arch.* 2017:642, 2017.

[41] M.H. Pearl. Generalized inverses with entries taken from an arbitrary field. *Linear Algebra Appl.*, 1:571–587, 1968.

[42] L.J. Pang and Y.-M. Wong. A new (t, n)-multisecret sharing scheme based on Shamir's secret sharing. *Appl. Math.*, 167:840–848, 2005.

[43] J. Pieprzyk and X.M. Zhang. Ideal threshold schemes from MDS codes. In *Information Security and Cryptology — Proc. ICISC 2002*, Lecture Notes in Computer Science, Vol. 1172, pp. 67–78. Springer, Berlin, 2003.

[44] S. Roman. *Coding and Information Theory*. Springer, 1992.

[45] MathStackExchange Post; https://math.stackexchange.com/quest ions/1614276/a-special-class-of-commutative-rings (Accessed on 29 February 2020).

[46] A. Shamir. How to share a secret. *Comm. ACM*, 22:612–613, 1979.

[47] H.-M. Sun and S.-P. Shieh. Construction of dynamic threshold schemes. *Electronic Lett.* 30:2023–2026, 1994.

[48] R. Yilmaz. *Some Ideal Secret Sharing Schemes*, Master thesis, Bilkent University, Ankara, Turkey, 2010.

[49] C.K. Wu and E. Dawson. Existence of generalized inverse of linear transformations over finite fields. *Finite Fields Appl.*, 4:307–315, 1998.

[50] C.-C. Yang, T.-Y. Chang and M.-S. Hwang. A new (t, n)-multisecret-sharing scheme. *Appl. Math. Comput.*, 151:483–490, 2004.

[51] J. Yuan and C. Ding. Secret sharing schemes from three classes of linear codes. *IEEE Trans. Inform. Theory*, 52(1):206–212, 2006.

[52] H. Zekraoui. Propriétés Algébriques des G^k-inverses des Matrices. Ph.D. dissertation, University of Batnai Algeria, 2011.

[53] H. Zekraoui. Some applications of coding theory. In *Cryptography, Codes and Ciphers: Cryptography and Coding IV*, pp. 33–47, 1995.

Chapter 5

Applications

5.1. On Key Distribution in MANETs

In this first application of secret-sharing schemes, we present a key distribution protocol that does not use a trusted third party. This protocol could for example be used by vehicles when they are on a highway. Incoming vehicles have to get a key while outgoing vehicles lose their key. The idea is that each vehicle is a node in the network and can participate in the key distribution protocol. The set of vehicles represents a Mobile *Ad-Hoc* Network (MANET).

MANETs are self-configuring networks of mobile nodes without the presence of static infrastructure. They can also be heterogeneous, which means that all nodes do not have the same capacity in term of resources (power consumptions, storage, computation, etc.). A good example is given by military battlefield networks. In that case, mobile devices have different communications capability such as radio range, battery life, data transmission rate, etc. Some nodes are then more vulnerable to attacks and may be considered as less reliable than others. Moreover, MANETs do not have a fixed size: nodes can join or leave the network dynamically. When joining the network, nodes need public and private keys (we assume the network has the computational ability to allow asymmetric cryptography). In absence of a central administration, key management must be self-organized by the nodes. Nodes obtain their keys with the help of other nodes, called *master*. Networks generally use a threshold scheme: a node must request at least $t + 1$ master nodes out of n in order to obtain its key.

153

Key management represents a big concern in MANETs. Identity-based cryptography (IBC) has been considered in many recent papers (for example [25, 32, 36]) in order to avoid the use of a heavy public key infrastructure (PKI). It is well known that IBC can simplify systems that manage a large number of public keys.

In this section, we explain [4] why identity-based is an appropriate concept for key management in MANETs. Then we analyze and compare key distribution solutions based on secret-sharing schemes. Section 5.2 introduces identity-based cryptography schemes and lists the advantages of using IBC in MANETs. Secret-sharing schemes are introduced in Section 5.3. In this section, we describe and evaluate different solutions to distribute the trusted third party (TTP).

5.1.1.   Identity-based cryptography in MANETs

5.1.1.1.   *Description*

In 1984, Shamir asked for a public key encryption and signature scheme in which the public key can be an arbitrary string. These schemes are called identity-based cryptography schemes (IBC). Shamir [53] easily constructed an identity-based signature (IBS) scheme using the RSA function, but he was unable to construct an identity-based encryption (IBE) scheme, which became a long-lasting open problem. In 2001, Boneh and Franklin used Weil pairing to introduce the first ID-based encryption scheme [5].

In an IB scheme, the public key of a user is directly derived from his identity. It can be an email address, and in the case of a MANET, the MAC address of the device or any identity bounded to the hardware of the device. Encrypting a message only requires to have the correct public key and some public parameters of a trusted party called Private Key Generator (PKG). There is no need to obtain public key certificate and it is possible to encrypt a message before the private key is computed. A user, who would like to decrypt a message, obtains his private key from the PKG. More precisely, an IB–Encryption scheme consists of four algorithms:

(1) *Setup* generates global system parameters and a master-key;
(2) *Extract* uses the master-key to generate the private key corresponding to an arbitrary public key string ID;

(3) *Encrypt* encrypts messages using the public key ID;

(4) *Decrypt* decrypts messages using the corresponding private key.

Algorithm *Extract* is achieved by the PKG and IBE systems provide key escrow since the PKG knows all private keys. In a MANET which has no central administration, the PKG must be distributed so that there is no single node that knows the secret master key. Secret-sharing schemes implement such distribution.

5.1.1.2. *Pairings*

Let $\mathbb{G}$ be a cyclic (additive) group of a prime order q and $\mathbb{G}'$ be a multiplicative group of the same order q. The group $\mathbb{G}$ is the group of points of an appropriate elliptic curve. A map $e : \mathbb{G} \times \mathbb{G} \to \mathbb{G}'$ is called a cryptographic bilinear map if it satisfies the following properties:

(1) Bilinearity: for all $P,\ Q \in \mathbb{G}$ and $a,\ b \in \mathbb{Z}$, $e(aP,\ bQ) = e(P,\ Q)^{ab}$;
(2) Non-degeneracy: $e(P, P)$ is a generator of $\mathbb{G}'$ and therefore $e(P, P) \neq 1$
(3) Computable: there exists an efficient algorithm to compute $e(P, Q)$ for all $P, Q \in \mathbb{G}$.

The security of ID-based schemes are based on the assumed hardness of the computational Diffie-Hellman (CDH) problem in G.

Let $s \in_R Z_q^*$ be the master key of the system. The corresponding public key is $P_{\text{pub}} = sP$.

Security of pairing-based schemes is based on problems which are considered more difficult than DLP over $\mathbb{Z}_q$. This is because known algorithms to solve these problems are exponential (or sub-exponential in some special cases). Hence, for the same security, these schemes use smaller keys. For example, RSA signature using a key of 1024 bits can be compared in term of security to BLS signature [6] using a key of length 160 bits. Even though the computational cost of a pairing is still high, computations are done in a smaller group and there exist now efficient implementations. Tate pairing, which has better computational performances than Weil pairing, has already been implemented on smartcards. In [51], it is demonstrated that, on smartcards, pairings can be calculated as efficiently as classic cryptographic primitives. It is then realistic to use IBC in MANETs. Moreover, pairing-based cryptography provides us with many interesting primitives. For example, in the domain of authentication, there are many kinds of short specific signatures, such as group signatures, blind signatures, multi-signatures, or ring-signatures (see [26, 39]).

Note that a library (written in C), called pairing-based cryptography (see [7]), is maintained online and propose-efficient implementation of pairings.

5.1.1.3.　*Features of IBC schemes in MANETs*

In this section, we present some features of IBC schemes that can be implemented in MANETs. Some of them can improve the management of a MANET. Indeed, with such schemes there is no need for a certificate authority, the revocation process is simplified and there exists a secret key between each pair of nodes which allows the nodes to communicate without using asymmetric cryptography:

Self-authenticating public key:　Users do not need certificates to authenticate public keys. Moreover, there is no need to exchange public key since there are known in advance. Communication overhead and memory space are then reduced. The public key Q_i is predetermined in the following way. Let H be a map-to-point hash function: $H : \{0,1\}^* \to \mathbb{G}$ and Id_i be the identity of node N_i, the public key is $Q_i = H(Id_i) \in \mathbb{G}$. The corresponding private key is $D_i = sQ_i$.

Key renewal:　It is also possible to limit the validity period of the public key by concatenating an expiry date. Then we have $Q_i = H(Id_i||'date')$. The validity period has to be carefully chosen to minimize both the cost of key renewal and the probability of key compromise. When the key is compromised before the end of expiry date, the following format can be adopted (for more detail, see [32]): $Q_i = H_i(Id_i||'date'||version\#)$ and the version number must be broadcasted to all nodes.

Symmetric keys:　When the network is fully operational, each node knows its own private key and the public key of any other node. Nodes could then communicate using asymmetric cryptography. However symmetric cryptography is more suitable in MANETs since the computational cost is lower. It is interesting to note that every pair of nodes (N_i, N_j) can compute a secret key K_{ij} without interacting. Node N_i computes $e(D_i, Q_j)$ and node N_j computes $e(D_j, Q_i)$. These two values are equal since $e(D_i, Q_j) = e(sQ_i, Q_j) = e(Q_i, sQ_j) = e(Q_i, D_j) = K_{ij}$ (here the pairing is symmetric).

Delegation of duties: This is another interesting feature that can be implemented in MANETs. Assume a node N has several node assistants each being responsible for a given particular task. Node N gives one private key to each of his assistants corresponding to the assistant's responsibility. Each assistant can then decrypt messages whose subject line falls within its responsibility, but it cannot decrypt messages intended for other assistants. Here, messages are encrypted with the same public key and a keyword corresponding to a given responsibility. The message can only be read by the assistant responsible for that subject.

5.1.2. Secret-sharing schemes without trusted party

5.1.2.1. *Secure secret-sharing schemes*

MANETs generally belong to a unique entity like a company or a military administration. In that configuration, an external server TTP plays the role of a PKG and can distribute keys D_i to all nodes before joining the network. Then, nodes can easily communicate using asymmetric or symmetric cryptography, as indicated before. But sometimes, the network must be fully self-organized. There is no trusted server to distribute keys to nodes and the master key of the PKG must not be known by any single entity. The idea is to construct a system in which each node of a fixed subset of nodes knows a part of the secret. This subset of nodes is the distributed representation of the PKG.

Secret-sharing schemes are used to distribute a secret, which, in our case, is the master key s of the PKG. Every node gets a share s_i of the secret and the private key D_i of a node can be computed by the collaboration of $t + 1$ nodes. In its seminal paper [52], Shamir's idea is based on the fact that the knowledge of $t + 1$ points of a given polynomial $f(z) = \sum_{k=0}^{t} a_k z^t \in_R F_q[z]$ (q being a large prime number) of degree t allows us to compute the coefficient $a_0 = f(0)$. The simplified protocol has the following steps:

(1) TTP picks at random a polynomial f of degree t;
(2) TTP sends to each user i a point $(i, f(i))$ as a share;
(3) the secret key a_0 can be recovered by collision of any group of $t+1$ users using Lagrange interpolation.

As we consider fully self-organized network, the TTP must be distributed. In that case, n nodes play the role of the TTP. These nodes are called master nodes. Each master node picks at random a polynomial f_i ($i = 1, \ldots, n$) of degree t and the sum of all these polynomials play the role of the polynomial f: $f = \sum_i f_i$. The polynomial f is indeed never constructed by any entity. Let h be a hash function: $h : \{0,1\}^* \to \mathbb{Z}_q$. We set $h_i = h(Id_i)$. The simplified protocol has the following steps:

(1) node N_i picks at random a polynomial f_i of degree t;
(2) node N_i sends $f_i(h_j)$ to node N_j for $j = 1, \ldots, n$. The share of node N_j is $s_j = \sum_i f_i(h_j) = f(h_j)$.

If at the end of this phase, a node N_j (master or not) needs its private key. It sends to $t+1$ master nodes its identity $Id_j \in \mathbb{G}$ and receives $f(h_i).Q_j$, i being the index of the set of $t+1$ nodes. Node N_j computes then its private key: $D_j = \sum_i \gamma_j f(h_i).Q_j$, where γ_j denotes appropriate Lagrange interpolation coefficients.

Shares must be periodically refreshed. To do it, each master node N_i picks at random a new polynomial g_i such that $g_i(0) = 0$ and sends the value $g_i(h_j)$ to node N_j. The new share of node N_j is $f(h_j) + g(h_j) = (f + g)(h_j)$, and the secret is left unchanged.

In 1991, Pedersen [48] proposed a verifiable secret sharing protocol without third party, using Feldman's protocol [28]. It acts as a distributed key generation in *discrete-log*-based system. Let g be an element of order q in $\mathbb{Z}_p^*$, where $q|(p-1)$. This protocol makes use of n polynomials $f_i(z) = \sum_{k=0}^{t} a_{ik} z^k \in_R F_q[z]$, n being the number of users. More precisely, node N_i:

(1) picks at random a polynomial f_i of degree t;
(2) broadcasts $g^{a_{ik}}$ for $k = 0, \ldots, t$;
(3) sends $f_i(h_j)$ to user N_j for $j = 1, \ldots, n$. The share of node N_j is $s_j = \sum_i f_i(h_j)$.

The private key (the secret) is $s = \sum_{i=1}^{n} a_{i0}$ and the corresponding public key is $y = \prod_i y_i$, where $y_i = g^{a_{i0}}$. We note that s can (only) be computed using any set of $t+1$ correct shares, as

$$s = \sum_{i=1}^{n} a_{i0} = \sum_{i=1}^{n} \left(\sum_j \gamma_j f_i(h_j) \right) = \sum_j \gamma_j s_j,$$

where γ_j denotes appropriate Lagrange interpolation coefficients and j belongs to any set of $t+1$ correct shares.

In 1999, Gennaro *et al.* [29] show that Pedersen protocol is not secure as an adversary can influence the distribution of keys to a non-uniform distribution. They show how an active attacker controlling a small number of parties can bias the values of generated keys. They propose a new protocol, called DKG, which they prove secure. They introduce in the beginning of the protocol an initial commitment phase where each node commits to its initial choice a_{i0} in a way that prevents the attacker from later biasing the output distribution of the protocol. This commitment phase is called Pedersen Verifiable Secret Sharing or Pedersen-VSS [49]. The distributed protocol DKG performed by n nodes generates n private outputs called the shares, and a public output. It satisfies the following requirements of correctness:

(1) Any subset of $t+1$ shares provided by honest nodes define the same unique secret key s.
(2) All honest nodes have the same value of public key.
(3) The secret s is uniformly distributed in $\mathbb{Z}_q$.

Moreover, no information on s can be learnt by an adversary (except for what is implied by the public value). In the following, we describe the protocol of Gennaro *et al.* in the context of Elliptic Curve Discrete Logarithm Problem (ECDLP). We call it ECDKG. This key distribution solution is adopted in [36] for *ad-hoc* networks. The value s is the secret (the master key) and P_{pub} is the corresponding public key of the distributed PKG.

Let $P \in \mathbb{G}$ and $P' \in (P)$ where (P) denotes the subgroup generated by P. We assume that ECDLP is hard in $\mathbb{G}$.

5.1.2.2. *ECDKG protocol*

Generating s

(1) Each node N_i performs a Pedersen-VSS of a random value z_i:

  (a) Node N_i chooses two random polynomials $f_i(z), f'_i(z) \in \mathbb{F}_q[z]$ of degree t:

$$f_i(z) = \sum_{k=0}^{t} a_{ik}z^k, \quad f'_i(z) = \sum_{k=0}^{t} a'_{ik}z^k.$$

  Let $z_i = a_{i0}$, node N_i broadcasts

$$C_{ik} = a_{ik}P + a'_{ik}P',$$

  where $k = 0, \ldots, t$. Remark that $C_{ik} \in \mathbb{G}$. Node N_i computes the shares

$$f_{ij} = \sum_{k=0}^{t} a_{ik}j^k \quad \text{and} \quad f'_{ij} = \sum_{k=0}^{t} a'_{ik}j^k$$

  for $j = 1, \ldots, n$ and sends f_{ij} and f'_{ij} to node N_j.

  (b) Each node N_j verifies the shares he received from the other nodes by checking the equality

$$f_{ij}P + f'_{ij}P' = \sum_{k=0}^{t}(C_{ik})j^k.$$

  If the check fails for an index i, node N_j broadcasts a complaint against node N_i.

  (c) Each node N_i who received a complaint from node N_j broadcasts the values f_{ij} and f'_{ij} that satisfy the equality.

  (d) Each node marks as disqualified any node that either received more than t complaints in step (1(b)) or badly answered to a complaint in step (1(c)).

(2) Let Q be the set of qualified nodes. This set is built by all the nodes (it is shown in [29] that all honest nodes find the same set).

(3) The private key is $s = \sum_{i \in Q} z_i$. And each node N_i sets its share as

$$s_i = \sum_{j \in Q} f_{ji} \quad \text{and} \quad s_i' = \sum_{j \in Q} f_{ji}'.$$

It is important to note that s is never explicitly computed.

Extracting the public key $P_{\text{pub}} = sP$

(4) Each node $i \in Q$ broadcasts $A_{ik} = a_{ik}P$ for $k = 0, \ldots, t$.
(5) Each node N_i verifies the correctness of the received values by checking the following equality:

$$f_{ij}P = \sum_{k=0}^{t} (A_{ik})j^k.$$

If the check fails for an index i, node N_j complains against node N_i by broadcasting the values $f_{i,j}$ and $f_{i,j}'$ that satisfy the first equality but not the second one.

(6) For nodes N_i who receive at least one such complaint, the other nodes run the reconstruction phase of Pedersen-VSS to effectively compute $z_i, f(z), A_{ik}$ for $k = 0, \ldots, t$. All nodes in Q compute $P_{\text{pub}} = \sum_{i \in Q} A_{i0} \in \mathbb{G}$.

Private key construction

(1) Node N_i sends Id_i to $t + 1$ nodes;
(2) Each node N_j sends $f(h_j).Q_i$ to node N_i;
(3) Node N_i computes $D_i = \sum_j \gamma_i f(h_j).Q_i$, where γ_i denotes appropriate Lagrange interpolation coefficients.

The security of this protocol is analyzed in [29].

5.1.2.3. *Properties and improvements*

In this protocol, there exist two types of nodes: master nodes and ordinary nodes. Only master nodes are able to deliver shares. If a node is unable to reach more than t master nodes, it cannot obtain its private key. A node which obtained less than $t + 1$ shares could try to move in order to reach new master nodes and get the missing shares. But this solution is not satisfactory in practice and furthermore, during the evolution of the network, the total number of master nodes may decrease to less than t. It is then important to replace a master node which leaves the network. A trivial solution is that before leaving the network, any master node sends to an ordinary node of its choice its polynomial. Hence, the number of master nodes in the network is left unchanged. But this solution only applies when nodes are honest. Moreover, a master node may not be able (for example, it may be out of order) to transfer data to an ordinary node just before leaving the network.

5.1.2.4. *Protocol using a bivariate polynomial*

In [24], Daza *et al.* propose a more satisfactory solution. In their scheme, there exist three types of nodes: master nodes, *parent* nodes and ordinary nodes. Master and parent nodes both have the capacity to provide shares to construct private key. Moreover, master nodes can distribute special shares to an ordinary node so as it becomes a parent node. In other words, ordinary nodes can become parents if they request $t + 1$ master nodes. Their idea is to choose a bivariate polynomial instead of a monovariate polynomial. More precisely, each master node N_i chooses a random symmetric bivariate polynomial

$$f_i(x, y) = \sum_{k,j=0}^{t} a_{k,j}^i x^k y^j.$$

As usual, we have $f = \sum f_i$ and the share of node N_j is $s_j = f(0, h_j) = S_j(0)$ (if we denote $S_j(x) = f(x, h_j)$). The second variable is only used to provide the special shares. The protocol is as follows:
Suppose an ordinary node m wants to become parent.

(1) Node N_m selects a group of $t + 1$ master nodes.
(2) Each master node N_i from the group sends to node N_m the value $f(h_i, h_m) = S_i(h_m) = S_m(h_i)$.
(3) Node N_m has enough shares to be able to construct $S_m(x)$ using Lagrange interpolation.
(4) Its share of the secret is $s_m = S_m(0)$.

It is important to note that a parent node obtains a monovariate and not a bivariate polynomial. Hence, it can provide shares but not special shares. This scheme partly solves the problem: it increases the probability for an ordinary node to be connected to a sufficient number of parent or master nodes. On the other hand, if the number of master nodes becomes less than t, no new parent nodes can be created.

When evaluating the efficiency of this scheme, we must take into account the complexity of the protocol. During the initial phase, master nodes exchange polynomials instead of values from $\mathbb{Z}_q$. Moreover, in their paper, Daza *et al.* suppose that master nodes are honest which is not always realistic. In the case where master nodes are not all honest, a Pedersen-VSS commitment protocol should be used during the initialization phase.

This protocol represents a good solution for a MANET where master nodes have strong communications capability and reliability but limited mobility. In that case, ordinary nodes may sometimes be too far from a master nodes to obtain shares and parent nodes may become essential. The initial phase is done once for all and the distribution of shares is similar to the one of the monovariate polynomial protocol.

5.1.3. Hierarchical threshold secret sharing

Let us consider a network with two groups of nodes: leader nodes and ordinary nodes. Moreover, suppose that the policy of the network imposes the following rule: in order to obtain its private key, a node must request at least k other nodes of which $k_1 < k$ are leader nodes. This configuration can be implemented by extending Shamir interpolation: instead of only considering shares as points of a polynomial f, one may consider shares as points of some derivatives of f: $(i, f^{(n)}(i))$. The secret can be recovered using Lagrange–Sylvester interpolation. In our example, the node must obtain $l \geq k_1$ points $(i, f(i))$ and $k - l$ points of the derivative $(i, f'(i))$, where f is a polynomial of degree $k-1$. This example can be generalized to hierarchical schemes of $t > 2$ groups, but it is easy to see that parameters of the scheme (here l, k, t) must be carefully chosen since interpolation does not always have a solution. Lagrange–Sylvester interpolation is also called Birkhoff interpolation. It has been studied, for example in [55].

The use of hierarchical threshold schemes has been mentioned in [40], for a two level hierarchy *ad-hoc* network. The initial polynomial is bivariate and shares are monovariate polynomials. The initialization phase is done offline by a dealer. Nodes have to carry out heavy computations for verifications. The paper does not study in detail the initialization phase and its security. In practice, for self-organized networks, the initialization phase is even more costly in term of communications and computations. The bivariate polynomial, which is in fact a two-dimensional matrix should be obtained in a distributed way. In a given subset of nodes, each node should pick at random a matrix and send a polynomial to all nodes. Moreover, the scheme should take into account compromised nodes and include a commitment phase like Pedersen VSS during the initialisation phase. Therefore, hierarchical threshold schemes do not seem to represent a realistic solution for MANETs as long as they do not have strong communicational and computational capabilities.

However, hierarchical threshold schemes can be a suitable solution for other purposes. For example, they may be used to share the secret of the nuclear button. In that case, the secret could be recovered by the collaboration of k personalities like the President, at least k_1 generals and some colonels. Hierarchies can also become more complex using multivariate polynomials. These schemes are indeed very interesting but they do not provide a realistic solution for key distribution in MANETs.

5.1.4.　Conclusion

In this paper, we showed that MANETs can be classified into those which have a central authority and those which do not. Networks of the first group have access to an external trusted party during the initialization phase. This TTP can send their private keys to all nodes. Networks of the second group are fully self-organized. However, within this group, there are two types of networks:

(1) Networks where any node has always access to at least $t+1$ master nodes. In that case, Gennaro's protocol is the most appropriate.
(2) Networks where some nodes may become isolated from master nodes. In this configuration, Daza's protocol represents the best solution.

Regarding hierarchical schemes, we stressed that schemes based on Birkhoff interpolation are very costly in the eyes of the nature of MANETS. Indeed, MANETs often have limited computational and communication abilities while hierarchical schemes are very costly during the initialization phase. We believe that these schemes are not suitable to MANETs.

Finally, let us mention that we focused on threshold sharing schemes and we did not mention other solutions like the ones based on PGP (see for example [33]) which are now well known but difficult to compare to the schemes we considered.

5.2. Absolute Time for Round-Based Timestamping Schemes

The second application we choose to present is secure timestamping because it is a cryptographic primitive of high importance. The aim of a time-stamping system is to provide a *proof-of-existence* of a digital document at a given time. This system is important to ensure integrity and non-repudiation of digital data for a long-time period. Most of existing provable timestamping schemes is based on the notion of round (a period of time) into one single value and publishes it in a widely distributed media (e.g. a newspaper). In this configuration, the TSA does not provide absolute time and furthermore the TSA can tamper timestamps in a round before the round token be published. The round token is obtained after the end of the round.

5.2.1. Introduction

Nowadays, the use of digital documents is growing rapidly. It thus becomes very important to ensure their security when they are stored/exchanged on the open network environment. Cryptographic primitives, including digital signatures, help to provide ongoing assurance of authenticity, data integrity, confidentiality and non-repudiation. Besides that, it is also important to be able to certify that an electronic document has been created at a certain date.

Timestamping protocols, which prove the existence of a message/ document at a certain time, are mandatory in many domains like patent submissions, electronic votes or electronic commerce, where the possible collisions are related to direct monetary (or even political) interests. Moreover, timestamping also assures the secure maintenance of documents with a long lifetime. This is helpful to solve problems related to repudiation of signatures. Indeed, a digital signature is only legally binding if it was made when the user's certificate was still valid. In reality, to prevent eventual compromise concerning a private key, key pairs used in public key cryptosystems have a limited lifetime of the signatures, which can be shorter than the document time-to-life, and therefore the digital signature for itself is not sufficient to guarantee non-repudiation. Even, in order to repudiate a signature, a malicious signer may claim that his credentials were already compromised when the signature issued. In a non-repudiation service, we must be able to determine, at a later time, if a document was signed (using the owner's private signature key) within the validity period of the certificate. The timestamping scheme can provide this service.

The first idea on timestamping is naive. Whenever a client have a document to be timestamped, he or she transmits the document D to timestamping service (TSS), the service timestamps D and retains a copy of the document for safe-keeping and verifying. These protocols have a lot of problems: privacy, bandwidth, storage and incompetence. Then, cryptographic tools as secure *collision-resistant* hash functions and digital signatures are used to improve the naive solution. However, those solutions are to use a trusted service (with a precise clock) that provides data items with current time value and digitally signs them [1]. The assumption of unconditionally trusted service hides a risk of possible collisions that may not be acceptable in applications. The risks are especially high in centralized applications. The first attempts to eliminate trusted services from timestamping schemes were introduces by Haber and Stornetta in [30]. They proposed two rather different approaches: linking and distributed trust. The former relies on a centralized server model that has to be trusted. The idea behind this scheme is to prevent the server from forging fake timestamp tokens by linking linearly the timestamps in a chronological chain. The later is to distribute the required trust among the users of the service.

5.2.1.1. *Absolute versus relative temporal authentication*

The main security objective of timestamping schemes is temporal authentication. Existing timestamping schemes provide two types of temporal authentication: *absolute authentication* [1, 30] and *relative authentication* [8, 12, 17, 19]. Absolute authentication provides absolute timestamps positioning the document at a particular point in time, based upon the time given by a trusted, mutually agreed upon source. Existing absolute authentication schemes presuppose that the TSS is a trust entity. While relative authentication provides relative timestamp containing information that only allows verifying if a document was timestamped before or after another document. For the relative scheme, the existence of a trusted entity is not necessary, therefore, there are mechanisms which guarantee that a document will always be timestamped with the current date and hour even if the TSS is malicious. For applications like patent submissions, electronic votes, ticket bookings, etc. the relative authentication is enough to be applicable. However, the absolute timestamp is very important for some applications (e.g. for contracts, bills, etc.). In this case, we need exactly know when a contract (or a bill) was signed or created.

5.2.1.2. *Existing timestamping schemes*

SIMPLE SCHEMES: A simple timestamping scheme is typically as the above naive solution. Such a scheme can use cryptographic tools as hash functions, digital signatures to guarantee the confidentiality, the integrity of documents. The timestamp tokens are independent to each other. Simple schemes are straightforward and easy to implement. On the other hand, the main weakness of this scheme is that the TSA has to be trusted unconditionally. Since the TSA is the one that guarantees the correctness of the time parameter, a malicious TSA can back-date or forward-date timestamps.

LINKING TIMESTAMPING SCHEMES: The first linking scheme which links linearly timestamps was proposed by Haber and Stornetta [30]. The linear linking scheme poses a very high demand on cooperation among clients, the verification cost thus will be very expensive. Moreover, in order to prevent *fake sub-chain* attacks which were showed in [34], it may impose a long computation time before a trusted timestamp is encountered on the chain, it is thus *impractical*. Later, various improvements for the linking scheme have been proposed in [8, 9, 12, 17, 19, 31]. The behind idea is to make use of the notion of round: a round can be a given number of requests, a period of time or a combination of both. At the end of each round, a timestamp is calculated which depends on all requests submitted during that round and on the previous token round. This also allows reducing the amount of information to be stored (for verification) and to improve system scalability. Subsequently, round tokens are regularly published in a widely distributed media (e.g. a newspaper). After the publication, it becomes impossible to forge timestamps (either to issue fake ones afterward, or modify already issued ones), even for the TSA.

The main *drawbacks* of round-based schemes are as follows: (i) The TSA which provides relative temporal authentication does not associate *absolute time* with a document. Indeed, time attached to documents is that of round, such a scheme only allows us to respond the question: *"who gets it first"* [60]. (ii) Timestamp for a document is only generated and sent to the client at the end of round. Thus, the TSA can fraud timestamps if the round is not yet finished. We can consider a following example: let $H_1, \ldots, H_n$ be the requests during a round. Before "officially" closing the round, the TSA may add (or re-order) requests and then generates fake timestamps.

DISTRIBUTED TIMESTAMPING SCHEMES: In such a scheme, the trust is required among the users of the service [30] or among the network of trusted servers [14, 15, 59]. In Haber-Stornetta's scheme [30], Alice who would like to timestamp a document sends her request to set of k users of the service and receives in return from these users a signed message that includes the time t. Her timestamp consists of k signatures. The main drawback of this protocol is the need of enough people available to answer the Alice's request.

A distributed approach based on a network of TSAs is proposed by Bonnecaze *et al.* [14, 15] and Tulone [59]. In general, these schemes use the threshold cryptography by fault-tolerantly distributing the secret information (e.g. the key which is used to sign the document) among a cluster of trusted servers. A subset of the network of TSAs sign and attach the time t to the document when a request arrives. In order to make back-dating possible, all involved TSAs have to become part of the malicious attack. Distributed schemes thus decrease the dependence on the TSA and also increase the availability and resistance to Denial of Service attacks. Even though it is secure, the high number of interactions between servers makes the scheme difficult to implement.

Another drawback of both of two above approach is the lifetime of the signatures which was signed and sent to clients by trusted servers (or by the users of service). If the keys pair of a signer is expired, valid timestamps will not be verified.

5.2.1.3. *Contribution*

We approach the problem of timestamping with the goal of constructing round-based timestamping schemes which can provide absolute authentication. Ideally, we would like to construct schemes in which the final timestamp will immediately be sent to a client after his request and the round token is calculated and published before beginning of each round. In order to obtain this goal, we use a special type of hash functions, called *chameleon hash functions*, rather than a regular hash function.

Chameleon hash function was introduced by Krawczyk and Rabin in [37] for the purpose of constructing chameleon signatures. A chameleon hash function associated with a hashing key HK and a trapdoor key TK allows us easily to generate collisions when TK is known. Formally, let $\mathcal{H}_r : \{0,1\}^m \times \{0,1\}^r \mapsto \{0,1\}^k$ be a chameleon hash function, it is easy to find r such that $\mathcal{H}_r(m,r) = \mathcal{H}_r(m',r')$ when (HK,TK) and (m,m',r') are given, however, it is hard to find two messages m, m' and two auxiliary numbers r, r' such that $\mathcal{H}_r(m,r) = \mathcal{H}_r(m',r')$ when only HK is given. Our technique is similar to that used to construct online/offline signatures [27, 56]. Roughly speaking, our timestamping procedure is divided by rounds, each round consists of two phases: the first phase generating timestamps and round token is performed offline before the round is began; the second online phase is performed one the document to be timestamped is known.

In this section, we present two such timestamping schemes. The first scheme use a TSA and the trapdoor key TK of the TSA do not compromise until the end of the round. In the second scheme, we eliminate the trust on TSA by distributing the trapdoor key on a network of trusted TSAs. The idea for sharing secret key is similar to the previous distributed timestamping schemes, however our scheme is basically based on rounds. In addition, our second scheme does not face the problem related to the limited lifetime of secret keys as the schemes in [14, 15, 59].

5.2.1.4. *Related works*

Absolute timestamping approach is also addressed in [1], however this solution poses some security problems as discussed above. This solution is thus *impractical*. Then, absolute authentication is provided by the distributed timestamping schemes, however, this approach have to face the problem related to the limited lifetime of secret keys. In [60], Villemson determined the importance of the absolute time and resolved a part of the problem by proposing an interval timestamping scheme. The behind idea in his thesis is that *"If you cannot do it exactly, try to be as precise as possible and prove that the event took place during some interval time"* [60]. In this paper, we point out that round-based timestamping scheme can also provide the absolute authentication.

5.2.1.5. *Organization*

The rest of the section is organized as follows. We first introduce basic notations and chameleon hash functions, then, we recall the notion of timestamping scheme and its security model, we present our construction and analyze its security. Finally, we describe our scheme based on threshold cryptography for the purpose of eliminating the trust on the TSA and we conclude.

5.2.2. **Preliminary**

In this section, we introduce the basic notations and cryptographic tools used in this paper.

5.2.2.1. *Notations*

We denote by $\{0, 1\}^*$ the set of all (binary) strings of finite length. If X is a string, then $|X|$ denotes its length in bits. If X, Y are strings, then $X\|Y$ denotes an encoding from which X and Y are uniquely recoverable. If S is a set, then $X \in_R S$ denotes that X is selected uniformly at random from S. For convenience, for any $k \in N$ we write $X_1, \ldots, X_k \in_R S$ as shorthand for $X_1 \in_R S, \ldots, X_k \in_R S$.

5.2.2.2. Cryptographic tools

Authenticated data structure: Authenticated data structures provide cryptographic proofs that their answers are as accurate as the author intended, even if the data structure is being maintained by a remote host. In this section, we briefly recall the most known authenticated data structure proposed by Merkle [44], called *Merkle tree.*

A *Merkle tree* is a binary tree with an assignment of a string to each node: $n \mapsto P(n)$, such that the parent's node values are one-way functions of the children's node values.

$$P(n_{\text{parent}}) = \mathcal{H}(P(n_{\text{left}}) \| P(n_{\text{right}})),$$

where $\mathcal{H}$ denotes the one-way function, a possible choice of such a function is SHA-1 in practical.

The *authentication path* of a leaf $leaf_i$, denoted $auth_i$, consists of the interior nodes that are siblings on the path from the root to the leaf $leaf_i$.

Chameleon hash function: The principal cryptographic tool we use is a *chameleon hash function*. Informally, a chameleon hash function is a special type of hash function, whose collision resistance depends on the user's state of knowledge: Without knowledge of the associated trapdoor, the chameleon hash function is resistant to the computation of preimages and of collisions. However, with knowledge of the trapdoor, collisions are efficiently computable.

Definition 5.2.1. A *chameleon hash function* [37], also called *trapdoor hash function*, is associated with a public (hashing) key, denoted HK, and a corresponding private key (the *trapdoor* for finding collisions), denoted TK. The chameleon hash function, denoted $\mathcal{H}_r$, can be computed efficiently given the value of HK. On input a message m and a random string r, the function generates a hash value $\mathcal{H}_r(m, r)$ which satisfies the following properties: Efficiency, *Collision resistance, Trapdoor collisions* and *Uniform probability distribution.*

- **Collision resistance:** Given any probabilistic polynomial time malicious entity A that does not know the private key TK, but only the public key HK, define its advantage to be the probability of finding (m_1, r_1) and (m_2, r_2) such that $\mathcal{H}_r(m_1, r_1) = \mathcal{H}_r(m_2, r_2)$. We require the advantage of A to be negligible.

- **Trapdoor collisions:** There exists a polynomial time algorithm A such that on inputs the pair (HK, TK), a pair (m_1, r_1), and a message m_2, then A outputs r_2 such that $\mathcal{H}_r(m_1, r_1) = \mathcal{H}_r(m_2, r_2)$.
- **Uniform probability distribution:** If r_1 is distributed uniformly, m_1, and (m_2, r_2) such that $H(m_1, r_1) = H(m_2, r_2)$, then r_2 is computationally indistinguishable from uniform over R.

Chameleon hash functions can be constructed from the hardness of factoring, discrete logarithm problem. Readers can see [37] for more details.

5.2.3.   Timestamping scheme and its security requirements

5.2.3.1.   *Timestamping schemes*

A timestamping scheme is generally made up of three parties: *client*, *TSA* and *verifier*. We consider the notion presented in [16] for round-based timestamping schemes. A timestamping scheme consists of a triple (Com, Cert, Ver) of efficient algorithms:

Commitment: The commitment algorithm Com takes a set X of requests sent by clients as input and outputs a commitment $R = \mathsf{Com}(X)$ by *aggregating* X due to an *authentication data structure*. This algorithm is executed by the TSA.

Certificate generation: The certificate generation algorithm Cert takes a set X and an element $x \in X$ (a request of the client) as input and generates a certificate $C_x = \mathsf{Cert}(X, x)$. In hash tree-based schemes, certificates are authentication paths. This algorithm is also executed by the TSA.

Verification: The verification algorithm Ver, which is executed by a verifier, takes a request x, a certificate C_x and a commitment R as input and checks whether x is a member of X. It outputs 1 (accept) or 0 (refuse). It tests the following equation holds: $\mathsf{Ver}(x, C_x, R) = 1$.

There exist two major methods to aggregate requests (generate the commitment) in a round. The first method uses a tree-like data structure such as the Merkle tree (e.g. in [8, 30]), the threaded authentication tree [20] or the skip list [11]. This method allows us to reduce to a logarithmic factor the amount of information to be stored and the verification consists in rebuilding a half of the tree. In the other methods, the TSA uses a one-way accumulator [10] which represent an (algebraic) alternative to the aforementioned data structures. Using these functions, the size of timestamps and computation time are constant with respect to the number of requests in the round. Besides that, the verification process can be done in only one operation. Accumulator functions which are generally used are modular exponentiation.

5.2.3.2. *Security requirements*

The security objectives of timestamping schemes is to guarantee the properties: *correctness, data integrity* and *availability*. The first property requires that the verification succeeds only if T_x is correct. The second means that an adversary cannot tamper the timestamp by back or forward-dating it, or modify the request associated to it, or insert an old timestamp in the list of timestamps previously issued. The final property means that timestamping and verification must be available despite processes failures.

There exist two major types of attacks on timestamping protocols: *back-dating attacks* and *forward-dating attacks*. The former is that an adversary may try to "back-date" the valid timestamp. This is a fatal attack for applications in which the priority is based on descendant time order (e.g. patents ...). The adversary may corrupt the TSA and may try to create a forged but valid timestamp token. In the later, an adversary may try to "forward-date" the timestamp without the approval of the valid requester. This is a fatal attack for applications in which the priority is based on ascendant time order (e.g. will ...).

The forward-dating attacks can be prevented by requiring the client's identity which allows us to determine who had timestamped the document. This type of attacks was analyzed more details by Matsuo and Oguro in [43]. The simple protocol is clearly not secure against back-dating attacks if TSA is corrupted, but the linking protocol is since a verifier can check the validity by computing the chain of hash values using published hash values. The strongest security condition against back-dating attacks for a timestamping scheme is presented by Buldas and Laur [18] which is defined using the following attack-scenario with a malicious Server:

(1) TSA computes and publishes a commitment R. Note that TSA is assumed to be *malicious*, so there are no guarantees that R is created by applying Com to a set X of requests.

(2) Alice, an inventor (client), creates a description $D_A \in \{0,1\}^*$ of her invention and protects it somehow, possibly by filing a patent or obtaining a time stamp.

(3) Some time later, the invention D_A is disclosed to the public and the TSA tries to steal it by showing that the invention was known to the TSA long before Alice timestamped it. He creates a slightly modified version D'_A of D_A (at least the author's name should be replaced).

(4) Finally, the TSA back-dates a hash value $x' = H(D'_A)$ of the modified invention document, by finding a certificate $C_{x'}$, so that $\text{Ver}(x', C_{x'}, R) = 1$. The TSA can then use this timestamp to claim his rights to the invention.

5.2.4. Construction

5.2.4.1. *Timestamping scheme*

Let k be a security parameter, $\mathcal{H} : \{0,1\}^* \mapsto \{0,1\}^k$ be a collision-resistant hash function (e.g. SHA-1) and $\mathcal{H}_r : \{0, 1\}^k \times \{0, 1\}^r \mapsto \{0,1\}^k$ be a chameleon hash function, where k is the security parameter. Let $\mathbb{G}$ be a cyclic group and g be a arbitrary generator of $\mathbb{G}$. In describing, we use the Merkle tree and the log-discrete-based chameleon hash function $\mathcal{H}_r = \mathcal{H}_r(g^m h^r)$ [37], where $h = g^x$, g, h are the hash keys and x is the trapdoor key of $\mathcal{H}_r$. We also denote $\mathcal{M} = \{0,1\}^k$ and $\mathcal{R} = \{0,1\}^r$.

Setup: Before each round, the TSA:

(1) Generates a keys pair: The TSA chooses at random $x \in_R \mathcal{Z}_p$ as the trapdoor key, and then computes $h = g^x$. The hashing keys are g, h.

(2) Uniformly chooses 2^n pairs of messages and auxiliary numbers $(m'_1, r'_1), \ldots, (m'_{2^n}, r'_{2^n}) \in_R \mathcal{M} \times \mathcal{R}$ at random.

(3) Uses the chameleon hash function $\mathcal{H}_r$ to compute hash digests $h_i = \mathcal{H}_r(m_i', r_i')$ for all $i \in 1, \ldots, 2^n$.

(4) Computes and publishes Merkle tree root R whose leaves are above hash digests. The TSA also publishes the hashing keys g, h of the chameleon hash function $\mathcal{H}_r$.

(5) Generates a sequence of authentication paths $auth_i$, one for each leaf. The pairs (m_i', r_i') and $auth_i$ must be stored securely.

Note that in constructing the Merkle tree we only use the chameleon hash function $\mathcal{H}_r$ to compute premiers hash digests h_i (leaves of the tree) and use the collision-resistant hash function $\mathcal{H}$ to compute hash digests at higher levels.

Timestamping: The Stamping Protocol used to generate a timestamp works as follows:

(1) The client ith of the round Alice sends her identity and the hash value of the document $m_i = \mathcal{H}(D_i)$ she wants to have timestamped: she sends ID_A, m_i.

(2) The TSA selects an unused triple $(m_i', r_i', auth_i)$, erase it from its secure storage, and then finds a collision of the form $\mathcal{H}_r(m_i', r_i') = \mathcal{H}_r(\mathcal{H}(m_i \| t), r_i)$ by using the trapdoor key x, $r_i = \frac{m_i' - \mathcal{H}(m_i \| t)}{x} + r_i'$.

(3) The TSA then returns the timestamp certificate

$$C_i = (i, ID_A, m_i, r_i, t, auth_i)$$

to Alice, where i is the certificate serial number, and t the current date and time for the round and $auth_i$ is the authentication path of leaf i (for the purpose of reconstructing this timestamp).

(4) Alice receives the certificate and checks that it contains the hash of the document he asked a timestamp for and the correct time (within reasonable limits of precision).

At the end of the round, the TSA discards the trapdoor key x. We use hash digest of $m_i \| t$ instead of m_i in the chameleon hash function to avoid attacks concerning time change of a malicious prover.

Verification: A verifier who questions the validity of the timestamp C_i for the document D_i will:

(1) Check that the hash value $m_i = \mathcal{H}(D_i)$ corresponds to the document D_i.
(2) Obtain the published hashing keys g, h of the TSA and the published round token R for this timestamp.
(3) Compute the value of the leaf i: $h_i = \mathcal{H}_r(\mathcal{H}(m_i\|t), r_i) = \mathcal{H}_r(g^{\mathcal{H}(m_i\|t)}h^{r_i})$ check that it is part of the data that reconstructs the round token R.

5.2.4.2. *Main features*

From efficiency point-of-view, our timestamping scheme is comparable to those based on Merkle tree. We assume that the cost of the hash functions is fixed constants. In our scheme, Merkle tree used is complete binary tree and authentication paths of each leaf are pre-generated by the TSA. After receiving a request, the TSA calculates r finding a collision of the form $\mathcal{H}_r(m', r') = \mathcal{H}_r(m, r)$ and returns immediately to the client a timestamp, this cost is negligible. Thus, efficiency of our scheme directly depends on construct the Merkle tree and authentication paths. Unlike other Merkle tree-based schemes, our scheme provides absolute time for the documents timestamped. In addition, we allow the clients to verify timestamps before the end of the round.

In our scheme, the number of requests of the round is predetermined as an exponent n of 2 before the round is began. Thus, n should be carefully chosen. Our scheme requires the trapdoor key is securely stored only one round (even several rounds).

5.2.4.3. *Totally ordered timestamping scheme with skip-list*

In the timestamping scheme proposed above, we use a Merkle tree for aggregating requests in a round. This authentication data structure is computationally efficient. However, basically Merkle tree based timestamping schemes do not prove order of requests in a round. A malicious TSA can give any time (after the time of round token) for a fake timestamp in current round. In this section, we present a modified timestamping scheme based on skip-lists.

Skip-lists is introduced by Pugh in [50] as an alternative data structure to search trees. The main idea is to add pointers to a simple linked list in order to skip a large part of the list when searching for a particular element. Blibech and Gabillon [12] defined an *authenticated dictionary* based this structure for the purpose of timestamping scheme. Their scheme is totally ordered, i.e. we can compare order of two timestamps even in the same round. Skip-list-based timestamping scheme is computationally efficient as Merkle tree based schemes (see [12] for more details).

Unlike Merkle tree, in order to prove membership of an element in the authenticated dictionary in [12], the *traversal chain* consists of a *tail proof* and a *head proof* which does not allow an adversary to re-order timestamps.

5.2.5. Security analysis

The security of our scheme reduces directly to the security of chameleon hash functions and the security of the Merkle tree (that depends on the property "collision-resistant" of hash functions).

We analyze the security under the following preconditions that are weaker the security condition of Buldas *et al.* [18] reviewed in Section 5.2.3.2. In Section 5.2.6, we also describe how to eliminate trust in the TSA in our scheme with distributed servers.

5.2.5.1. *Security preconditions*

We require that the hashing key of TSA do not be compromised until the end of the next round. This does not violate the limited lifetime requirement for secret keys. The TSA should be competent to keep his keys uncompromised during a short time. In addition, we also assume that the cryptographic tools used (Merkle tree and chameleon hash function) is not broken during a round.

Before analyzing the security of our scheme against back-dating and forward-dating attacks, we consider the following theorem:

Theorem 5.2.2 (Collision resistance). *A computationally bound adversary cannot construct two authentication paths $auth_i$ and $auth_i'$ verifiable against the same commitment R if the hash functions used $\mathcal{H}$ and $\mathcal{H}_r$ are collision-resistant.*

Proof. Suppose that an adversary can, in fact, construct an efficient proof collision with proofs $auth_i$ and $auth_i'$ against common commitment R at the same position i. That is, the adversary may find either a collision of the chameleon hash function $\mathcal{H}_r$ without knowledge of the trapdoor key or a collision of the hash function $\mathcal{H}$ for the authentication path of leaf i on the Merkle tree. Both of them are impossible if the chameleon hash function $\mathcal{H}_r$ and the hash function $\mathcal{H}$ used for constructing the Merkle tree are collision resistant.   □

The following security proof of our timestamping scheme follows directly from the security of the above theorem. It is demonstrated in the following theorem.

Theorem 5.2.3. *The proposed timestamping scheme is secure against back-dating and forward-dating if Theorem 5.2.2 is holds.*

5.2.5.2. *Back and forward-dating attacks*

Back-dating: Consider the following situation, Alice, an inventor, needs to timestamp her patent d at time t. After some time, the invention is disclosed to the public. Bob, an adversary tries to steal the right to Alice's invention. He slightly modifies Alice's invention (at least the author's name should be replaced), and tries to back-date it relative to Alice's invention. Bob is successful if he can construct a timestamp of the modified invention d' such that it can be verified at time t' $(t' < t)$. Bob can then use this timestamp to claim his rights to the invention.

An adversary (who can collude with the TSA or not) tries to back-date a document (invention) using a published round token and/or some valid timestamps of this round he received at time t' in the past. We consider two cases: Alice discloses her invention when the round related to the timestamped invention does not still terminate and when the TSA had terminated. In the first case, the TSA is required to do not reveal the trapdoor key as security pre-conditions. On the contrary, we allow the adversary to collude with the TSA. In both two cases, in order to back-date the invention, the adversary may find a collision of the authentication path for this document. This is impossible if Theorem 5.2.2 holds.

Forward-dating: Consider a client who has sign-timestamped the hash of his will which initially favours the adversary. After some time the will is updated, writing the adversary out and then is sign-timestamped again. Assuming that the adversary has access to the hash of the original will, he can once again re-register the hash of the original will. The TSA timestamps the hash of the "first" will and then send to the adversary a token which can be used to prove authenticity of the "first" will.

As we presented in Section 5.2.3.2, these attacks can be prevented by using the client's identity (see a more details discussion in [43]).

5.2.5.3. *Other attacks*

Besides above attacks, an adversary can also make attacks concerning time reference of the timestamping scheme such as: masquerade, delay, replay. In order to prevent these attacks, we should use the Network Time Protocol (NTP). Reader can see [42] for a discussion more details.

Malicious clients can also use DoS (Denial of Service) attacks on a timestamping service. A DoS attack in this context is an attempt to make the TSS unavailable to its clients (e.g. an attempt to "flood" the network, to prevent a particular client from accessing the service, etc.). In [59], Tulane described how to employ the puzzle techniques against DoS attacks on a timestamping system. Her puzzle mechanism is a local mechanism controlled by the server and activated by it only in response of higher server load. When activated, the server replies to *getTime* by computing a puzzle for the client to solve.

5.2.6. **Eliminating trust in the TSA**

In this section, we describe a round-based distributed timestamping system for the purpose of eliminating trust in the TSA. The trapdoor key is stored at distributed server partially. The TSA consists of two types of servers: a reception server and hash servers. The former will receive requests and return timestamps to clients. The later consists of some servers, each of them keep a part of the trapdoor key of the TSA and will make a partial collision of the chameleon hash function. We also show that our scheme is robust against corrupted TSAs. When it is detected that some parts of the trapdoor key may be stolen, the current trapdoor key is promptly canceled. The basic idea for distributing the trapdoor key is make use of the threshold cryptography. Before each round, the trapdoor TK and hashing keys HK and (m_i', r_i') pairs are generated. Then, TK and r_i' will be distributed to hash servers. After, we use the threshold cryptography to generate hash digests h_i and construct the Merkle tree. When a client send a document to timestamp, a subset of the hash servers finds a trapdoor collision and then returns a timestamp certificate to the client. The protocol works in details as follows:

Let $\mathcal{S}$ be the set of hash servers, $\mathcal{H}_r(m, r) = \mathcal{H}_r(g^{r+x^m}) = \mathcal{H}_r(g^r h^m)$ be a chameleon hash function based on discrete logarithm, where $h = g^x$, x is trapdoor key and g, h are hash keys. This chameleon hash function being a variant of that in Section 5.2.4.1 was presented and proved the security in [23] based on *one-more-discrete-logarithm* assumption.

Key generation. In describing of the key generation, we make use of the Distributed Key Generation (DKG) protocol proposed by Gennaro *et al.* in [29] which generates securely keys for discrete-log-based threshold cryptosystems.

(1) Use the DKG protocol to create $h = g^x$, where $x \in_R \mathbb{Z}_p$ is the trapdoor key and $P_i \in \mathcal{P}$ receives the share x_i for a degree t polynomial $p_x(y) \in \mathbb{Z}_p[y]$ such that $p_x(0) = x$.
(2) Publish the hash keys g, h, each hash server $P_i \in \mathcal{P}$ retains x_i.

5.2.6.1. *Setup*

(1) Use the DKG protocol to create $g^{r_j'}$, where $r_j' \in_R \mathbb{Z}_p$. Each hash server $S_i \in \mathcal{S}$ receives the share r_{ji}' for a another degree t polynomial $p_{r_j'}(y) \in \mathbb{Z}_p[y]$ such that $p_{r_j'}(0) = r_j'$.
(2) Use the DKG protocol to create $h^{m_j'}$, where $m_j' \in_R \mathbb{Z}_p$. Each hash server $S_i \in \mathcal{S}$ receives the share m_{ji}' for a another degree t polynomial $p_{m_j'}(y) \in \mathbb{Z}_p[y]$ such that $p_{m_j'}(0) = m_j'$.
(3) Use the DKG protocol to generate shares z_{ji} for each hash server $S_i \in \mathcal{S}$ of a degree $2t$ polynomial $p_0(y) \in \mathbb{Z}_p[y]$ such that $p_0(0) = 0$.
(4) Now $g^{r_j'}$ and $h^{m_j'}$ are both known to the servers, so the hash digest $h_j = \mathcal{H}_r(m_j', r_j') = \mathcal{H}_r(g^{r_j'} h^{m_j'})$ is computed.
(5) Compute h_j for $j = 1, \ldots, 2^n$.

(6) Compute and publish tree root whose leaves are above hash digests. The TSA also publishes the hashing key (g, h) of the chameleon hash function $\mathcal{H}_r$.

(7) Generate a sequence of authentication paths $auth_j$, one for each leaf. These paths are stored by the reception server.

For constructing the Merkle tree, we use a cryptographic hash function $\mathcal{H}$ (e.g. SHA-1) as described in Section 5.2.4.1.

Timestamping: The Stamping Protocol used to generate a timestamp works as follows:

(1) Alice, the client jth of the round sends her identity and the hash value of the document $m_j = \mathcal{H}(D_j)$ she wants to have timestamped: she sends ID_A, m_j.

(2) The reception server chooses a subset of hash servers $\mathcal{S}' \subset \mathcal{S}$ of size $2t + 1$, computes $m = \mathcal{H}(m_j \| t)$. Each hash server $S_i \in \mathcal{S}'$ computes $col\text{-}1_i = r'_{ji} - x_i m$ and $col\text{-}2_i = x_i m'_{ji} + z_{ji}$ which is S_i's share of the trapdoor collision. Then S_i sends $col\text{-}1_i, col\text{-}2_i$ to the reception server.

(3) Define $f_i(y) = \prod_{S_k \in \mathcal{S}' \setminus P_i} \frac{k-y}{k-i}$, as in the definition of Lagrange interpolation. The trapdoor collision is computed as follows:

$$r_j = \sum_{S_i \in \mathcal{S}'} (col\text{-}1_i + col\text{-}2_i) f_i(0)$$

$$= \sum_{S_i \in \mathcal{S}'} (r'_{ji} - x_i m + x_i m'_{ji} + z_{ji}) f_i(0)$$

$$= r'_j + x m'_j - x m.$$

(4) Each hash server $S_i \in \mathcal{S}'$ discards its share m'_{ji}, r'_{ji}, z_{ji}.

(5) The TSA (reception server) then returns the timestamp certificate $C = (j, ID_A, m_j, r_j, t, auth_j)$ to Alice, where j is the certificate serial number, and t the current date and time for the round and $auth_j$ is the authentication path of the message m_j on the Merkle tree (for the purpose of reconstructing this timestamp). This is the timestamp for Alice's document D_j.

(6) Alice receives the certificate and checks that it contains the hash of the document she asked a timestamp for and the correct time (within reasonable limits of precision).

Unlike the scheme presented in Section 5.2.4.1, in this scheme the secret of the trapdoor key is shared by the network of servers, we do not thus need change the trapdoor key after each round.

Verification: A verifier who questions the validity of the timestamp C for the document D_i will:

(1) Check that the hash value $m_i = \mathcal{H}(D_i)$ corresponds to the document D_i.
(2) Compute the value of the leaf i: $h_i = \mathcal{H}_r(\mathcal{H}(m_j \| t), r_i)$ check that it is part of the data that reconstructs the timestamp for the round.

Furthermore, the scheme is robust against dishonest hash servers. As pointed out in [23], we can verify values $col\text{-}1_i, col\text{-}2_i$ for the purpose of detecting incorrect shares. In this section, we briefly recall the proof of Crutchfield *et al.* in [23].

(1) Verifying $col\text{-}1_i$: Because $g^{r'_{ji}}$ and g^{x_i} are known values from the DKG protocol, we can compute for each hash server $S_i \in S', g^{r'_{ji}} \cdot (g^{x_i})^{-m_j} = g^{r'_{ji}-x_i m_j}$ and confirm that $g^{col\text{-}1_i} = g^{r'_{ji}-x_i m_j}$ as desired.
(2) Verifying $col\text{-}2_i$: We can apply Chaum and Pedersen's zero knowledge proofs (ZKP) for equality of discrete logarithms [22]. Let $d = g^{x_i}, e = g^{m'_{ji}}$ and $f = g^{col\text{-}2_i-z_{ji}}$. Each hash server S_i uniformly chooses $r \in Z_p$ at random and computes $H(g, d, e, f, g^r, e^r) = c$, where H is a random oracle and c is the challenge. S_i computes $v = x_i c + r$ and broadcasts the pair (c, v). Finally, all servers compute and confirm that $H(g, d, e, f, g^v d^{-c}, e^v f^{-c}) = c$.

If any of the shares is deemed incorrect, then broadcast a complaint against S_i. If there are at least $t + 1$ complaints, then clearly S_i must be corrupt since with at most t malicious players, there can be at most t false complaints.

Unlike the timestamping scheme in [57] and timestamping schemes based on threshold signature in [13, 15, 59], our scheme is basically based on rounds and the round tokens are regularly published in a widely distributed media. For verifying timestamps, the clients need only trapdoor keys g, h, that is published along with the round token. Thus, our scheme has not to face security problems related to the limited lifetime of digital signatures. We can renew the hash keys g, h and trapdoor key x after several rounds.

5.2.7. Conclusion

In this paper, we presented round-based secure timestamping schemes which provide absolute times for documents timestamped. The main trick technique used in our constructions is to make use of chameleon hash function. The authenticated data structure (Merkle tree) is constructed before each round, the timestamp is thus responded immediately after receiving a request from a client. This idea is similar to that used online/offline signatures. The first scheme is monoserver, we thus need the trust during a round to guarantee the secret of the trapdoor key. We also presented the second distributed scheme which is based on threshold cryptography for eliminating trust in the TSA.

5.3. An Image Secret-Sharing Method Based on Shamir Secret Sharing

As a third application, we choose to focus on image sharing. The effective and secure protection for important message is a primary concern in commercial and military applications [58]. Numerous techniques, such as image hiding and watermarking, were developed to increase the security of the secret.

The image secret-sharing approaches are useful for protecting sensitive information [58]. The main idea of secret sharing is to transform an image into n shadow images that are transmitted and stored separately. The original image can be reconstructed only if the shadow images that participated in the revealing process form a qualified set [61]. The (k, n)-threshold image-sharing schemes were developed to avoid the single point failure. Hence the encoded content is corrupted during transmission. In these schemes, the original image can be revealed if k or more of these n shadow images are obtained. Moreover, a set of users with complete knowledge of $k - 1$ shares cannot obtain the original image.

Blakley [3] and Shamir [52] independently proposed original concepts of secret sharing in 1979. In these (k, n)-threshold schemes encode the input data D into n shares, which are then distributed among k recipients. D can be reconstructed by anyone who obtains a predefined number k, where $1 \le k \le n$, of the images.

Naor and Shamir [45] extended the secret-sharing concept into image research and referred it as visual cryptography. Visual cryptography requires stacking any k image shares (or shadow images) to show the original image without any cryptographic computation. The disadvantages are (i) image shares have larger image size compared to the size of the original secret image and (ii) the contrast ratio in the reconstructed image is quite poor [2]. A better image secret-sharing approach was presented by Thien and Lin [58]. They used Shamir's secret-sharing scheme to share a secret image with some cryptographic computation. The method significantly reduces the size of the secret image and the secret image can be reconstructed with good quality.

Ramp secret-sharing schemes form another type of secret-sharing schemes [38, 47, 54]. In ramp schemes, a secret can be shared among a group of participants in such way that only sets of at least k participants can reconstruct the secret and $k - 1$ participants cannot [35].

5.3.1. Review of Shamir's secret-sharing scheme

Shamir [52] developed the idea of a $0 \le x_1 \le x_2 \le \cdots \le x_n \le p-1$-threshold-based secret-sharing technique ($k \le n$). The technique allows a polynomial function of order $(k - 1)$ constructed as,

$$f(x) = s_0 + s_1 x + s_2 x^2 + \cdots + s_{k-1} x^{k-1} \pmod{p},$$

where the value of s_0 is the secret and p is a prime number. The secret shares are the pairs of values (x_i, y_i), where

$$y_i = f(x_i), 1 \le i \le n \quad \text{and} \quad 0 \le x_1 \le x_2 \le \cdots \le x_n \le p - 1.$$

The polynomial function $f(x)$ is destroyed after each shareholder possesses a pair of values (x_i, y_i) so that no single shareholder knows the secret value s_0 [2].

Actually, no groups of $(k - 1)$ or fewer secret shares can discover the secret s_0. That is when k or more secret shares are available, then we may set at least k linear equations $y_i = f(x_i)$ for the unknown s_i's.

The unique solution to these equations shows that the secret value s_0 can be easily obtained by using Lagrange interpolation [52].

5.3.2. Proposed method

In this section, we have examined the application of some secret-sharing schemes [21]. We have worked with a new approach to construct secret-sharing schemes based on field extensions in [41]. In this section, we generalize the results of [41].

5.3.3. Application of some secret sharing schemes

Digital image consists of by transporting images in the nature through the agency of sensors to the computer. Digital images are sampled signals at regular intervals. These sampling points are called the pixel. The image is a two-dimensional matrix which consists of pixels. It should be determined that how many bits of each pixel value will be stored when this matrix is constructed. This value is called the bit depth. For an image with a bit depth of 8, the maximum value that a pixel can have is 255.

In general, it is used three bands to obtain a color picture. These bands have same size and each matrix represents a different color component.

Each color component corresponds to red, green and blue.

5.3.4. Proposed scheme

Consider the matrix I is an image with height of h and wideness of w. The height corresponds to row number of matrix and the wideness corresponds to column number. Let the secret space be M_q for a pixel, where

$$M_q = \{a \mid 0 \leq a \leq q - 1, a \in \mathbb{Z}\}.$$

This set consists of the elements of the matrix I.

Let the secret be the image I and the threshold structure be (k, n). In this case, it can be constructed a secret-sharing scheme as follows:

$$I = [a_{ij}] = \begin{bmatrix} a_{11} & a_{12} & \cdots & a_{1w} \\ \vdots & \vdots & & \vdots \\ a_{h1} & a_{h2} & \cdots & a_{hw} \end{bmatrix}_{h \times w}, \quad a_{ij} \in M_q. \tag{5.3.1}$$

The matrix $P(x)$ is generated by using I consisting of height of h and wideness of $\lceil \frac{w}{k-1} \rceil$:

$$P(x) = [p_{ij}(x)] = \begin{bmatrix} p_{11}(x) & p_{12}(x) & \cdots & p_{1w'}(x) \\ \vdots & \vdots & & \vdots \\ p_{h'1}(x) & p_{h'2}(x) & \cdots & p_{h'w'}(x) \end{bmatrix},$$

$$h' = h, \ w' = \left\lceil \frac{w}{k-1} \right\rceil. \tag{5.3.2}$$

$$p_{ij}(x) = rx^{k-1} + \sum_{t=0}^{k-2} a_{i'j'} x^t \in M_q[x],$$

$$i' = i, \ j' = (j-1) \cdot (k-1) + (k-t), \ r \in M_q - \{0\}. \tag{5.3.3}$$

The a_{ij} entry corresponds to ith row and jth column of matrix I.

It is clear that the degree of polynomial p_{ij} is $(k-1)$. The columns of the matrix I are divided into pieces that has length of $(k-1)$. jth piece in the ith row is represented by the vector $H_{ij} = \{h_1, h_2, \ldots, h_{k-1}\}$. It is used the vector H_{ij} to construct the element p_{ij} $(1 \le i \le h', 1 \le j \le w')$ of the matrix $P(x)$.

The first entry of H_{ij} is located ith row and $[(j-1)(k-1)+1]$th column of the matrix I.

The leading coefficient of polynomial $p_{ij}(x)$ is randomly chosen from $M_q - \{0\}$. The coefficient of term which is the degree of t $(0 \le t \le k-2)$ of polynomial $p_{ij}(x)$ is chosen as $(k-t-1)$th element of H_{ij}.

This corresponds to $[(j-1)(k-1)+(k-t)]$th column in the ith row.

The matrix $P(x)$ is written as the elements of matrix $T(x)$ by using Algorithm 1 [41].

$$T(x) = [t_{ij}(x)] = \begin{bmatrix} t_{11}(x) & t_{12}(x) & \cdots & t_{1w'}(x) \\ \vdots & \vdots & & \vdots \\ t_{h'1}(x) & t_{h'2}(x) & \cdots & t_{h'w'}(x) \end{bmatrix},$$

$$t_{ij}(x) \in (\mathrm{GF}(q))[x] \tag{5.3.4}$$

It is determined an ID number for each participant. The secret piece is obtained by equality (5.3.3) for each participant and $u_i \in M_q$ $(1 \leq i \leq n)$. These ID numbers are transformed to the $v_i \in \mathrm{GF}(q)$ $(1 \leq i \leq n)$ by Algorithm 1 [41]. Then the matrix R_i $((1 \leq i \leq n))$ is transformed to the matrix $T(x)$ as follows:

$$R_i = T(v_i), \quad 1 \leq i \leq n, \tag{5.3.5}$$

$$R_i = \begin{bmatrix} t_{11}(v_i) & t_{12}(v_i) & \cdots & t_{1w'}(v_i) \\ \vdots & \vdots & & \vdots \\ t_{h'1}(v_i) & t_{h'2}(v_i) & \cdots & t_{h'w'}(v_i) \end{bmatrix}_{h' \times w'}. \tag{5.3.6}$$

This polynomial matrix is written as the matrix Y_i by using Algorithm 2 [41]:

$$Y_i = \begin{bmatrix} a_{11} & a_{12} & \cdots & a_{1w'} \\ \vdots & \vdots & & \vdots \\ a_{h'1} & a_{h'2} & \cdots & a_{h'w'} \end{bmatrix}_{h' \times w'}. \tag{5.3.7}$$

5.3.5. Secret retrieval procedure

To reach the secret, at least k pieces of secret must be known. On the other hand, the number of elements of $W = \{u_i | t_i \in M_q - \{0\}, 1 \leq i \leq n\}$ must be at least k.

In the ordered pair $(u_{t_i}, Y_{u_{t_i}})$, the order of participant in the W is denoted by i, and the order in the set of participants of participant t_ith in the W is denoted by u_{t_i}.

$Y_{u_{t_i}}$ is the secret piece which is given to participant with ID of u_{t_i}. These ordered pairs are transformed to the ordered pairs $(v_{t_i}, R_{u_{t_i}})$ by using Algorithm 1 in [41].

It is used to Lagrange interpolation for the ordered pairs $(v_{t_i}, R_{u_{t_i}})$. Hence it is obtained the matrix $T(x)$ again. Then it is found the matrix $P(x)$. The image is constructed with the coefficients of this polynomial.

Example 5.3.1. Let the secret space be M_{256} and the irreducible polynomial be $f(x) = x^8 + x^4 + x^3 + x^2 + 1 \in (\mathrm{GF}(2))[x]$ to construct $\mathrm{GF}(256)$.

It can be constructed a $(3, 5)$-threshold scheme by using the following matrix I:

$$I = \begin{bmatrix} 254 & 241 & 189 & 189 & 241 & 254 \\ 254 & 189 & 254 & 254 & 189 & 254 \\ 197 & 210 & 210 & 210 & 210 & 197 \\ 178 & 192 & 209 & 209 & 192 & 178 \\ 172 & 186 & 196 & 196 & 186 & 172 \\ 157 & 168 & 168 & 168 & 168 & 157 \end{bmatrix}_{6\times6}. \tag{5.3.8}$$

The matrix $P(x)$ can be constructed as follows.

The leading coefficient is randomly selected and the other coefficients are chosen from matrix I:

$$P(x) = \begin{bmatrix} (2x^2 + 254x + 241) & (8x^2 + 189x + 189) & (64x^2 + 241x + 254) \\ (128x^2 + 254x + 189) & (x^2 + 254x + 254) & (8x^2 + 189x + 254) \\ (16x^2 + 197x + 210) & (128x^2 + 210x + 210) & (28x^2 + 210x + 197) \\ (196x^2 + 178x + 192) & (57x^2 + 209x + 209) & (59x^2 + 192x + 178) \\ (x^2 + 172x + 186) & (159x^2 + 196x + 196) & (56x^2 + 186x + 172) \\ (244x^2 + 157x + 168) & (209x^2 + 168x + 168) & (170x^2 + 168x + 157) \end{bmatrix}. \tag{5.3.9}$$

The coefficient of polynomial in the matrix $P(x)$ is moved to $GF(256)$. Therefore, it is obtained the elements of matrix $T(x) = [t_{ij}(x)]$, $(t(x) \in (GF(q))[x])$.

$$t_{11}(x) = (\theta)x^2 + (\theta^7 + \theta^6 + \theta^5 + \theta^4 + \theta^3 + \theta^2 + \theta)x$$
$$+ (\theta^7 + \theta^6 + \theta^5 + \theta^4 + 1),$$

$$t_{12}(x) = (\theta^3)x^2 + (\theta^7 + \theta^5 + \theta^4 + \theta^3 + \theta^2 + 1)x$$
$$+ (\theta^7 + \theta^5 + \theta^4 + \theta^3 + \theta^2 + 1),$$

$$t_{13}(x) = (\theta^6)x^2 + (\theta^7 + \theta^6 + \theta^5 + \theta^4 + 1)x$$
$$+ (\theta^7 + \theta^6 + \theta^5 + \theta^4 + \theta^3 + \theta^2 + \theta),$$

$$t_{21}(x) = (\theta^7)x^2 + (\theta^7 + \theta^6 + \theta^5 + \theta^4 + \theta^3 + \theta^2 + \theta)x$$
$$+ (\theta^7 + \theta^5 + \theta^4 + \theta^3 + \theta^2 + 1),$$

$$t_{22}(x) = (1)x^2 + (\theta^7 + \theta^6 + \theta^5 + \theta^4 + \theta^3 + \theta^2 + \theta)x$$
$$+ (\theta^7 + \theta^6 + \theta^5 + \theta^4 + \theta^3 + \theta^2 + \theta),$$

$$t_{23}(x) = (\theta^3)x^2 + (\theta^7 + \theta^5 + \theta^4 + \theta^3 + \theta^2 + 1)x$$
$$+ (\theta^7 + \theta^6 + \theta^5 + \theta^4 + \theta^3 + \theta^2 + \theta),$$
$$t_{31}(x) = (\theta^4)x^2 + (\theta^7 + \theta^6 + \theta^2 + 1)x + (\theta^7 + \theta^6 + \theta^4 + \theta),$$
$$t_{32}(x) = (\theta^7)x^2 + (\theta^7 + \theta^6 + \theta^4 + \theta)x + (\theta^7 + \theta^6 + \theta^4 + \theta),$$
$$t_{33}(x) = (\theta^4 + \theta^3 + \theta^2)x^2 + (\theta^7 + \theta^6 + \theta^4 + \theta)x + (\theta^7 + \theta^6 + \theta^2 + 1),$$
$$t_{41}(x) = (\theta^7 + \theta^6 + \theta^2)x^2 + (\theta^7 + \theta^5 + \theta^4 + \theta)x + (\theta^7 + \theta^6),$$
$$t_{42}(x) = (\theta^5 + \theta^4 + \theta^3 + 1)x^2 + (\theta^7 + \theta^6 + \theta^4 + 1)x$$
$$+ (\theta^7 + \theta^6 + \theta^4 + 1),$$
$$t_{43}(x) = (\theta^5 + \theta^4 + \theta^3 + \theta + 1)x^2 + (\theta^7 + \theta^6)x + (\theta^7 + \theta^5 + \theta^4 + \theta),$$
$$t_{51}(x) = (1)x^2 + (\theta^7 + \theta^5 + \theta^3 + \theta^2)x + (\theta^7 + \theta^5 + \theta^4 + \theta^3 + \theta),$$
$$t_{52}(x) = (\theta^7 + \theta^4 + \theta^3 + \theta^2 + \theta + 1)x^2 + (\theta^7 + \theta^6 + \theta^2)x$$
$$+ (\theta^7 + \theta^6 + \theta^2),$$
$$t_{53}(x) = (\theta^5 + \theta^4 + \theta^3)x^2 + (\theta^7 + \theta^5 + \theta^4 + \theta^3 + \theta)x$$
$$+ (\theta^7 + \theta^5 + \theta^3 + \theta^2),$$
$$t_{61}(x) = (\theta^7 + \theta^6 + \theta^5 + \theta^4 + \theta^2)x^2 + (\theta^7 + \theta^4 + \theta^3 + \theta^2 + 1)x$$
$$+ (\theta^7 + \theta^5 + \theta^3),$$
$$t_{62}(x) = (\theta^7 + \theta^6 + \theta^4 + 1)x^2 + (\theta^7 + \theta^5 + \theta^3)x + (\theta^7 + \theta^5 + \theta^3),$$
$$t_{63}(x) = (\theta^7 + \theta^5 + \theta^3 + \theta)x^2 + (\theta^7 + \theta^5 + \theta^3)x$$
$$+ (\theta^7 + \theta^4 + \theta^3 + \theta^2 + 1). \tag{5.3.10}$$

Let the IDs of participants be $u_1 = 1$, $u_2 = 2$, $u_3 = 3$, $u_4 = 4$ and $u_5 = 5$. These elements correspond to $v_1 = 1$, $v_2 = \theta$, $v_3 = \theta + 1$, $v_4 = \theta^2$ and $v_5 = \theta^2 + 1 \in \mathrm{GF}(256)$

The pieces of participants are as follows:

$$R_1 = T(1),$$
$$R_2 = T(\theta),$$
$$R_3 = T(\theta + 1), \tag{5.3.11}$$
$$R_4 = T(\theta^2),$$
$$R_5 = T(\theta^2 + 1).$$

These elements correspond to the following matrices in M_{256}:

$$Y_1 = \begin{bmatrix} 13 & 8 & 79 \\ 195 & 1 & 75 \\ 7 & 128 & 11 \\ 182 & 57 & 73 \\ 23 & 159 & 46 \\ 193 & 209 & 159 \end{bmatrix}, \quad Y_2 = \begin{bmatrix} 24 & 250 & 28 \\ 102 & 27 & 185 \\ 5 & 81 & 12 \\ 142 & 138 & 195 \\ 251 & 23 & 37 \\ 120 & 134 & 66 \end{bmatrix},$$

$$Y_3 = \begin{bmatrix} 228 & 79 & 173 \\ 24 & 228 & 12 \\ 208 & 3 & 194 \\ 248 & 98 & 56 \\ 86 & 76 & 167 \\ 17 & 255 & 64 \end{bmatrix}, \quad Y_4 = \begin{bmatrix} 14 & 243 & 105 \\ 138 & 49 & 176 \\ 252 & 85 & 119 \\ 238 & 5 & 2 \\ 32 & 246 & 217 \\ 29 & 163 & 117 \end{bmatrix},$$

$$Y_5 = \begin{bmatrix} 242 & 70 & 216 \\ 244 & 206 & 5 \\ 41 & 7 & 185 \\ 152 & 237 & 249 \\ 141 & 173 & 91 \\ 116 & 218 & 119 \end{bmatrix}. \qquad (5.3.12)$$

At least three participants can recover the image by combining their shares by using Lagrange interpolation in [41].

5.3.6. Advantages

It is known that a file in the computer environment can be expressed with a bit string. A bit string consists of 8 bits is called a byte. A byte gets value in the range (0–255) and is an element of M_{256}.

A file D consisting of m bytes can be expressed as a vector such that $D = \begin{pmatrix} a_1 & a_2 & \cdots & a_m \end{pmatrix}$ $(a_i \in M_q)$.

Consider any file (text, image, video, etc.) by using the proposed scheme, the file is also secret.

The operations of secret-sharing schemes can be applied to this file. The participants know that the secret is the image. The secret-sharing scheme is defined over GF(256). So it is a lossless scheme.

As in the Shamir's scheme if the operations were done in GF(251), then the large values than 250 would be lost. That is, the file will be corrupted. So the entire file could be lost. At result, the image could not reconstruct again.

5.3.7. Security analysis

In a secret-sharing scheme, there exists the possibility that some participants lie about the value of their shares in order to obtain some illicit benefit. Therefore, the security against cheating is a key point in the implementation of secret-sharing schemes.

Our image sharing method has been constructed based on Shamir secret sharing. We send the matrix as an secret image and then the participants use the Lagrange interpolation to recover the secret. Since Shamir's scheme is ideal and perfect, this method is the best of the others by means of security. So our method is reliable.

5.3.8. Conclusion

We proposed an image secret-sharing method based on Shamir secret sharing. We have two techniques: (i) Secret sharing scheme using matrix projection and (ii) Shamir's secret sharing scheme.

A secret image can be successfully reconstructed from any k image shares but cannot be revealed from any $(k-1)$ or fewer image shares. The size of image shares is smaller than the size of the secret image. Our scheme is defined over GF(256). So it is a lossless scheme which is another advantage of our scheme. So the proposed scheme stands well, in terms of security.

References

[1] C. Adams, P. Cain, D. Pinkas and R. Zuccherato. Internet X.509 public key infrastructure time-stamp protocol (TSP), 2001.

[2] L. Bai, S. Biswas, A. Ortiz and D. Dalessandro. An image secret sharing method. In *9th Int. Conf. Information Fusion*, Italy, 2006.

[3] G.R. Blakley. Safeguarding cryptographic keys. In *Proc. AFIPS 1979 National Computer Conf.*, USA, pp. 313–317, 1979.

[4] A. Bonnecaze and A. Gabillon. On key distribution in MANETs. 2009 Fifth International Conference on Signal Image Technology and Internet Based Systems. doi:10.1109/SITIS.2009.64

[5] D. Boneh and M. Franklin. Identity-based encryption from the weil pairing. In *Advances in Cryptology — Proc. CRYPTO*, 2001.

[6] D. Boneh, B. Lynn and H. Shacham. Short signatures from the weil pairing. In *Proc. Asiacrypt 2001*, Lecture Notes in Computer Science, Vol. 2248, pp. 514–532. Springer-Verlag.

[7] D. Boneh *et al.* PBC library. http://crypto.stanford.edu/pbc/.

[8] D. Bayer, S. Haber and W.S. Stornetta. Improving the efficiency and reliability of digital time-stamping. In *Sequences II: Methods in Communication, Security, and Computer Science*, pp. 329–334, London, UK, 1993. Springer-Verlag.

[9] J. Benaloh and M. de Mare. Efficient broadcast time-stamping. Technical Report 1 TR-MCS-91-1, Clarkson University Department of Mathematics and Computer Science, August 1991.

[10] J. Benaloh and M. de Mare. One-way accumulators: a decentralized alternative to digital signatures. In *EUROCRYPT '93: Workshop on the Theory and Application of Cryptographic Techniques on Advances in Cryptology*, pp. 274–285, Secaucus, NJ, USA, 1994. Springer-Verlag New York, Inc.

[11] K. Blibech and A. Gabillon. Chronos: An authenticated dictionary based on skip lists for timestamping. In *Proc. 12th ACM Conf. Computer Security (Workshop Secure Web Services)*, George Mason University, Fairfax, VA, USA, November 2005.

[12] K. Blibech and A. Gabillon. A new timestamping scheme based on skip lists. In *ICCSA* (3), pp. 395–405, 2006.

[13] A. Bonnecaze. A multi-signature for time stamping scheme. In *SAR/SSI 06: The 1st Conf. Security in Network Architectures and Information Systems*, Seignosse, France, June 2006.

[14] A. Bonnecaze, P. Liardet, A. Gabillon and K. Blibech. Secure time-stamping schemes: A distributed point of view. *Ann. Telecommun.*, 61(5–6):662–681, May–June 2006.

[15] A. Bonnecaze and P. Trebuchet. Threshold signature for distributed time stamping schemes. *Ann. Telecommun.*, 62(11–12), November–December 2007.

[16] A. Buldas and A. Jurgenson. Does secure time-stamping imply collision-free hash functions? In W. Susilo, J.K. Liu and Yi Mu, editors, *ProvSec, Lecture Notes in Computer Science*, Vol. 4784, pages 138–150. Springer, 2007.

[17] A. Buldas, P. Laud, H. Lipmaa and J. Villemson. Time-stamping with binary linking schemes. In *CRYPTO*, pp. 486–501, 1998.

[18] A. Buldas and S. Laur. Do broken hash functions affect the security of time-stamping schemes? In *ACNS*, pp. 50–65, 2006.

[19] A. Buldas and H. Lipmaa. Digital signatures, timestamping and the corresponding infrastructure. Technical Report, Kberneetika AS, 2000.

[20] A. Buldas, H. Lipmaa and B. Schoenmakers. Optimally efficient accountable time-stamping. In *Public Key Cryptography*, pp. 293–305, 2000.

[21] S. Çalkavur and F. Molla. An image secret sharing method based on Shamir secret sharing. *Current Trends Comput. Sci. Appl.*, 1(2), 2018.

[22] D. Chaum and T.P. Pedersen. Wallet databases with observers. In E.F. Brickell, editor, *CRYPTO*, Lecture Notes in Computer Science, Vol. 740, pp. 89–105. Springer, 1992.

[23] C. Crutchfield, D. Molnar, D. Turner and D. Wagner. Generic online/off-line threshold signatures. In M. Yung, Y. Dodis, A. Kiayias and T. Malkin, editors, *Public Key Cryptography*, Lecture Notes in Computer Science, Vol. 3958, pp. 58–74. Springer, 2006.

[24] V. Daza, P. Morillo and C. Rfols On dynamic distribution of private keys over MANETs. *Electronic Notes Theoret. Comput. Sci.*, 171(1):33–41, 2007.

[25] H. Deng, A. Mukherjee and D. Agrawal. Threshold and identity-based key management and authentication for wireless ad-hoc networks. In *ITCC'04*, Vol. 1, pp. 107–115, 2004.

[26] R. Dutta, R. Barua and P. Sarkar. Pairing-based cryptographic protocols: A survey. In *Cryptology ePrint Archive*, Report 2004/064, 2004.

[27] S. Even, O. Goldreich and S. Micali. On-line/off-line digital signatures. *J. Cryptology*, 9(1):35–67, 1996.

[28] P. Feldman. A practicable scheme for non-interactive verifiable secret sharing. In *Proc. 28th FOCS*, pp. 427–437, 1987.

[29] R. Gennaro, S. Jarecki, H. Krawczyk and T. Rabin. Secure distributed key generation for discrete-log based cryptosystems. *J. Cryptology*, 20(1):51–83, 2007.

[30] S. Haber and W.S. Stornetta. How to Time-Stamp a Digital Document. In *CRYPTO'90: Proc. 10th Annual Int. Cryptology Conf. Advances in Cryptology*, pp. 437–455, London, UK, 1991. Springer-Verlag.

[31] S. Haber and W.S. Stornetta. Secure names for bit-strings. In *ACM Conf. Computer and Communications Security*, pp. 28–35, 1997.

[32] K. Hoeper and G. Gong. Bootstrapping security in mobile ad hoc networks using identity-based schemes with key revocation. In *Ad-Hoc, Mobile, and Wireless Networks*, Lecture Notes in Computer Science, Vol. 4104/2006, pp. 224–237, 2006.

[33] J.-P. Hubaux, L. Buttyn and S. Capkun. The quest for security in mobile ad hoc networks. In *Proc. 2nd ACM Int. Symp. Mobile Ad Hoc Networking & Computing*, pp. 146–155, 2001.

[34] M. Just. Some timestamping protocol failures. In *NDSS 98: Proc. Symp. Network and Distributed Security*, pp. 89–96, San Diego, CA, USA, March 1998.

[35] W.A. Jackson and K. Martin. A combinatorial interpretation of ramp schemes, 1996.

[36] A. Khalili, J. Katz and W. Arbaugh. Toward secure key distribution in truly ad-hoc networks. In *Proc. 2003 Symp. Applications and the Internet Workshops*, p. 342.

[37] H. Krawczyk and T. Rabin. Chameleon signatures. In *NDSS*, 2000.

[38] K. Kurosawa, K. Okada, K. Sakano, W. Ogata and S. Tsujii. Nonperfect secret sharing schemes and matroids. In *Advances in Cryptology*, Berlin.

[39] D. Le, A. Bonnecaze and A. Gabillon. Multisignatures as secure as the Diffie-Hellman problem in the plain public-key model. In *Third Int. Conf. Pairing-Based Cryptography*, Pairing, 2009, Stanford University, USA, August pp. 12–14, 2009.

[40] C. Ma and R. Cheng. Key management based on hierarchical secret sharing in ad-hoc networks. In *Inscrypt'07*, Lecture Notes in Computer Science, Vol. 4990, pp. 182–191, 2008.

[41] F. Molla and S. Çalkavur. A new approach to construct secret sharing schemes based on field extensions. *European J. Pure Appl. Math.*, 2018.

[42] H. Massias and J. Quisquater. Time and cryptography. Technical Report, Universit'e catholique de Louvain, 1997.

[43] S. Matsuo and H. Oguro. User-side forward-dating attack on timestamping protocol. In *Proc. 3rd Int. Workshop for Applied Public Key Infrastructure (IWAP'04)*, pp. 72–83, 2004.

[44] R.C. Merkle. *Secrecy, authentication, and public key systems*. PhD thesis, 1979.

[45] M. Naor and A. Shamir. Visual cryptography II: Improving the contrast via the cover base. *Security Protocols*, 1189:197–202.

[46] M. Naor and A. Shamir. Visual cryptography. In *Advances in Cryptology, EUROCRYPT'94*, Berlin.

[47] W. Ogata and K. Kurosawa. Some basic properties of general nonperfect secret sharing schemes. *J. Universal Comput. Sci.*, 4(8):690–704, 1998.

[48] T. Pedersen. A threshold cryptosystem without a trusted party. In *Advances in Cryptology, Eurocrypt'91*, Lecture Notes in Computer Science, Vol. 547, pp. 522–526, 1991.

[49] T. Pedersen. Non-interactive and information-theoretic secure verifiable secret sharing. In *Advances in Cryptology, Crypto'91*, Lecture Notes in Computer Science, Vol. 576, pp. 129–140, 1991.

[50] W. Pugh. Skip lists: a probabilistic alternative to balanced trees. *Comm. ACM*, 33(6):668–676, 1990.

[51] M. Scott, N. Costigan and W. Abdulwahab. Implementing cryptographic pairings on smartcards. In *Cryptographic Hardware and Embedded Systems — CHES 2006*, Lecture Notes in Computer Science, Vol. 4249/2006, pp. 134–147, 2006.

[52] A. Shamir. How to share a secret. *Comm. ACM*, 22:612–613, 1979.

[53] A. Shamir. Identity-based cryptosystems and signature schemes. In *Proc. CRYPTO'84*, Lecture Notes in Computer Science, Vol. 196, pp. 47–53, 1984.

[54] K. Srinathan, N.T. Rajan and C.P. Rangan. Non-perfect secret sharing over general access structures. In *Progress in Cryptology-INDOCRYPT*, pp. 409–421, 2002.

[55] T. Tassa. Hierarchical threshold secret sharing. *J. Cryptology*, 20:237–264, 2007.

[56] A. Shamir and Y. Tauman. Improved online/offline signature schemes. In J. Kilian, editor, *CRYPTO*, Lecture Notes in Computer Science, Vol. 2139, pp. 355–367. Springer, 2001.

[57] A. Takura, S. Ono and S. Naito. A secure and trusted time stamping authority. In *IWS 99: Internet Workshop*, pp. 88–93, Osaka, Japan, 1999. IEEE Computer Society.

[58] C.C. Thien and J.C. Lin. Secret image sharing. *Comput. Graphics*, 26(5):765–770.

[59] D.Tulone. A secure and scalable digital time-stamping service. In *Proc. IEEE Int. Conf. Communications (ICC): Network Security and Information Assurance Symp.*

[60] J. Villemson. *Size-efficient interval time stamps*. PhD thesis, University of Tartu, Estonia, 82 pp., 2002.

[61] K.S. Wu. A secret image sharing scheme for light images. *EURASIP J. Adv. Signal Processing*.

Index

Printed in the United States
by Baker & Taylor Publisher Services